RESISTANCE, REBELLION AND REFUSAL IN GROUPS

New International Library of Group Analysis

Series Editor: Earl Hopper

Stone - Contributions of Self Psychology to Group Psychotherapy

Gans - Difficult Topics in Group Psychotherapy: My Journey from Shame to Courage

RESISTANCE, REBELLION AND REFUSAL IN GROUPS
The 3 Rs

Richard M. Billow, Ph.D.

Routledge
Taylor & Francis Group
LONDON AND NEW YORK

First published 2010 by
Karnac Books Ltd.

Published 2018 by Routledge
2 Park Square, Milton Park, Abingdon, Oxon OX14 4RN
711 Third Avenue, New York, NY 10017, USA

Routledge is an imprint of the Taylor & Francis Group, an informa business

Revised, reworked, and excerpted material from the following journal articles and book chapters I authored appears in the following chapters.

Chapter 1: (2009) The radical nature of combined psychotherapy. *International Journal of Group Psychotherapy*, *59*: 1–28.

Chapter 2: (2004) Truth and falsity in group. *International Journal of Group Psychotherapy, 54*: 321–345; (2004) A falsifying adolescent. *Psychoanalytic Quarterly, 73*: 1041–1078.

Chapter 3: (2004) The dual identity of the group leader. *Group, 28*: 51–56. (2005) The two faces of the group therapist. *International Journal of Group Psychotherapy*, 55: 107–187.

Chapter 4: (2006) The Three R's of group: Resistance, rebellion and refusal. *International Journal of Group Psychotherapy, 56*: 259–284.

Chapter 5: (2010) On resistance. *International Journal of Group Psychotherapy. 60.*

Chapter 6: (2005) Truth seeking and abandonment: group processes of resistance, rebellion and refusal. *Group, 29*: 453–467; (2010) Anarchy. *Group Analysis, 43.*

Chapter 7: (2005) Discussion of "A sinking depression." In: L. Motherwell & J.J. Shay (Eds.), *Complex Dilemmas in Group Therapy—Pathways to Resolution*. New York: Bruner-Routledge, pp. 144–147; (2007) On refusal. *International Journal of Group Psychotherapy, 57*: 419–449.

Chapter 8: (2009) Modes of leadership: Diplomacy, integrity, sincerity, and authenticity. In: R.H. Klein, C.A. Rice, & V.L. Schermer (Eds.), *Leadership In A Changing World* (Chapter one). Lanham, MD: Lexington Books, pp. 29–47; (2010) Modes of therapeutic engagement: Part I: Diplomacy and integrity. *International Journal of Group Psychotherapy, 60*: 1–28; (2010) Modes of therapeutic engagement: Part II: Sincerity and authenticity. *International Journal of Group Psychotherapy, 60:* 29–58.

British Library Cataloguing in Publication Data

A C.I.P. for this book is available from the British Library

ISBN-13: 9781855757745 (pbk)

Typeset by Vikatan Publishing Solutions (P) Ltd., Chennai, India

I dedicate this volume to the members of
our Monday, Tuesday, and Wednesday psychotherapy groups,
past and present. Each member, each session,
and each group is special, evolving in unique ways,
in precious moments of time that cannot
be replaced or recaptured.

CONTENTS

FOREWORD

Resistance, Rebellion and Refusal in Groups

For over four decades, Richard Billow Ph.D. has been associated with the Derner Institute of Advanced Psychological Studies at Adelphi University in Long Island, New York. Clinical Professor and Director of the Post-Graduate Program in Group Therapy, he has shared the intellectual vitality of his seminars with many group analysts. A Member of the American Group Psychotherapy Association, the Eastern Group Psychotherapy Society, and the International Association for Group Psychotherapy and Group Process, Dr. Billow is a renowned teacher of psychoanalysis and group analysis at Universities, Institutes and Societies throughout the world. Fellow group analyst and psychoanalyst, he has brought his new book *Resistance, Rebellion and Refusal in Groups* to the New International Library of Group Analysis. As the Editor of NILGA, I am especially pleased to have been involved with the publication of this book.

In conjunction with its companion volume *Relational Group Psychotherapy: From Basic Assumptions to Passion*, Billow (2003) has made a major contribution to the theory of psychoanalytical group therapy, and in particular to the development of the relational perspective in various clinical modalities. He appreciates the shift that has occurred in psychoanalysis and group analysis from attempts to decipher the myth of Oedipus to attempts to answer the riddle of the Sphinx. This has informed his struggles to learn more about the heart of the human condition, which is always a function of what group analysts call our 'location' within the social, cultural and political worlds. This has, in turn, provoked further efforts to elucidate more valid ways of living within established orders. This existentialist project is not only a matter of resisting the ritualised and imitative understandings proffered by and through interpretations within the traditional and often idealised hierarchy of the psychoanalytical dyad; it is also a matter of courageous working through in the countertransference. On this basis it is inevitable that established orders might be both understood and changed.

As his own man, Richard Billow has made a personal integration of the work of Bion and Foulkes, Kernberg and Kohut, and a number of psychoanalysts and group analysts. On this basis, he is concerned here with the non-reductive exploration of what he has termed diplomacy, integrity, sincerity and authenticity as component processes in the four modes of therapeutic interaction. He brings into focus nothing less than the common humanity of therapist and patient. Driven to seek a deeper understanding of our unwillingness and inability to suffer the psychic pain associated with the discovery of social-psychological truths, and, hence, to achieve insight into them, he may well have suggested a potential theory of phases of group development involving the continuing and spiralling shifts and oscillations from insight to action filtered through the ability to endure truth.

Richard reminds us of the importance of 'combined' individual and group therapy. It is often overlooked that in the same way that we should not conceptualise individuals as opposed to their groupings, but instead recognise that they are interdependent on one another, we should not couch debates about the validity of group therapy in terms of group therapy as opposed to individual therapy, but instead recognise the specific modality of individual and group therapy combined. Although during the 1960s and 1970s many of us practiced in this way, combined therapy has been neglected in the United Kingdom and throughout Europe. Continuous, long term twice weekly group analysis, on the one hand, and more intensive 'block therapy', on the other, have become the most commonly practiced forms of group analysis, especially in connection with the training of group analysts. Combined therapy is difficult to manage, finding suitable times for meeting all the members of the group individually as well as the group as a whole, allowing for variation in the ability of the patients to meet their financial needs and responsibilities, extensive training required in individual and group work, etc. Combined therapy also challenges the capacities of the therapist to be both loyal and neutral in his dealings with each and every individual patient with whom he has forged unique relationships, while being full engaged with the group as a whole. Being able and willing to work with considerable transparency is absolutely essential. Yet, combined therapy offers powerful clinical experiences. It challenges the narcissism of being special through having to acknowledge the necessity to share, and deserves renewed recognition and appreciation.

More personally, I acknowledge with pleasure the benefits that I have had from being in relationship with Richard. He is a stimulating critic who always focuses on finding the best in people and their ideas. I am proud to have him as a friend and colleague. His work illustrates the value of the open and honest negotiation of co-constructed, social psychological truths, both within life and within the clinical encounter. I would, however, be very much remiss if I did not at least mention that Richard is an inspired collector of modern paintings, sculptures and artefacts, and that if he did not heed the call of his clinical practice, he would be better known as an aficionado of the slopes of both Northern and Southern hemispheres, than as an inspired clinician, teacher and author.

Earl Hopper, Ph.D.
28 June 2010

Billow, R.M. (2003). *Relational Group Psychotherapy: From Basic Assumptions to Passion*. London: Jessica Kingsley Publishers.

Billow, R.M. (2009). Editor of Special Issue: Models of Combined Psychotherapy: Current Trends in Theory and Technique. *The International Journal of Group Psychotherapy*, 59, 1.

ACKNOWLEDGMENTS

Charles Raps, PhD, has shared the adventure of this project from its inception, which involved patiently listening to my difficulties in pinning down the concept of "authenticity," my dissatisfactions with traditional usages of the term, "resistance," and my conviction that something as yet undefined was going on in our struggles with our patients and groups, and within ourselves, to bring "truth" to experience. He has debated, clarified, and contributed to the ideas of *Resistance, Rebellion and Refusal in Groups: The 3Rs* and to the cogency of the clinical examples. As with my companion volume, *Relational Group Psychotherapy: From Basic Assumptions to Passion*, Dr. Raps has served as brilliant "uber-editor," and few words and fewer thoughts have escaped improvement from his meticulous reading and creative responses to each draft of the manuscript.

Earl Hopper, PhD, editor of the New International Library of Group Analysis, has been an intellectual lodestar, one who takes group and students of group seriously. I have profited immensely from his longstanding interest and involvement in my work. As he did for *Relational Group Psychotherapy,* he has provided challenging feedback, stimulating ideas, and perused the final manuscript carefully. I am honored by his invitation to join the distinguished list of authors of the New Library and appreciate his shepherding its publication by Karnac.

Les Green, PhD, has been an ongoing source of support and guidance. As editor of the *International Journal of Group Psychotherapy*, he oversaw the drafts and revisions of the *Journal* articles that form the backbone of *The 3 Rs*. I thank him for supplying first-rate anonymous reviewers for my submissions, for organizing their helpful and often lengthy evaluations, and for providing his own.

I appreciate the ease in working with Oliver Rathbone, the publisher of Karnac Books, Lucy Shirley, Publishing Assistant, and James Darley, our copy editor.

The following organizers and organizations provided opportunities to sharpen my work, by inviting me to present to colleagues and students from different subcultures and cultures: David Scharff MD and Jim Poulton PhD, *International Psychotherapy Institute*, in Salt Lake City and New York; Robert Weber PhD, *Northeastern Society for Group Psychotherapy*, Boston; Robert Schulte MSW and Molly Donovan PhD, Mid-*Atlantic Group Psychotherapy Society*, Bethesda, MD; Virginia, *Widener University*, Philadelphia; Pnina Rappoport PhD and Suzi Shoshani MSW, *Imagine 2006 Conference*, Tel Aviv and Jerusalem; Esther Stone MSW, *International Association of Group Psychotherapy*, an energetic force behind the conferences in Sao Paulo, Rome, and elsewhere; Pirkko Grönlund PhD and Marja Turtiainen MSW, *Group Psychotherapy Association of Finland*, Helsinki; Chris Garner PsyD and Rudy Troyer LCSW, *Louisiana Group Psychotherapy Society*, New Orleans; Erwin Lebner, Nikolaj G. Neznanov, and Maria Ammon, *World Association for Dynamic Psychiatry* and the *German Academy for Psychoanalysis*, Munich, Germany; and Lars Bo Jørgensen, *Group Analytic Society* and the *Institute of Group Analysis*, Copenhagen, Denmark.

The Eastern Group Psychotherapy Society and the American Group Psychotherapy Association have been durable host organizations, providing a community of receptive colleagues, stimulating annual meetings, and scholarly journals to strive for.

I thank my colleagues for inviting my participation in their book and conference projects: Drs. Malcolm Pines, Earl Hopper, Martin Livingstone, Jerome Gans, Robert Klein, Cecil Rice, Andrew Eig, Bernard Frankel, Lise Motherwell, Josepth Shay, Jeffrey Kleinberg,

Sharan Schwartzberg, Robi Friedman, and Vic Schermer, M.A. and Leyla Navaro, M.A.

The Derner Institute of Advanced Psychological Studies of Adelphi University has been an intellectual and emotional home. I have benefited from over 40 years of interaction with my colleagues and generations of students in the doctoral program of clinical psychology and in the postgraduate programs of psychoanalysis and psychotherapy. Directing our postgraduate group program has given me access to an especially creative and vocal population of candidates, and they have been responsive participants as I presented my ideas and applied them to our experiential learning groups. Drs. Melinda Blitzer, Andrew Eig, Holly Gotta, Heather Perrin-Boyle, Mark Sammons, and Lisa Stern, and Elizabeth O'Connor, MSW, have collaborated on our presentations at annual meetings of the American Group Psychotherapy Association. I have had cooperation and support from respectively, the former and present dean of the Derner Institute, Drs. Robert Mendelsohn and Jean Chin, and the former and present director of the postgraduate programs, Drs. Joseph Newirth and Mary Beth Cresci.

Throughout the lengthy process of writing, and rewriting, my wife Elyse has provided a loving, supportive home environment, while maintaining her own clinical practice and activities and still managing to be a good reader of my work. Our children Jennifer, David, and Brette, son-in-law Bryon, and granddaughter Jordyn Semantha, lift spirits and keep scholarly and clinical ambitions in their proper perspective.

PROLOGUE

Making a "hat"

However you live, there's a part of you
Always standing by, mapping out a sky.
Finishing the hat.
Starting on a hat.
Finishing the hat.
Look I made a hat
Where there never was a hat.

—Lyrics by Stephen Sondheim,
Sunday in the Park with George

For me, the urge to write, like an urge in psychotherapy—arises as a response to a feeling of irritation. Something troubles me that I cannot quite identify. It begins to occupy my mental space, and I find myself "standing by," even when I am otherwise and enjoyably engaged. Irritation, like any kind of pain, concentrates on itself, pulling its owner away from one kind of lived-in moment to another. The type of irritation I am describing is not altogether unpleasant, a demanding background noise—seductive, but also isolating. When I am fortunate, I "map out" a source of my irritation, and as

I give it some attention, it begins to find its own being. With relief, I reconnect to others.

In writing *Relational Group Psychotherapy: From Basic Assumptions to Passion,* I made a "hat." Yet, again the siren and an irritating question: What is key in relational group psychotherapy, that is, in the vision of relational group psychotherapy to which I aspire? I latch upon the word, "authenticity," and try to let it breathe, to see how and if it develops with nuance and complexity.

If authenticity is key to group theory and process, how to approach and describe its manifestations, oppositions, contradictions, and also, its component intersubjective elements? "I trust you totally, but I can't believe what you are saying," a patient reports. "I have a sickening, pit-in-the-stomach feeling. I don't know if it's because I am telling the truth or lying" reports another. And from a third individual: "This is your job as the therapist; how do I know how you really feel?"

These communications—known to all of us as therapists and patients—alerted me that the concept of authenticity could not be easily separated from notions of truth/falsity, integrity, sincerity, and credibility. I needed to understand how these intersubjective elements fluctuated in the immediacy of the clinical situation, affecting the group member, therapist, and group-as-the-whole. If *resistance,* as classically understood, is involved, does it reside primarily in the speaker, the listener, their interaction, or also in the sociopolitical context of the professional relationship?

I continued to think about psychotherapy, and like many of our contemporaries, I was dissatisfied with conceptualizations of the "they and me" sort, formulations emphasizing pathology and the regressive potentials of individuals who become our patients and of the groups that they form. Racker (1968) decimated the "healthy/mature analyst-neurotic/infantile patient" myth. In hyphenating "transference-countertransference," contemporary psychoanalysis has found a common relational ground. We now think of intersubjective interactions, ongoing ego activities (Bird, 1972) that function on varying levels of awareness/nonawareness, contributing to the therapeutic alliance and meaning-making, and to the circumlocutions, enactments, ruptures, and impasses, avoidable and not.

I am committed to the modality of combined dyadic-group treatment (*Chapter one*). It is foundational in my thinking, therapeutic mindset, and professional identity, and hence informs the writing of *Resistance, Rebellion and Refusal in Groups: The 3 Rs*. Combined psychotherapy is a logical extension and natural fit with relational theory, given its emphasis on destabilizing absolutist thinking, reducing patient-analyst asymmetry, and fostering a collaborative truth-seeking process (O'Leary & Wright, 2005).

The combined modality extends the field of psychoanalytic observation, participation, and interpretation beyond the dyad. Group members are witnesses to and collaborators in combined treatment, and their voices may be as authoritative, informed, and psychologically evolved as their therapist's. Even more than dyadic relational psychotherapy, combined treatment advances Racker's (1968) call for "social reform," and the demolishment of the traumatogenic "patriarchal order" and "inequality in the analyst-analysand society" (p. 132).

The "Bionion shift" in contemporary psychoanalytic theory—placing the drive to know (*K*) in a position of pre-eminence, even over drives of love and hate (*L* and *H*)—continues to influence both my formulations and how I address them. Bion's ideas regarding the structure of thought, the role of affect, the inexorable compromise between truth and falsity, and the tension between conservative and creative social forces, add metapsychological and clinical depth to relational group psychotherapy.

Bion's work imprinted a mode of clinical thinking in which I attempt to evaluate clinical communications, my own as well as others', in terms of their level of development and their use or purpose in establishing, questioning, investigating, challenging, or obstructing meaning. Bion concluded that despite the human need to become aware of emotional truth, which spurs growth and development, the individual and group function with falsity, producing barriers to knowledge. In groups, small and large, falsity motivates conformist thinking and behavior and the development of rigid, stultifying "*Establishments*" (Bion's (1970) term). He thus concentrated on the negative and pathological aspect of falsity, and its relationship to lying and the liar.

But I am suspicious of binary, either/or judgments. I saw that falsity could be removed from its associations only with pathology or principles of right and wrong. Falsity can be seen as a necessary and protective device in thinking and communication. It is too simple merely to contrast truth with falsity, and to limit the realm of authenticity to the former.

Conversely, certain truths, and certain modes of truth seeking, may be experienced as destructive to the self or to the other, and so not beneficial. Even when factual, truth may be challenged as misleading, irrelevant, or inappropriate, a buffer against genuine mental interaction, and hence, false.

I came to think of many forms of interpersonal behaviors—including those involved in psychotherapy and in group organization and process—as a series of moves and countermoves to express, redirect, modify, or block the search for truth. With this vantage, I began to re-think the concept of resistance, which tends to be utilized as an umbrella term, encompassing nonconscious[1] processes, transference, stages of group development, distortions, and psychopathology. Resistance has specific pathways, and all-important adaptive and social contexts, intersubjective dimensions not explicitly developed by Freud, Bion, or other psychoanalytic and group theorists.

While pre-rational, irrational, and nonconscious factors are always involved, of course, "resistance" may refer to the response to the the person, manner, or group process of conveying truth, and which truth is the proposed object of interest, rather than truth-seeking itself. It is useful to distinguish among different strategies and different motives to forestall or otherwise challenge the process of developing emotional awareness. I thought the terms "rebellion" and "refusal" brought out these crucial facets of therapeutic and group relationships. Such factors need to be examined and negotiated, segregated from overweening preconceptions, assumptions, and clinical approaches traditionally associated with "resistance."

Individuals and groups resist, and also rebel against or refuse to participate in truth-seeking for all sorts of motives, including some that are quite reasonable and others that are typical of the therapeutic

---

[1]Throughout this volume, I use the term "nonconscious" rather than "unconscious," to avoid structure metaphors and to accommodate theories that have expanded upon the repression-based model of mental organization (e.g., Bion, 1965; Bromberg, 2001; Bucci, 2001). As Strachey (1957, p. 165) reminds us, the word "unconscious" does not have a German equivalent, and is best understood as a passive participle. The apposite translation of Freud's *bewusst* and *unbewusst* are, respectively, "consciously known" and "not consciously known."

situation. Hence, *resistance, rebellion* and *refusal: the 3 Rs,* intrapsychic and interpersonal regulators, through which we negotiate and make palatable versions of truth. *Rebellion* and *refusal* may function as pathways of *resistance,* qualitatively distinct phenomena, or both, depending on the context and point of view.

The therapist, in striving for authenticity, functions with curiosity: a genuine interest to learn about ourselves and others and the relationships we create in the dyadic, group, or combined setting of our practices. Still, we are not sole arbiters of truth and are not the only or necessarily the best judge of ourselves or our effects on others. We bear the tension between truth and falsity, and like any other individual or group member, we can understand a great deal about another, oneself, and the group at large, without pursuing that which is painfully immediate and most meaningful. Not only do we remain in conflict regarding pursuing truth, we respond characteristically and countertransferentially when experiencing opposition to our own truth-seeking needs.

Modes of therapeutic engagement (*Part III*) that emphasize *diplomacy, integrity,* or *sincerity* establish and reaffirm our bonding with, but also separation from, others. In being professional we take on different, seemingly contradictory roles, such as conservator or challenger of group process. At the same time, the relational psychotherapist eschews role-playing, and reaffirms the personal element, which includes attending to our own conflicts involving truth seeking and acknowledging unavoidable dynamics of falsity. *Authenticity* involves "passion" (Billow, 2002; 2003c), then becoming informed by tolerating and integrating one's most basic and powerful feelings. It is the ideal that the group therapist may achieve and foster with varying degrees of constancy and success.

The plan of the book

The subject of this book involves three *Rs*—a tightening of the definition of *resistance* and reorganization of related phenomena under the headings *rebellion* and *refusal* —followed by an examination of four relational modes or stances the therapist may assume: *diplomacy, integrity, sincerity* and *authenticity*. My own thinking, insofar as it represents a contribution, both of original ideas and a clearer exposition as well as modification of some of Bion's, has grown and developed from my experiences as a combined therapist. Hence, my book begins with an argument for combined psychotherapy. I believe that the richest expression of psychoanalysis as a body of knowledge, a relational discipline and a clinical practice, is most fully realized in combined therapy. I have learned and grown both professionally and personally from the many patients who have concurred that their own developmental and reparative paths involved the experience of combined therapy.

As in *Relational Group Psychotherapy: From Basic Assumptions to Passion,* I confer on the therapist's emotional experience a primary influence upon the formation and evolution of the group structure, culture, and process. The group therapist remains in the center of the action. Hence, I begin in *Chapter one* by exploring the mindset of the group therapist, how the commitment to combined psychotherapy radically influences what the group therapist thinks and does.

In *The 3 Rs,* I bring greater emphasis to what I believe to be the essential therapeutic task: to address the hunger for truth, an appetite stimulated by the group itself (*Chapters two* and *three*). How various members assess and respond to the drive for truth, in the immediate context of the group, creates the clinical phenomena of *resistance, rebellion* and *refusal.*

Part II explores the theory, technical considerations, and clinical applications of the *3 Rs*: *resistance, rebellion* and *refusal. Chapter four* introduces concepts and provides a clinical example of how the pathways may operate in interaction. *Chapters five, six,* and *seven* explore each construct separately and in depth. *Part III,* integrating the insights from *Parts I* and *II,* considers specific courses of therapeutic intervention: *diplomacy, integrity, sincerity,* and *authenticity* (*Chapter eight*). The *Appendices* hopefully will supply useful summaries of essential ideas.

All chapters include case examples, to illustrate how the contemporary psychotherapist may disentangle and address the relational modes I describe. The chapters concentrate on key players and key group interactions or phases. Differences are acknowledged and respected, the attempt being to "normalize" what appears to be deviant by empathic understanding and by universalizing diversity, and showing how it may apply to all members (the leader included). In my opinion, the therapist always is implicated, and hence, technical issues and decisions regarding issues of "truth," intersubjectivity, presentation of self, and self-disclosure remain a continuous therapeutic preoccupation.

I suspect all formulations and case presentations in some ways are retrofitted to the personality of the formularizer. Therefore, I leave it to the reader to decide if my concepts, categories, and clinical illustrations provide useful rationales, or self-deceptive rationalizations (or both), for the theoretical and therapeutic stances I have adopted. My "hats" fit my head. Most likely, they will need altering to fit yours.

Chapter descriptions

Part I: Truth and falsity in group

Chapter one: The Group Never Leaves the Room: The Radical Nature of Combined Psychotherapy. I consider the combination of individual and group psychoanalytic psychotherapy to be radical, that is, foundational and primary in the mindset, stance, and identity of the committed psychotherapist. The therapist's commitment in thought and action to combined practice influences all aspects of professional life. It imbues my thinking, my "'truths" —the theories, formulations, and case examples in *The 3 Rs*.

Hence, the radical: the idea as well as the shared history of combined psychotherapy are rooted within the complexities and intensities of the multiple transference-countertransferences, intrapsychic defenses, interpersonal strategies, and inevitable enactments of all members of one's practice. Combined individual-group psychoanalytic therapy is a natural fit and extension of contemporary relational psychoanalytic theory and practice.

Case anecdotes illustrate (a) the psycho-social impact of *Establishment* psychoanalysis and Group Analysis on the therapist practicing combined treatment; (b) the intertwining of dyadic-group experience on manifest and latent content, inference making, and interpretation; (c) how the "group" never leaves the room, i.e., the salutary effects on the therapist's thinking and clinical relationships of the idea as well as the reality of group, even with those patients not exposed to combined treatment; and (d) resistances specific to combined treatment.

Chapter two: Truth, Significance, and the Role of Falsity. The universal tension and juxtaposition between truth seeking and truth evasion are explored in a contemporary relational context. Bion's key concept of "*psi*," or psychic evasiveness, refocuses group theory, supplementing intra- and inter-psychic perspectives with sociopolitical analysis. To some extent the psychotherapy group exists as a political *Establishment* (Bion, 1970) and thus corresponds to *psi*.

Using three illustrative case examples, I consider the nature and nurture of truth evasion, along with the purposes it serves in individual and group psychology and the forms it may take in group psychotherapy. The therapist must maintain a disruptive-creative influence on group process (*Chapter three*), but like other group members, he or she instead may accept and promote falsity. Whereas the therapist ensures the integrity of the culture, the members, and not solely the therapist, break up old relational patterns and experiment with new ones. Dynamic, evolving groups aid the leader in life-affirming truth seeking, eventually challenging *Establishment* tendencies and exposing falsity.

Chapter three: The Two Faces of the Group Therapist. The group therapist wears two faces: spokesperson of the *Establishment* and spokesperson of significant truth. To run vital groups, these two roles of group leadership must stand in dialectic relationship to each other. The therapist introduces principles and practices that normalize group relations and provide a sense of cohesion, continuity, and regularity. However, to be constructive and promote significant new truth, the group therapist must also be deconstructive, and encourage and support the group's questioning and challenging the very principles and practices that he or she asserts. A case example illustrates how the group leader is also two-faced in another sense of the term, since he or she may be false and insincere—or perceived as such—when being either the conservator or challenger of group process and culture.

Part II: Resistance, rebellion and refusal

Chapter four: Introducing the 3 Rs of Relational Group Psychotherapy. As with my earlier volume, my intention in *The 3 R's* is to provide clarifying concepts, without suggesting certainty or finality in assessing self, other, and the group interactions. Indeed, in making distinctions and introducing complexity, one calls attention to—without necessarily reconciling—the ambiguous, multifaceted nature of individual and group psychology.

The 3 Rs describe three basic patterns of interaction—*resistance, rebellion* and *refusal*. These conventional terms are shown to operate also outside the domain of pathology, encompassing analyst and analysand in situations of potential discovery, debate, independent thinking, and fresh modes of relating. Individuals resist, rebel, and refuse for all sorts of motives, including some that are reasonable and others that are typical of the therapeutic situation.

Resistance remains an umbrella term, and I think it is better to use it in a specific sense: resisting nonconscious (truths) from being developed and becoming conscious. I propose utilizing the terms *rebellion* and *refusal* for alternative relational strategies. As stated earlier, *rebellion* and *refusal* may function as specific pathways of *resistance*, or qualitatively distinct phenomena, or both together, depending on the context and point of view. A case example illustrates the shifting, often overlapping interactions among the three modes and their subcategories.

Chapter five: Resistance. As a basic, and ongoing, mental process, *resistance* always involves symbolizing. Stimulated by psychosocial circumstance, resistance accumulates internally and interpersonally, often preceded by unspecific and unpredictable sources of arousal: not only nonconscious, pre-rational, and irrational, but also conscious, environmental, interpersonal, and sociopolitical. In the human struggle to process and integrate difficult and often painful emotional truth, resistance develops, emerges, and evolves; it is communicated and understood within relational contexts.

I present five assertions about resistance. Resistance (a) regulates the development, expression, and usefulness of emotional truth; (b) is motivated by the basic conflict between thinking and not thinking; (c) reveals interplay between truth and falsity; (d) involves multiple levels and types of intersubjective interplays ("enactments"), including transference; and (e) is not "lifted," but rather works towards truth and is continuous.

Chapter six: Rebellion. While *rebellion* represents a mental attitude, it eventuates in various strategies of social action differentiated by their processes and outcomes: *defiance, secession/exile, anarchy*, and *revolution*.

Defiance represents a type of palpable and phasic pressure exerted against ongoing process and content. In *secession/exile*, reciprocal allegiances and attachments are threatened or ruptured. *Anarchy* refers to psychic interludes of breakdown of core defenses and established modes of feeling and thinking, which may be a consequence of effective group process. However, certain groups and individuals cannot adequately tolerate or work through turbulent experience, and anarchy may endanger the group or individual members. In *revolution*, rebellious premises and solutions aim to bring a group, subgroup, or individual member to a new phase, which may be positive and/or negative.

In each situation, it is important to understand the core beliefs that spur rebellion. Especially relevant is the therapist's role, both in contributing to and negotiating the group or group member's rebellion, and in instigating one's own. In a well-working group, conflicts of therapeutic assumptions and values are continual; uncovering and negotiating incongruities in tactics, pragmatics, and goals are essential aspects of group process.

Chapter seven: Refusal. *Refusal* manifests a willful nonparticipation in offering or responding to material that can be symbolized. All communication has an element of refusal, which occurs at various levels of persistence, intensity, and legitimacy. Clinical examples are provided to discriminate *refusal* from *resistance*, and to describe three categories of mental and group experience: (a) *refusal to perceive external experience*; (b) *refusal to think about what one knows*; (c) *refusal to think about what one does not know*.

Therapeutic impasses may relate to limitations of the therapist's creativity and flexibility in thinking about and dealing with *refusals*, including one's own. To move group relationships (psychic and interpersonal) forward and expand the boundaries of what can be thought about and talked about, the group leader needs to encourage thinking about refusal, yet also convey respect for the reasons behind it. Not only are our words important in the process, but also the therapist's attitude and success in achieving a mode of authentic connection that lessens the anticipation of intrapsychic or interpersonal pain.

At times, *refusal* transforms into *resistance*, as members put into words, action, and/or dream imagery the motives for characteristic patterns of refusal. At other times, *refusal* leads to *rebellion* and a renegotiation of the therapeutic contract, stated and/or enacted. Some *refusals* persist; *refusal* remains an option for therapist and all group members at various degrees of legitimacy.

Part III: Modes of therapeutic interaction

***Chapter eight: The four modes of therapeutic interaction*.** The topic of *Part III* (*Chapter eight)* concerns strategies of therapeutic discourse, four relational modes of speaking and listening, adopted with and without awareness: *diplomacy, integrity, sincerity,* and *authenticity*. They inform the therapist in his or her efforts to seek, confront, and modify truth. The four modes are offered as conceptual tools, to help the therapist build therapeutic relationships, respond to challenges and impasses, and advance group process and insight. They are navigated to cement bonding, build trust, allow troubled relationships to evolve and resolve, and strengthen the abilities to think and relate.

Diplomacy is concerned with the uses and allocations of power, in establishing and maintaining relationships and alliances. In being diplomatic, the therapist is both political and strategic: trying to influence the group to use its power in cooperative interrelationships rather than to express power in forms of retaliatory *rebellions* or *refusals*. Patience—timing and tact—would seem to characterize diplomacy; however, spontaneity, emotional openness, transparency (self-disclosure), and confrontation may be effective, even requisite, in bringing meaning to the psychotherapeutic situation.

In engaging through the mode of *integrity*, salience resides in the therapist's moral and ethical principles, in reference to his or her professional, political, ethnic and religious affiliations. Integrity involves strength and consistency, but also flexibility. Judgments of integrity interface and may conflict with ethical and moral beliefs of certain cultures and subcultures of the group participants and of the larger social matrix. More often than we may appreciate, no one set of rules or principles can do justice to all group circumstances, and the therapist must negotiate conflicting systems of ethics.

Sincerity is categorical—either you are sincere or not. In my conceptualization, sincerity derives from the developmental stage of idealization, preceding the full-fledged working through of the "depressive position," as described by M. Klein. In this phase prior to emotional maturity, others are capable of being recognized and preserved mentally as loved objects. However, splitting rather than mature thinking remains prominent as a mode of organizing experience ("either/or"; "good/bad" thought and feeling).

In contrast with *sincerity, authenticity* represents the achievement of working through the depressive position, its hallmark being the experience of ambivalent feelings while maintaining a balanced and humane outlook. Sincerity and authenticity can coexist, but authenticity monitors the expressions of sincerity such that idealizations and devaluations do not predominate. Authenticity involves mental integration of conflicting feelings, thoughts, wishes, and motives, directed to loved objects and also competitors, and even enemies. Translated into Bion's (1961) group terminology, sincerity remains wedded to "*basic assumption*" mentality while authenticity encompasses "*work group*" thinking as well.

The description of the four relational modes are accompanied by case examples from group therapy and extended with a political illustration from George W. Bush's presidency. *Diplomacy, integrity, sincerity,* and *authenticity* may be shown to operate or fail to operate in the relationship of political leaders to their groups.

PART I

TRUTH AND FALSITY IN GROUP

CHAPTER ONE

The group never leaves the room: The radical nature of combined psychotherapy

I consider the combination of individual and group psychoanalytic psychotherapy to be radical, that is, foundational and primary in the mindset, stance, and identity of the committed psychotherapist. It imbues my thinking and the theory and case examples in *The 3 Rs*. The combined modality actualizes many of the precepts of relational psychoanalysis, a movement Mitchell (1993) proclaimed "revolutionary," leading to a "paradigm difference" (Hoffman, 2006), and so, it is radical in that sense too.

Relational life involves a duality. The human being needs groups, and not only dyadic relationships, to secure a psychological identity, to organize and ground thinking, and to grow emotionally. But the tendency to establish organization and structure may lead to rigid customs, hierarchies of status and power, and conformity, what Bion (1970) referred to as a truth-avoiding *Establishment*. As I will explain in *Chapter three*, an effective leader wears two faces: conservator and revolutionary. He or she introduces principles and practices that normalize dyadic and group relations and provide a sense of cohesion, continuity, and regularity. Yet, to be constructive and seek the qualities of emotional truth that lead to growth, such an individual is also deconstructive, encouraging the individual and the group to question and challenge the very principles and practices that he or she asserts.

Combined treatment confronts and even subverts many of the conventions and conventional ideas of individual and group psychoanalytic psychotherapy. Destabilizing the theory, training, and practice of both *Establishment* psychoanalysis and Group Analysis, combined psychotherapy thus is radical in the sense of innovative and divergent, and warrants sustained attention from training institutions, journals, and clinical practitioners.

Toward a metadiscipline of combined psychoanalytic psychotherapy

The theory and practice of psychoanalytic psychotherapy preceded group psychotherapy. Likewise, most theorists and practitioners conceive of and recommend group psychotherapy following individual therapy. Of course, the natural sequence of the therapeutic relationship is first, individual, then group, since therapist and patient initially meet and assess each other in the dyadic setting. Whereas this sequence is both historical and clinically practicable, nothing inherent in theory or practice prohibits thinking holistically and moving toward a metadiscipline of combined psychoanalytic psychotherapy.

Combined psychotherapy is not "pure" psychoanalysis, as defined by such traditional extrinsic features (Gill, 1994) as the dyadic setting, session frequency, use of the couch, and so forth. Arguably, combined psychotherapy may be considered psychoanalytic, particularly if we accept that "the wide scope of the current forms of psychoanalytic therapy allows room for many ideas, which do not even have to be restricted to the field of psychoanalysis in the stricter sense" (Thoma & Kachele, 1994a, p. 188). Even the most classical of analysts acknowledged, "No patient has ever been analysed with a technique in which interpretations alone have been used" (Eissler, 1958, p. 223).

Freud himself introduced the possibility in describing the two intrinsic features of psychoanalysis; these are key factors also for psychoanalytically oriented practitioners of combined therapy. "The theory of psycho-analysis is an attempt to account for two striking and unexpected facts of observation which emerge whenever an attempt is made to trace the symptoms of a neurotic back to their sources in his past life: the facts of transference and of resistance. Any line of investigation which recognizes these two facts and takes them as the starting-point of its work has a right to call itself psycho-analysis" (Freud, 1914d, p. 16).

As a unique modality, combined psychotherapy is not merely the aggregate of its component forms, individual and group treatment. Its proponents consider it more potent in value and depth than individual psychoanalysis: It is a separate approach in its own right. In this volume, I present issues and considerations that hopefully will clarify its indications, contraindications, mechanisms of action, developmental stages, and techniques.

The traumatic history and ongoing loneliness of the combined psychotherapist

Neither *Establishment* Psychoanalysis nor Group Analysis embraces combined psychotherapy. Despite Freud's curiosity and writings about groups and group process, the idea of integrating group treatment into psychoanalysis—or psychoanalysis in group treatment—remains taboo in the respective psychoanalytic and Group Analytic Establishments. Their institutes do not include combined treatment in the course of training and certification.

In mainstream psychoanalysis, a "striking avoidance" of the topic and essential literature of small and large groups exists in the institutes (Kernberg, 2000), in national and international meetings (Schachter, 1988), and in the prominent journals. To give a recent example, in a Special Issue of *Psychoanalytic Psychology* (2006) entitled "The Relevance of Sigmund Freud for the 21st Century," none of the 16 articles considered combined treatment or group psychoanalysis. In the one article diverging from a traditional dyadic framework, Twemlow and Parens (2006) devised a model curriculum for psychoanalytic institutes to produce community psychoanalysts. They recommended an experience of group dynamics for their hypothetical candidates, following Bion's framework, assuring the reader that "it is not necessary to have many hours of such exposures since the regression in groups and their basic assumption can be produced in a group exercise of not more than two hours in length" (Twemlow & Parens, 2006, p. 447)!

While psychoanalysis proper holds the dyadic mode sacrosanct, Group Analysis franchises the group exclusively. Foulkes, the founder and leading theoretician of Group Analysis, attempted to derive conceptualizations from group theory and to eschew formulations from individual psychotherapy, which served "to blur the sharpness of our observation and distort it" (Foulkes & Anthony, 1957, p. 250). Group is "the ultimate primary unit of consideration, and the so-called inner processes in the individual are internalizations of the forces operating in the group to which he belongs" (Foulkes, 1971, p. 212).

But Foulkes also wrote that "group-analytic psychotherapy ... is a form of psycho-analytic psychotherapy, and its frame of reference is the group as a whole. Like all psychotherapy it puts the individual into the centre of its attention" (Foulkes, 1964, p. 39). Dalal (2000) excoriated Foulkes for not taking the group "seriously," to the extent to which he was not sufficiently group-centric. And indeed, while Foulkes suggested that individual analysis, if needed, take place after completion of group treatment, later in his career he practiced a "back door" combined approach. Group members were seen individually in turn, one per week, and so, approximately bi-monthly (Hobdell, 1991, p, 137).

Three anecdotes involving combined psychotherapy

Breaking taboo. During an international meeting, in which I served as leader of a supervisory group, a recent graduate of a European Group Analytic institute mentioned casually: "I have several clients in my practice I would love to put in group!" "You don't have room?" I inquired naively. The young caseworker, while respecting my "expert" status, responded incredulously: "You can't do that! Can you? We send our clients to other groups, when they're available." "'We?'" I asked, "'your agency?" "No, my training institute," he replied, and with some trepidation, which I understood as his fear of incriminating me, he inquired: "You put your individual clients in group?" I reassured him that there were other technical models that he could learn about and even consider utilizing, since there seemed to be no injunction from his employer against them. Still, I felt like the proverbial snake. Tempted now by *Knowledge* of (the existence of) combined psychotherapy, this young clinician no longer rested comfortably in his *Garden* of group analytic orthodoxy.

Exiled by my own psychoanalytic journals. During a five-year period I published eight articles in two prominent psychoanalytic journals, all of which were adapted and contributed to my book on relational group psychotherapy. After a suitable interval, I inquired of both editors whether they were considering the book for possible review. One editor did not respond, but the second cordially agreed to send *Relational Group Psychotherapy—From Basic Assumptions to Passion* to the journal's book editor. The latter individual informed me that the journal reviewed psychoanalytic books and it was not its custom to review books on group. He asked me to justify its possible inclusion, which I did. He then thanked me for sending a copy of the book, but broke off further correspondence. As in the previous example involving the Group Analysis graduate, I felt I had broken a taboo and now was *exiled* as a rebel (see *Chapter six*). Broadcasting the idea of combined psychoanalytic therapy defied institutional orthodoxy.

Fear of humiliation by the Establishment. A senior psychoanalyst invited a younger colleague to contribute a paper to a symposium on "Women and Anger." She was complimented by and interested in the offer to present at a major psychoanalytic conference. However, she was afraid to broach her idea, which was to explore transference-countertransference configurations of anger as they varied in her individual and group work. She was relatively comfortable acknowledging and exploring her responses to several "difficult" patients. But, could she disclose the reality of a combined practice to her respected colleague, the other panelists, and the audience of orthodox psychoanalytic practitioners?

Discussion

At the prospect of innovation and change, large groups such as psychoanalytic, political or religious organizations, may become "paranoiagenic" (Kernberg, 2000), and take conservative or counter-revolutionary stances (Bion, 1970). The psychotherapist practicing combined psychotherapy may possess a wider and more intensive scope of theory, training, and supervision, and a different set of experiences than the traditional psychoanalyst or group analyst. Still, we are not immune to a social context determined, to some extent, by oligarchic and authoritarian training and certifying Establishments.

At best, supported by like colleagues and inclusive organizations such as the AGPA or IAGP (International Association of Group Psychotherapy), we ally ourselves in professional subgroups. At worst, to avoid ostracism, we conceal the truth concerning an important aspect of our professional identity or find ourselves exiled in outgroups.

Brief literature review of combined psychotherapy

Given its short history, with the first paper published only 60 years ago (see Porter, 1993), combined psychoanalytic psychotherapy has an established system of theory and belief. Looking back almost two decades, when the last flurry of papers and symposia were presented on the subject of combined psychotherapy, we see the influence of ego psychology, the faith in diagnosis and developmental level, confidence in the existence of proper technique, and an assumption of clinical authority, even certainty.

While acknowledging the less than perfect fit, authors described with some confidence how the two modalities provided different points of access to psychological reorganization and growth. Individual psychotherapy allowed for a deeper intrapsychic and historical exploration, free association, and the opportunity to deal with shameful secrets; while group psychotherapy provided the arena for broad, interpersonal exploration, behavioral risk, and the exploration of a wide variety of transferences (Porter, 1993). Individual therapy invited "vertical transferences" to authority and parents, while group therapy promoted "horizontal transferences" to peers; sibling rivalry, envy, and jealousy—triangular transferences—may be prominent (Rutan & Stone, 2001).

The therapist's technical tasks of individual versus group therapy were conceptualized in terms of developmental stages. For example, regarding the oral stage: individual therapy provided object constancy and supported development of basic trust and security, while group therapy modified stranger anxiety and sensory overload. Anal sadistic impulses, repressed and unavailable in the individual treatment, to preserve the therapist, may be played out in group, wherein the therapist or other members may be perceived as totally bad. Dyadic therapy afforded privacy and safety for the exploration of Oedipal issues and sexuality without a group of competitors, while group recapitulated the drama of the family of origin, sibling rivalry, envy, and jealousy (Rutan & Alonso, 1982, pp. 268–269; also, Praper, 1997).

Diagnostic categories and other personality descriptors fueled recommendations for or against combined treatment (Bellak, 1980; Porter, 1993; Scheidlinger & Porter, 1980; Wong, 1979). The authors observed how combined treatment differentially influenced transference and the therapeutic alliance with patients at various level of ego development. Either setting could provide a "holding environment," or complementary positive pole, in which to contain the anxiety and negativity generated by the other setting. Usually however, individual therapy provided the safer context, for need gratification and/or emotional anchorage, and group, the challenging context, for confrontation of maladaptive behaviors and defense. When successful, group and individual therapy take on a growing reciprocity wherein each becomes a forum for exploring reactions to the other setting (Rutan & Alonso, 1982, p. 271).

Slavson and Schiffer (1975) advised that severely parentally deprived or overprotected children first required individual treatment before they could deal with multiple group relationships. Pfeifer and Spinner (1985) cautioned that the complexity of combined treatment could threaten children with impoverished egos, while enriching alliances with healthier children. Still, they found advantages in the use of combined therapy with "ego-impaired" children, in that primitive defenses, such as splitting, could be therapeutically corralled to manage an otherwise negative transference (and countertransference) and weak therapeutic alliance.

Regarding adult treatment, Caligor, Fieldsteel, and Brok (1984) recommended adding group only after certain traditional goals of individual therapy have been accomplished, e.g., personality integration, awareness of transference, and solid working alliance. Dissonance induced by two different modalities may overwhelm a patient's defenses. Some patients cannot tolerate competition for the primary object (Wong, 1979). Still, the consensus in this literature remained that, with the exception of "severe" cases, combined treatment was the treatment of choice for neurotic and characterological disorders (Porter, 1980; 1993).

Some authors appreciated group psychotherapy as a way out of therapeutic impasse, as when an adolescent patient exhibited inability to manage intense transferential feelings (Pfeiffer & Spinner, 1985, p. 17), or when both an alexithymic patient and the therapist found the individual sessions boring and unproductive (Swiller, 1988). However, adding group in these situations worked against Rutan and Alonso's (1982) admonition against making the "fundamental error" of adding another modality rather than resolving the "stuck" therapy within that relationship.

Discussion

In acknowledging the collective wisdom of these masterly papers, book chapters, and books, let us keep in mind the principle that our perceptions and thinking are based on preexisting ideas and theories, constructions of "truth," rather than direct apprehension of external reality (Gill, 1984). Sorting differences between dyadic and group psychotherapy may be a natural inclination and has appealing face validity, supported by clinical experience and self-report.

Rutan and Stone (2001), for example, described how each modality offers something that the other does not, and provides new information. While the patient's communications have relevance in both individual and group therapy, "nonetheless, some material clearly relates to one modality more than the other" (p. 208). I would amend their sensible observation to read: "some material *seems* to relate to one modality more than the other."

Informed by the realities of the clinician's limited knowledge and indeterminacy of the sources of perception, judgment, and action, contemporary psychoanalysis no longer assumes that the origin of our data resides "in" analysand or analyst. Psychic patterns that become actualized and particularized are rooted in the interaction, hence the hyphenated transference-countertransference. The clinical situation is even more ambiguous in combined therapy, since psychic data—transference, countertransference, recovery of trauma, regressive and progressive experience—may seem to originate with and refer to the dyad, the dyad-in-the-group, the whole group, its stage or process, the subgroups, and so forth.

The "radical" or basal concept sidesteps the either/or of dyadic versus group. The multi-dimensionality of combined therapy may be thought of in terms of the dynamics of the container-contained (Billow, 2000c; 2003b; c). All individuals and all dyads exert pressure on the group, and likewise, the group exerts pressure on the dyads and on the mentality of each member. Thus, dyadic as well as other subgroup relationships are nested and contained within the whole group (and vice-versa).

The two modalities of combined therapy may be thought of and experienced as dialogic, antagonistic, complementary, or hierarchic. Each idea exists at various times and perhaps simultaneously in the mind of the therapist and other group participants. One setting may appear manifestly as a place for nurture, while the other, for challenging the therapist, but we must not assume that the manifest behavior necessarily reflects in toto the state of psychic affairs. The converse relationship may exist in nonconscious[1] and pre-rational and irrational states of mind. The two modalities of combined psychotherapy exist in material reality, but what is significant, if not completely determinable, is how they remained both unified and split apart in psychic reality.

Clinical example: Data remain rooted in the combined psychotherapy

Tory (in group): "I told Richard [therapist] I need to leave group, I'm having another baby and I don't have time to keep all my individual sessions and drive out here for group. Besides, my husband has a new job and I can't count on his being home. Even though Richard didn't say anything, I know he wants me to stay in group, to keep a good customer."

Tory's group cohorts became alarmed: "How are you planning on feeding the baby?" "Why no time?" "Why don't you get a 'live-in' or more baby-sitting help so you don't have to rely on your husband coming home?"

---

[1]To repeat *footnote 1* that appeared in the *Prologue,* throughout this volume I use the term "nonconscious" rather than "unconscious," to avoid structure metaphors and to accommodate theories that have expanded upon the repression-based model of mental organization (e.g., Bion, 1965; Bromberg, 2001; Bucci, 2001). Strachey (1957, p. 165) reminds us that the word "unconscious" does not have a German equivalent, and is best understood as a passive participle. The apposite translation of Freud's *bewusst* and *unbewusst* are, respectively, "consciously known" and "not consciously known."

Tory: "Rich said all this to me, but it didn't sound 'analytic.' I feel he's just manipulating me. I can accept it when it is from you."

Another group member, Peter (sardonic): "You can't trust Rich, but you trust group, so you want to leave group and spend your time with him?"

Tory: "Yes, exactly. I can't tell what my mother is really thinking. She always has a goal in mind. Like she complains about my sister and brother not visiting her, and I hear the message that I should take better care of her. It makes me want to be close to her, have her all to myself, even though I'm mad at her for being untrustworthy."

Peter (playfully ironic): "I don't trust Rich either, he 'tattle-tells' on me. He knows when I'm bullshitting the group, and I don't see him privately."

Tory: "I trust him with you, but not with me."

In the individual sessions that followed, Tory did not bring up the group session or talk about her conflicts about continuing group, nor did I. I did not feel an impulse to nag or harass her; I had confidence that she would struggle with issues of trust-distrust when, where, and how she wanted to. Several weeks later a member asked: "So are you staying?"

Tory: "I didn't expect such a caring response. You people are so smart. I guess I better. I hired a baby-sitter. I'm going to deduct it from Rich's bill."

Discussion

The experience and expression of psychic reality comprise the true subject of our psychotherapeutic investigations. The underlying psychic invariants and their repetitive as well as creative transformations operate in the context of combined treatment. We aim our investigation at the locus of what seems fresh and salient. Multiple dimensions of experience, that is, nonconscious/conscious, individual/dyadic/group, intrapsychic/interpersonal, are simultaneously explored. Of course, some elements of psychic experience are discovered and understood only retrospectively, while others still remain out of our awareness.

The group session provided the *manifest* context for Tory and Peter, particularly, to articulate, explore, and partially repair (and hence transform) an invariant: the trauma of untrustworthy dependency. To some extent, each individual has experienced this invariant of failure of maternal provision, which some theorists have posited as necessary for reality testing (Freud), psychological separation (Winnicott), and the discovery of the self (Kohut). Given Tory's history of parental neglect and deceit, we would expect the "shadow" of bad (internal) objects to fall on all her interpersonal relations, impact on both her desire and fear, and constitute an important dimension of her (split) transferences to the therapist, other group members, and the whole group.

Striking was the relationship with "the therapist of the dyad," which left her in the predicament Peter described: longing to depend on an undependable object. She trusted "the therapist of the group" to provide for other members such as Peter, but not for herself. Even her professed trust in the group was contradicted by her surprise at its maternal quality: "I didn't expect such a caring response."

In parallel to Tory's response to me, I did not entirely trust her. While I respected her, I often felt skeptical in listening to Tory when she evaluated her therapy and verbalized feelings about me. I was thus alerted countertransferentially that Tory, in partial identification, could be acting out her internalized unreliable mother. This mother could not be trusted to convey truth: so often, she did not mean what she said, or say what she meant.

Was Tory seriously thinking of leaving group? I did not and do not know. Once Tory took the courageous step of bringing to group her ambivalent attachments (feelings, thoughts, fantasies) to me as the group leader and to the group itself, I felt no imperative to initiate further discussion in our individual meetings. Besides, she was not thinking of leaving me, her "untrustworthy" individual therapist. I waited to see how, and if, she would negotiate the two fantasy therapists, if indeed she was seriously considering leaving group.

To the extent of her identification with her unreliable mother, Tory could not trust her own mind sufficiently to develop truth, which would comprise a coherent view of the therapist and the combined psychotherapy. She maintained several part object relationships: with her group therapist, the therapist of the other group members, and her own one-on-one therapist. Peter, as a prominent group spokesperson, served as an object who could think—both rationally and irrationally—and hence represented a caring figure: a bellwether of psychic truth. Notice that productive psychic derivatives arise from group members such as Peter who are witnesses to, even when not actual participants in, their own combined treatment.

Suitability for combined psychotherapy

I put forth that individuals who are capable of any psychotherapeutic treatment, broadly defined, are suitable for combined psychotherapy, even if they require a brief introductory phase of treatment. Obviously, combined psychotherapy remains limited by the fit between patient and prospective group, and the availability of group in one's practice or clinical placement. The prospective member is evaluated with an eye to the composition of the group; the important variables include age, presenting symptoms, psychological sophistication, diagnosis, ego functioning (Brabender & Fallon, 1993), severity, and to the setting (e.g., private practice, clinic, or hospital).

The therapist's commitment to and comfort with combined treatment influence how he or she introduces the group idea and utilizes convincing interventions to ensure successful entry and ongoing treatment. Lacan put it thus: "It is ultimately the analyst's desire which operates in psychoanalysis" (cited in Rowan & Harper, 1999, p. 190). The combined therapist "desires" combined treatment, but not necessarily for all members of the practice. Willingness of the therapist to offer and the patient—who most often does not consider combined treatment when appearing for consultation—to accept group are key factors, of course, and both may be ambivalent about the prospect. Hence, it is important to analyze "the resistance to joining the group—in the patient and in me [the therapist]" (Grotjahn, 1993, p. 58). Also influencing the therapist are the values and standards promulgated by the body of work briefly summarized above—the group entry requirements of those of us who write and speak and are creating the "bibles" of the discipline of combined therapy.

The group never leaves the room: A radical view of combined therapy

The therapist's commitment in thought and action to the idea of the combined practice impacts all aspects of his or her professional life Hence, the "radical" or foundational: the idea as well as the shared history of the clinician's practice of combined psychotherapy are rooted within the complexities and intensities of the multiple transference-countertransferences, intrapsychic defenses, interpersonal strategies, and inevitable enactments of all individuals in treatment. That is, because the group, as idea as well as experienced reality, exists in the mind of the committed psychotherapist, perforce it enters into therapeutic "space." Hence, the group is always present in the consulting room.

Four clinical anecdotes: The group never leaves the room

Group is present in the initial interview

Planning on returning to her combined clinical practice after a ten-week maternity leave, a therapist received a telephone request for marital therapy. Her preference was to delay adding clinical hours. At the same time she was concerned about the potential of group dropouts. She dreaded the thought of having to rebuild her two groups, as after her last childbearing experience. Perhaps she should see the couple and assess their availability for combined treatment, one in each of her groups, which would be unlikely, although ideal. She also felt guilty for having a hidden agenda—for wanting to float the idea of group psychotherapy and hence entering the consultation possessing "memory and desire."

The therapist was able during the assessment to assuage her anxiety and turn need to clinical advantage. Armed with her knowledge of and experience with group process, she observed the couple's marital interaction and the ongoing interview also through a group lens. Every dyad exists as a group and exhibits, among other group phenomena, Bion's *basic assumptions* (Grotstein, 2003). Now she had joined the couple's group, and she could experience, in situ, their availability for work, i.e., for emotional thinking, which opposes every couple's tendency for *fight/flight*, *pairing*, and parasitic *dependency*.

Discussion

For the therapist who practices combined psychotherapy, it is perhaps inevitable that in the initial interview and further evaluations, the therapist considers the referral also in terms of group dynamics and for group potential. The prospective or ongoing therapeutic relationship is affected, whether or not an invitation to combined treatment is ever offered, or accepted.

The therapist carries the dual relationship although the patient refuses individual treatment

A downcast 33-year-old was referred by his former therapist, the latest who "had not helped me with my problems, my depression. He suggested group." Jack described a history of learning disabilities, parental dependence, and social withdrawal: "My parents were told I would never go to college. But I had the best tutors and I made it. Now I have an executive position in one of my father's companies. My father was my basketball coach. I got so good I was scouted. But I quit in college after I saw how much better the other guys were. I also have a sexual problem and usually back away."

Certainly, Jack was not the best candidate for one of my groups of high-performing professionals, most of whom were, or had been, in combined treatment. And, given what I took—and interpreted—as his longing for a "coach," I suggested continuing in individual psychotherapy, before launching into group. But after several more consultations, Jack refused to make another appointment and insisted: "I've done individual; I don't know why, I think a group could help and I could help other people too." I countered: "But we have a problem, your 'premature quititis'." He laughed, catching on to my neologism and countering my skepticism: "Come on, I don't quit everything. I'm a good worker; I have a lot of good buddies."

Somehow, I felt myself becoming one of them. I had discovered in our few meetings that he was not as concrete or unassertive as he presented himself, and I told him so. "If you join one of my groups, I'm not letting you get away with talking about your 'problems' without trying to understand them." "What do you mean?" he asked. "There you go again," I replied.

Jack actually seemed pleased by my therapeutically adversarial stance, which I brought to group. I left it to other members to bridge to Jack in a more accommodative fashion, and after awhile, I congratulated him on stirring up pity. The other members understood intuitively when I declared my *refusal* to play Jack's "helper," a parental role that had defeated him and his previous therapists. But the group served as my helper. Anchored by my perception that the veteran members had established a warm initial bond with Jack, I felt I had the *diplomatic* (*Chapter eight*) leeway to be confrontational without alienating Jack or unduly disrupting group process. (I discuss this case further in *Chapter seven, Refusal*).

Discussion

The therapist derives information from every available source. In particular, the therapist maintains a dyadic relationship with each member of the group. Sometimes this relationship exists both within the group and in one-on-one sessions. Nonetheless, with those group patients who are not also in individual therapy, the dyadic relationship exists, as one among the many subgroups of the whole group. The group observes these relationships, and may provide counterpoint useful to the therapist's interventions, which are now nested in and so contained by the combined context.

The therapist carries the dual relationship although the patient refuses group psychotherapy

Reported in supervision: (a) "I lose interest in those patients who aren't also involved in group. I think of my groups as my family, and until patients are in a group, I don't feel we are really engaged." (b) "I get angry and feel rejected when a patient refuses my invitation to join one of my groups. I told one patient that if he did not at least try group for three months, I would not see him." (c) "I stopped haggling with that patient who insisted that he wasn't interested in my group. So I said: 'Look, I'm not going to fight you to the death at this time, but I'm going to keep bringing it up because I think it is in your best interests and if you come to the group for awhile, I think you will agree'."

Discussion

The therapist proposes what he or she believes to be an optimal therapeutic program, and is *refused*, perhaps for valid reasons, e.g., competing time commitments, or unsatisfactory prior group experience. Underlying *resistances*—to the extent to which they are implicated—such as involving anxiety, defensive structure, and conscious and nonconscious attitudes and fantasies—are not sufficiently resolved, despite competent analytic work.

In my opinion, the impact of the *refusal* has greater significance for the therapist than for the patient, who may maintain disinterest. The therapist still values the group idea and may even establish a fantasy relationship with the patient-in-group. At the same time, the therapist may experience and revisit feelings of sorrow, disappointment, rejection, anger, and recrimination towards the patient or oneself for the rejection of combined treatment. These were the feelings expressed in examples (3a) and (3b).

In my ongoing dyadic treatments, I continue to think about group, and utilize my fantasy of the patient-in-group, such as by speculating what the patient would learn by allowing the experience. For example: "You aren't nearly as 'paranoid' as you claim as your excuse for not joining. I'd bet you would take to group immediately, and they would take to you." Or, "I think you would find yourself not so alone, and gain confidence in group." And finally, "The group is a safe 'lab' to practice what we've been talking about here." The group idea—that is, the idea of group, and of joining a group—becomes a type of intervention, an aspect of an interpretation. And thus, a symbolic or fantasy combined psychotherapy is nested within the dyadic psychotherapies.

Of course, the therapist must meter references to and urging for group, so as not to fight, hector, or otherwise manipulate the patient. The therapist in example (3c) found a mode of tempering interventions, while still conveying an ongoing commitment to group for the patient.

Group "voices" are heard in the dyad

Sheila confined her group behavior to involvement with others, typically presenting little material from her outside life. I knew from our individual work that Sheila felt humiliated by revealing certain aspects of her second marriage, including a disadvantageous prenuptial agreement, her husband's insistence on sexual activity more than daily, and favoritism towards his children over hers.

At various times, members questioned Sheila, who responded hesitantly but cooperatively: "Well, what else do you want to know?" Eventually, the members noticed a pattern in the group's question-and-answer interchanges: I did not press Sheila to reveal the way I did others. They offered theories: I enjoyed our private relationship; I felt protective; Sheila did all her important work in individual therapy and remained in group because she found it interesting. They explained to Sheila (and to me) that the issue was not about "facts," but for her to engage more personally and spontaneously. "We care about you and what's going on week-to-week, just like you care about us."

There was important truth in everything the group said, which I acknowledged. Our "special" relationship was now exposed. I got some ribbing for not being perfect, playing favorites, and so forth, but mostly the members were touched by finding me "human after all" and pleased that I had feelings. I did not detect excessive jealousy or envious and destructive feelings, perhaps because Sheila also acknowledged the truth of the group's messages and in subsequent sessions became more revealing.

However, one member, Sam, remained resolutely curious about her "facts" and could become inappropriate and invasive. Sheila responded to him with cool annoyance. "You're never satisfied." Sam's hunger only increased as she withdrew her warmth and approval. Sheila's aloofness—a characterological *resistance*—was new to group and a side of her psychology that I had not experienced in our dyadic therapy. Serving as savior and protector had convinced me that we had an intimate and trusting relationship. Sam became the "voice" of her husband and of her devouring mother, from both of whom she had isolated herself, protectively and spitefully.

Discussion

Sheila and I could not evade the truths the group voiced, nor did we want to. They alerted us to neglected transference-countertransferential dynamics, such as my role in her psychic life as her beloved but passive father. We needed to get at her "unavailable" self, and the underlying, retaliatory aggression that drove her husband, and Sam, into frenzy. I could not remanufacture myself to be the bad maternal object; we appreciated Sam's voice, which even in the dyad stimulated her anger and negativity where I could not.

Group members respond to each other and to the therapist; and also, to the therapist's relationship with each patient (and subgroup), and to the therapist's moment-to-moment, session-to-session performance. The therapist practicing combined psychotherapy is beholden to the group, whose reactions, opinions, and fantasies infiltrate one's consciousness and nonconsciousness, and hence stimulate and help resolve one's (counter)resistances. When working one-to one, as with Sheila, I make mental reference to her in the group, and how various group members, myself included, have reacted and responded to her. The individual members and the group as a whole resonate in my subjectivity, affect my dyadic participation, and also, my solitude. I hear my groups' voices as I write these words.

Resistances, rebellions, and refusals specific to combined treatment

Resistances, rebellions, and refusals specific to combined treatment involve variants of splitting the modalities. Constraints are imposed on what may be conveyed, discussed, or analyzed, from one modality to the other. An individual may act as though engaged in two unrelated therapies. One therapy may be used against the other, to impact the therapist, the group, or a particular group member. As so often in psychotherapy, the content of any withheld, split off, or enacted material is less significant than the underlying motivations; these may comprise legitimate differences in values and beliefs (justifiable *rebellions and refusals*) as well as *resistances* related to the intersubjective context: the developing fantasies, affects, thoughts (transferences) and characterological defenses. The dyad/group split represents a technical problem then, relating to each of the *3 Rs*, and their combination, but also provides the opportunity to understand and articulate underlying rationales and symbolic meanings behind them.

Three clinical anecdotes: Resistances, rebellions, and refusals in combined treatment

A dyad/group split reveals the depth of a member's psychic splitting

Abby established in group that there were certain personal subjects that could be mentioned but were otherwise reserved for "private therapy." She justified her *rebellion* against a "basic rule" to share our work in the combined modality: she did not want to be chastized or to reopen the wounds of others. Several years passed before she acknowledged in group an extra-marital affair. It was "wrong" and Abby felt that the members would disapprove, although she realized that these were her attitudes and not supported by group data. Later she focused on Beatrice, a member who had divorced a philandering husband: "I don't want to remind you of your marriage, or for you to lose respect for me." Beatrice reassured her that she could tolerate hearing about the affair: "I know I'm getting better because I don't feel like raging and moralizing as I used to do."

So, it was not until Abby's fourth year that the members heard the details of what became a group non-event. Abby: "I thought it would make a big difference. My heart was pounding more than it ever has. There was nothing you [group members] said that I haven't heard from my private [dyadic therapy]. But I'm so relieved."

Abby now had extended to the group the privileges of her individual work: the members heard and could discuss the intricacies of Abby's situation. But the group discourses did not further any depth analysis of *resistance*: the symbolic meanings behind the affair and also her strategy of keeping knowledge of the affair from the group.

Indeed, similar to the affair itself, Abby's presentations were dramatic, emotionally stimulating, and mentally consuming, and that was the extent of the meaning that the group or the dyadic psychotherapy currently could bring. Ensconced within her "private" thought and behavior, she repetitively lived out—both in the actual affair and in her reports of the affair—certain affects and fantasies, splitting off awareness of symbolic meanings behind them, recurrent feelings of guilt, and her longing for social and emotional integration (reparation).

Discussion

Even in primary school, Abby developed secret relationships with her girlfriends that she kept from her invasive mother. Her secret *rebellion* against her mother continued in her mind, such that she fantasized playing with these children during lonely family weekends. As a consequence, "private" relationships—both actual and mental—came to preoccupy this bright and lively child and now adult, and also made her feel guilty. In splitting the therapies—secreting the dyadic work from the group—Abby continued the pattern of *rebellion* against her traumatogenic mother, represented symbolically by the whole group.

Sharing the details of the affair with the group was not curative, for it resolved neither her *rebellion* —the prominent "secreting" defenses, nor the underlying maternal trauma (the *resisted*). To some extent, Abby split off and *refused* the learning experience offered potentially by both modalities; it was not easy for her to renounce her *rebellion:* the private world of pain and pleasure in which she had *exiled* herself (see *Chapter six*).

Treating the other modality as if it did not exist

After several months in combined treatment, middle-aged Seth introduced his "story": "As you probably can tell, I'm a late developer. I'm usually 'up' but I just got married and a depression hit me hard. I also started a new job at the same time." The group attempted to work with Seth, but the discussion became intellectualized as Seth relayed a personal and clinical history almost verbatim from his dyadic presentation. But he omitted to tell the group a precipitant that he and I had agreed was dynamically significant. The newlyweds had bought their "dream house," and it was on the day of closing and receiving ownership that Seth's mood altered drastically.

I shared my surprise that Seth omitted "some other recent event," but he seemed bewildered. I then reminded him about his house purchase, without its importance seeming to register. But other group members had no difficulty putting psychic pieces together, and they offered interpretative variations—appropriate to the group context—of the theme of our individual work. The omission signified Sam's ambivalence. Was he going to set up house with us, or cling to his intellectualized story telling, and hence regressively *refuse* to emotionally face the issues impeding his maturation?

Discussion

Seth repeated the same "story," replicating words, affect, and comprehension in each setting. When participating in either modality, he minimized, or even denied hearing or understanding, the insights of the other. When interpretative hypotheses were offered once again, he responded as if hearing them for the first time.

As a young child, Seth established a pattern of self-defeating, pseudo *rebellion*. He would run away from his tumultuous home but, forbidden to cross the busy mainstreet, he returned humiliated and defeated, but at the same time, comforted by its familiarity and regressive warmth. He described himself as "always getting started, but never getting there." With an agile mind and a charismatic personality, Seth had lived a school and professional life of great potential, but little achievement. The group received Seth with high expectation, but they soon understood how he could remain with us without the emotional participation necessary to produce growth and change. His regressive splitting off of transformative experience constituted a pseudo *rebellion,* essentially a *refusal* to leave the regressively familiar. Shedding the potentially therapeutic effects of both modalities, and their interaction, left him unhappily "at home," but not a home of his adult choosing.

Using one modality against the other

After four years of group membership, Mark casually referred to "Johnnie," a stepson he had raised from age five until his divorce ten years later. The members were astonished: Mark had a relationship with his ex-wife's child that he had never mentioned!

Mark defended himself: "Richard knows all about it. We discussed him in individual many times. I guess I didn't think it was relevant." He responded casually and incuriously to the group's mounting indignation. But a member observed a gleam in his eye, and then several others suggested that he seemed to enjoy withholding and frustrating the group. "Well," he granted, "You all know I don't like to be pushed."

"So who's pushing you?" a member asked helpfully. But he *refused* the invitation to take the interaction further, which would have provided an opportunity for transference analysis (i.e., analyzing the *resistance*).

In the following individual session, Mark referred to the group experience, playfully taking me to task. "Why didn't you bring Johnnie up all these years? You got me in trouble."

I thought of Yalom's (1995) description of the patient who "may interact like a sponge in the group, taking in feedback and carrying it away to gnaw on like a bone in the safe respite of the individual therapy hour" (p. 407). Mark's mild reproach was a ploy to entice me to share his bone, to feast on the group and hence to triumph *rebelliously* against it. I reminded him of the group's detection of his pleasurable gleam: "You got yourself in trouble, not for not telling, but for not caring why. People are strange, they seem not to like it when they catch on to your disdain."

He detected a tone of disdain in my own voice, and gave a wide smile. "Like you're doing with me, you s.o.b.!"

I responded: "But here you're interested in what I say and how I say it. You want to pursue the dialogue. You don't get a kick out of cutting me off or tuning out."

Discussion

Mark was the first of the three apples of his father's eye. The four males acted as if they were no match against the lone female, the outcast wife-mother of a *fight/flight* family drama. As an adult, Mark maintained intimate, long-term friendships with males, while he tended to get angry or to go "dead" in heterosexual relationships. He desired women—to the extent of marrying three of them—yet each complained that he gradually withdrew, until he was not "there." Similarly his laissez-faire approach, coupled with angry outbursts, threatened to cause havoc among this busy executive's female secretarial staff.

Mark responded positively in the dyadic sessions to my confrontations regarding his passive-aggressive maneuvers, for there I was a trusted male friend. In contrast, he could be cautious and cagey in the group, and our dyadic relationship served as a refuge and also, a mode of retaliation. Although he genuinely cared about each member, the group-as-a-whole (including the therapist) stood for the treacherous yet contemptible mother.

Combined psychoanalytic therapy: A natural theoretical fit, yet radical extension of contemporary relational psychoanalytic practice

Combined treatment would seem to be a logical extension and natural fit with relational theory, given its emphasis on destabilizing absolutist thinking, reducing patient-analyst asymmetry, and fostering a collaborative, egalitarian process (O'Leary & Wright, 2005). For group members are witnesses to and collaborators in combined treatment, and their voices may be as authoritative, informed, and psychologically evolved as their therapist's. Even more than dyadic relational psychotherapy, then, combined treatment advances Racker's (1968) call for "social reform," and the demolition of the traumatogenic "patriarchal order" and "inequality in the analyst-analysand society" (p.132). However, to practice an analytically informed combined psychotherapy, core traditional concepts must be revised or adapted, and I refer to several briefly.

The expanded frame. Combined psychotherapy moderates the exclusivity and confidentiality of the patient-analyst relationship, since now other individuals are involved. The group witnesses and may participate in establishing normative arrangements between patient and therapist, including policies regarding attendance, fee, telephone and e-mail communication, and missed sessions. Depending on the therapist's orientation and on the group culture, extra-therapeutic contact among members may be discouraged, forbidden, or encouraged, as in the practice of an extra (leaderless) group session or an "aftergroup."

Transference-countertransference. The communal scope of combined psychotherapy elicits multiple intersubjective configurations, and hence, multiple transference-countertransferences and resulting action scenarios involving *resistance, rebellion* and *refusal.* "The psychoanalyst who lacks a group analytical orientation is unable to appreciate the full range of transference and countertransference processes that are inevitably split off from the psychoanalytical encounter: the 'third' object is not so much hiding beneath the couch, as barely coming into the room" (Hopper, 2009).

Not all transferences are directly focused on the analyst, of course, viz., member-to-member and member-to-whole group relationships (Kauff, 2009; Raps, 2009). Similarly, countertransference extends to subgroups and whole group, and is influenced by the intersubjective situations evolving in each treatment modality and their combination. All group members participate directly or indirectly in the combined treatment and thus, in the transference-countertransferences influenced by combined treatment.

Neutrality-anonymity. The relational group analyst endorses redefined concepts of neutrality and anonymity. Both terms refer to an affectively involved therapist who invites others to be alert to their contributions to all interactions. "It is the analyst's awareness of this unremitting influence of patient and analyst on each other and his attempt to make that influence as explicit as possible that constitute his 'neutrality'" (Gill, 1994, p. 50). The combined modality offers the opportunity to study multiple as well as mutual influences. The relational group therapist practicing combined treatment cannot but reveal certain values and personality characteristics. Most prominently, such an individual enjoys and trusts other human beings sufficiently to gather them together in a quasi-social situation. The therapist allows the dyadic as well as group therapy to be exposed, thought, felt, and challenged by others. He or she accepts a level of mutual risk-taking, self-exposure, uncertainty, and unpredictability. The clinician is multidimensional and not excessively role-bound, and sees the patient and the therapeutic situation as multifaceted. More than likely, then, the therapist has democratic ideals and shares authority and power.

Regression vs. progression. The interface of the two treatment modalities provides enhanced opportunities for experimentation, feedback, self-other awareness, in addition to introspection and retrospection. Analytic process thus is viewed as progressive as well as regressive, with the assumption that insight arises in the context of new experience, not merely by repeating and remembering.

Emphasis on implicit/performative features. Freud's (1916–1917) assertion that "nothing takes place in a psycho-analytic treatment but an interchange of words between the patient and the analyst" (p. 17) exists in an historical context. Thoma and Kachele (1994a) represent a contemporary viewpoint: "The overvaluation of remembering may be associated with a neglect of sensations linked with the body ego … the exclusion of psycho motoric and sensual communication and the concentration on verbal exchange (who may be unseen and hidden) contradicts human nature. Self-presentations rely on feedback that is emotionally modulated and employing all the senses" (p. 305).

Influenced by advances in infancy research and in understanding pre-and non-verbal communication, the relational therapist practicing combined treatment is alert to the performative dimensions of mental life. Dyadic and group analysis extends to facial communication, body positioning, spontaneous here-and-now interactions, and unfolding action-scenarios ("enactments", see Roth, 2009)—all influenced by the effects of the dual modalities.

Clinical anecdote involving a not-so-radical combined psychotherapist

In the midst of bullying another group member, Ralph apologetically acknowledged that he was "acting like Fox News," a reference to the conservative American television network. "That's what Rich calls me in individual [psychotherapy] when I get aggressive and finger-pointing."

While pleased that Ralph showed self-awareness, I unexpectedly felt embarrassed by his sharing of my "Fox News" trope. I knew that no one but me was ruffled by the exposure of my political bias that, while not completely submerged, stayed in the background of my therapeutic work. Apparently, I carried the fantasy—a remnant of classical psychoanalytic indoctrination—that I should function value-neutrally and be anonymous, personally and politically. "God forgive me, I'm an atheist," I thought to myself. For, in my nonrational being, I remained a mere rebel, and not radical or revolutionary. Still loyal to King Psychoanalysis, I had violated the edicts regarding anonymity and neutrality.

Discussion

The interface of the two modalities reveals multiple self-states (Bromberg, 1998). Like other members of the combined practice, the therapist may examine and work through unevolved modes of feeling, thinking, and communicating. Still, it remains much easier to preach an integrated, relational combined psychotherapy than fully to practice it.

Conclusion

To provide theoretical and clinical background to *The 3 Rs*, I have presented professional and clinical vignettes, exploring the worlds that combined therapy open up. The group impacts on the dyad, the dyad impacts on the group, and via mental activity, these impacts pertain even if the patient or client is not actually in treatment in both modalities.

Combined treatment does not obviate psychoanalytic process, but rather extends the field of observation, participation, and interpretation beyond the dyad. If one were to question participants, patients and analysts, who have experienced combined treatment, one would sample probably a near unanimous chorus of supporters. Why then, is combined therapy the exception, rather than the rule?

In the classical days of psychoanalysis, the privileges of authority and anonymity of the analyst were assumed and preserved. Bion-influenced Tavistock and systems-oriented groups likewise upheld these entitlements. However, to be properly trained and to function as a group analyst, one must tolerate self-exposure to groups, and this means surrendering entitlements even beyond those promulgated by relational theorists (Billow, 1999a; b).

The clinician who wishes least to protect analytic entitlements more likely will practice combined therapy; for in this milieu, he or she is most psychically revealed. Intimacies of the dyad are witnessed and reviewed in the group: the clinician, who is both the analyst and a group participant, must face the individual patient once again. My intuition suggests an allied reason combined therapy is not practiced more widely: although all individuals desire and need to be emotionally known, analysts and their *Establishments* refuse sharing the discovery process with each other, perhaps even more than with their patients.

CHAPTER TWO

Truth, significance, and the role of falsity

By virtue of their appearance in this book, my words are granted *Establishment* credibility, but each reader decides if they are significant. In a similar vein, our professional credentials give us voice and professional status, however, our group members decide if what we say is true, and further, significant.

The novelist William Burroughs (1985) captured an essence of what I will be getting at in *Resistance, Rebellion and Refusal in Groups: The 3 Rs:* "Truth is used to vitalize a statement rather than devitalize it. Truth implies more than a simple statement of fact. 'I don't have any whiskey,' may be a fact but it is not a truth." Significant truth vitalizes the self and relationships, such as I am attempting to establish with the reader; significant truth vitalizes the group, and society at large.

"Worse than being right or wrong is the failure of an interpretation to be significant" (Bion, 1970, p. 79). I qualify Bion's aphorism, for an interpretation—like any intervention—is an intersubjective construction. Its rightness,and its significance remain subjective without a final or fully objective assessment.

Bertrand Russell (1927) cautioned against the "tendency to use 'truth' with a big T in the grand sense, as something noble and splendid and worthy of adoration. This gets people into a frame of mind in which they become unable to think" (p. 265). Significant truth, I believe, is conceptual and emotional, but it involves a small "t." And, in communicating truth, we should keep it "as simple as possible, but not too simple" (Einstein).

Emotional meaning: "Truth" with the small "t"

I like to think about "t-ruth", or better, "truthing," as a verb, describing an evolving process, occurring in relationship to ourselves and others, of reaching for emotional awareness. We make truth by examining and re-examining communications in the immediacy of personal, group, and cultural-social context. In vital groups, truths—both conscious and nonconscious—are discovered, integrated, and reconfigured in the members' intrapsychic and interpersonal relationships, and in the structure and process of the group itself.

Always pertinent are the methods by which truth is reached and the uses to which it is put. Truth with a small "t" is local, socially constructed, and related to issues of power, status, cultural norms, and practice of the groups to which we belong. It may be immediate and cathartic, or discovered, even re-discovered over time, thought and felt about, and reworked in the course of intrapsychic and interpersonal experience.

Truth with the small "t" is neither certain nor unchanging. Therapist, patient, reader, or author, each monitors discourses for truth through the lens of subjectivity and asserts influence by adopting and responding to various aspects of clinical theory, narrative, and interaction that often are subtle and out of awareness. Consensus among the participants concerning what is said, what is meant, or its significance, may be absent.

Truth infinite—falsity ineliminable

Freud asserted that aversive unconscious truth—the repressed—was at the core of psychic disturbance. The analyst's task was to reveal the patient's unconscious to consciousness, whereby *resistance* was "lifted." "The patient's mental life is permanently changed, is raised to a high level of development and remains protected against fresh possibilities of falling ill" (Freud, 1916–1917, p. 451; see *Chapter five, Resistance*).

Bion (1965) proposed a striking theoretical realignment, by replacing the polarity unconscious-conscious with infinite-finite (Symington & Symington, 1996). "Truth" is unbound, and has no form, no categories, and remains unknown—hence Bion's notation: "*0*". According to this perspective, we make human truth—always with a small "t"—by transforming experience through different, evolving but finite perspectives: rational, pre-rational, and irrational, conscious, nonconscious, interpersonal, and intrapsychic.

As individuals, we hunger for such truth:

> There is a need for awareness of an emotional experience, similar to the need for an awareness of concrete objects that is achieved through the sense impressions, because lack of such awareness implies a deprivation of truth and truth seems to be essential for psychic health. The effect on the personality of such deprivation is analogous to the effect of physical starvation on the physique (Bion, 1962, p. 56).

But the truth has consequences, suffering the frustration of reaching truth, and accepting its consequences: the often-painful realizations that change the way one feels, thinks, and treats others and oneself. Bion also noted that the psychological need for truth strains the human being's mental abilities. We remain inadequate to perceive and bear too much truth. And thus, even the strongest among us evade the "need for awareness of an emotional experience," and collude with other group members to avoid truth-seeking.

"Psi": The dimension of "falsity"

While Freud and Klein mythologized an essential human struggle between the libidinal and aggressive drives—between life and death instincts and love and hate, Bion added the fundamental dialectic between the need for emotional truth and the need to avoid psychic pain. Bion asserted that an ineliminable (see Louw & Pitman, 2001) screen of protective falsity exists in all human relations, and to some degree, in any thought or communication. He called attention to a deceptive part of the personality and of groups:

To avoid anxiety and psychic pain, we practice concealment and lying.

Bion reserved a special category of thinking and of evasive response, designated by the Greek letter *psi* (Ψ), referring to statements "known by the initiator to be false, but maintained as a barrier against statements that lead to a psychological upheaval [i.e., growth and change]" (1970, p. 9). I wish to qualify this definition, "known by the initiator to be false." Falsity or "*psi*" may involve defenses against truth that is known but partially and not developed, or is premonitory, or split-off, or that remains without sufficient awareness despite available derivatives and adequate interpretation (see *Chapter seven, Refusal*).

Psi responses serve to assert a superiority of falsity over truth. Emotions as well as words can serve as *psi*. Bion (1970) gives the example of rage, "of which the fundamental function is denial of [awareness of] another emotion" (p. 20).

Psi communications carry a metamessage, "here is a truth," when the individual cannot tolerate or admit not understanding. Or, the individual may pretend not to understand, when he or she fears thinking about the truth and its consequences. The individual may omit, distort, or exaggerate relevant data, leading to confusion or drawing false inferences. Even when factually true, like Burroughs' "I don't have any whiskey," *psi* communications may serve falsity, by being misleading, inauthentic, irrelevant, or cliché, so providing a buffer against genuine mental interaction. *Psi* exists on individual, group, and societal levels, and may be understood in a developmental context.

Truth and falsity in human development

> The customary answers given the child…damage his genuine instinct of research and as a rule deal the first blow, too, at his confidence in his parents…he usually begins to mistrust grown-up people, and to keep his most intimate interests secret (Freud, 1907c, pp. 135–136).

To a significant degree, the capacity of the developing individual to tolerate truth seeking reflects the history of the caregivers' interest and success in responding to the child's truth needs. Only a certain amount of truth may be introduced into experience, and it is among the parents' first and most important tasks to protect the infant and growing child from too much or too little truth. From the start, parents introduce make-believe into the infant's world, creating (or in today's jargon, co-creating) "his majesty, the baby," and fostering mutually idealizing, bonding scenarios. However, to advance truth seeking, the parents must gradually dethrone the infant. We may hypothesize that certain depriving caregiving behaviors—for instance, those involving physical absence, delay of immediate satisfaction as in partial weaning, and so forth—stimulate thinking and a reality orientation. And so arrives a most painful truth: others exist as separate objects; they can be present or absent. Thus, thinking involves the experience of "missing," of anxiety and frustration; and truth, when it emerges, may be difficult to bear (see *Relational Group Psychotherapy, Chapter three*).

If the infant is constitutionally able and early caregiving experiences progress satisfactorily, it begins to take over parental functions of regulating truth. Through the development of reasoning and representational thought, the child learns to contain and articulate the reality of its own emotional experiences and to differentiate what is new and potentially valuable from what has become familiar and established. However, truth seeking remains an experimental process that involves a component of omnipotent and hallucinatory thinking, which is gradually but not totally worked through.

From the mature point of view, the infantile or neurotic self continues to falsify experience, to the extent the individual feels responsible for all that happens to oneself. Infantile or neurotic modes of thinking produce false premises based on guilt, shame, and personal agency. Bleandonu (1994) suggested that Bion's appellation, *psi*, likely referred to "proton pseudos," the "first lie" that Freud (1895d) located at the heart of hysteria. Indeed, Freud understood the etiology of neurosis as related to the individual lying to oneself. Cure was achieved by catharsis: the patient's finding and accepting the traumatic truth.

However, even the mature human being must continually work through a level of "primitive" emotionality and nonconscious fantasy to achieve separation from a world of subjective objects and events to think with some clarity and objectivity. Klein (1975) called this process achieving (and maintaining) the working through of the depressive position. Winnicott (1971) described the creative aspects of this process. We reach into ourselves before we grasp external reality: first creating an illusional object, then "destroying" it to discover "otherness." Solipsistic falsification provides a bridge, an entry to truth.

In childhood and adolescence—indeed, at all stages of development—to seek truth and to challenge the human tendency toward falsification, the individual requires authentic communicative interaction. In some measure, the *Establishment*, consisting of parents, school, religious and cultural institutions, government, media, and peers, represents and upholds reality, including the values and standards of the status quo. But the established order must also encourage challenge and dissent, and must stimulate and respond to emotional truth and the individual's search for it.

Parents and societal caregivers who unduly rely on *psi* may reward conventionality, to the neglect and discouragement of curiosity and experimental behavior (play). They may use truth for influence and control, for example, in order to impose a moral or political agenda. The established order, rather than providing a stable foundation from which the individual questions and explores inner and outer reality, may thus foster a resentful but inhibited "good baby," who emerges in adolescence with a conforming "good-citizen" or rebellious "bad-citizen" self, or both. In response to a psychosocial network that is suppressive, manipulative, or merely inadequate in fostering truth, the young adult may become evasive and tentative as a form of self-protection, and hide behind a "false self" (Winnicott, 1960). Truth—as well as the need for truth—remains unintegrated and dissociated.

The group leader monitors falsity

Bion's (1961) early group theory placed the conflict between truth and falsity squarely within the individual, who remains internally "at war," caught between wishes to preserve independence of mind and to participate with furtive "groupishness." The problem of truth exists both on the individual and group levels: the therapist interprets and attempts to affect the group-as-a-whole, but the target remains the mind of each individual.

Bion (1970) later added a sociopolitical dimension to the conflict between truth and falsity. He referred to groups as *Establishments*, to the extent to which they correspond to *psi* in their modus operandi. *Establishments* are unable to accept new information, seek to ignore, suppress, or negate anything new, and resort to lying rather than having their ideas disturbed. The explicit target of the therapist's interventions now included the group *Establishment*: the leader must "be destructive of the laws, conventions, culture, and therefore coherence, of a group within the group, if not of the whole group" (Bion, 1970, p. 64). The group therapist must actively and consistently challenge the group's tendency to represent and promulgate *psi*, the conforming, mind-deadening aspects of *Establishment* formation, culture, and process (*Chapter six, Rebellion*).

Case example: A group discovers deception

It was now many years since Rob, our senior member, first came into group, disconsolate, confused, and lonely, after a divorce from Rachel, who had found him hard and unreachable. In group therapy, Rob mellowed and matured. After a long mourning period, Rob began a series of romantic relationships, which he would recount to the group. Rachel remained in the picture, however, for the couple often was thrown together in planning and attending the many ceremonies of a family: the graduations, engagements, and marriages of the children. Rob reported that Rachel had come to praise and even bless the group, for her ex-husband was a changed man, warm, supportive, and good company. The group shared a fantasy that they would be reconciled.

"No, I don't think so," Rob protested, "although I have thought about it. She's still a good looking woman."

"And," a member egged him on.

"And maybe my best friend" Rob blurted.

"You seem embarrassed, like a young guy with a crush," said a female member to the 60-year-old Rob. "But it looks good on you. You're still a good looking man." Rob, who had become gallant and something of a group flirt, returned the compliment.

During the next several years, Rob returned intermittently to romance, and we began hearing of a tempestuous relationship with Maria whom, to our surprise, he was thinking of marrying.

However, months later, a distraught Rob told us how his intended fiancé suddenly broke it off. "I had never seen Maria in such a rage, and I can't understand it."

The group was confused and spent most of the session trying to piece together the history of Rob's liaison, and then to understand how it unraveled. Finally the subject turned to Rachel, but Rob insisted that she had nothing to do with the bewildering turn of events. "She consoled me, she was sorry that it didn't work out."

Rob's reply did not sit well with the membership. "Sounds like your ex is still your best friend. That wouldn't work for me," said one of the female members. "You're fooling yourself, Rob, and maybe Maria felt like a fool too." "'If we feel your vibes for Rachel, Maria must too." Rob stuck to his own position: Maria had a complicated family life; she was afraid of commitment; the couple had religious differences, and so forth.

We followed Rob's emotional recovery in the following months. Yes, he was feeling better. Yes, Rachel continued to be a support. They attended a mutual friend's anniversary party and they danced all night. They were spending Sundays at the beach. Their children were pleased and teased them. Yes, she was a turn-on.

And then, from a member: "Have you kissed her?"

"Yes."

"When?"

Rob took the moral high ground and insisted the details were not important. But certainly, they kissed hello and kissed good-bye. Friends do that. "What about on the beach?" a member insisted.

"It wasn't that kind of beach," Rob replied, "but I did rub her back with suntan oil."

The mood in the room was skeptical, as one member asked casually what Rob meant by "not that kind of beach."

"It was a nude beach," Rob replied, matter-of-factly. And then, all hell broke loose.

"What!" "You've been taking Rachel to nude beaches." "And rubbing her back." "Your best friend!" "We spent a whole session about Rachel and Maria, and you deceived us!" "I'm really pissed. You led us on, why would you do that!" "I can't believe I wasted my group time on Rob. Richard [the therapist], did you know about this? Why did you let him go on!" "How much kissing are you doing with Rachel, and what else?" "I can't stand this. He reminds me of my husband. When I ask him a question he acts like a defendant in a court of law. I never get a straight answer." "I'm tired of men lying to me, I thought it would be different in group." "Hey, I've been fucked over by women and men, it's not gender specific."

I finally broke in: "I don't know any more about Rob's relationship with Rachel than anyone else. We're all learning together, and I believe Rob is too. [to Rob, who had maintained his composure] Could you work with us and explain why you've been omitting and covering up crucial details?"

"I think I've been doing the same to myself. At first, I didn't want to admit that I could really want Rachel back. I didn't think she was interested, that I had a chance. I'm still afraid to think about what's happening, I don't trust it, and if I talk about it, it might go away."

"Have you been talking to Rachel about it?" a member asked.

"Not really, we've just been doing it—I mean seeing each other and making out, okay, a bit more, that's all." Rob continued: "I didn't want to deceive the group, but I've been embarrassed, I feel confused and ashamed that you've been right, and that I had something to do with Maria's breaking up. I thought she became irrationally jealous, and that I had picked another crazy woman."

Discussion

Within nonconscious and pre-rational and irrational realms of experience, nothing is false; simultaneously, our defenses allow us to deny everything. While Rob the realist had put his life back together, becoming a caring individual, the nonconscious Rob had become a bigamist. He wanted Maria and Rachel, and by maintaining different types of *psi* relationships, for a while he succeeded in husbanding both. Rob's reportedly Platonic friendship with Rachel had disguised his erotic involvement, from himself and the group, but not from Maria. Like the group, Maria became furious when she realized that her ardently conventional suitor was a two-timer.

In terms of group theory as presented in *Experiences in Group*, at various times the group process illustrated each of the *basic assumptions*: *dependency*, to the extent the group attempted to take care of Rob; *pairing*, when the membership seemed preoccupied with establishing a procreating couple, and *fight/flight*, the initial angry group response to the discovery of Rob's deception. *Work group* functioning predominated later in that session, and in those that followed, when the group, Rob included, took up the issue of falsity—in parents, mates, peers, children, and themselves—in psychological rather than moral terms.

In terms of Bion's later formulations regarding falsity, to some extent the group had established a collusive *psi* relationship with Rob, who functioned as the group elder, a figure of *Establishment*. Certain falsifying aspects of Rob's psychology and its relationship to the group had remained undiscovered and unexplored. The members eventually detected and challenged Rob's deceptions. For an anxious interlude, the group fractionalized ("aggregated" (Hopper, 2003b)), in response to the trauma of being lied to, before reintegrating via insightful discussions that expanded appreciation of psychic reality. Rob's position in the group changed, as well; without losing the group's respect, he was more frequently challenged and participated with greater openness.

Bion assumed that the therapist, to the extent he or she is able, functions as sole truth bearer. But in this example, the group itself carried out the function of confronting *psi* with truth. To advance group process and encourage psychological awareness, it is often necessary for the therapist to monitor boundaries and other aspects of group process, and to step in and reassert leadership. Still, truth evasion is universal, as is truth seeking, and the group therapist struggles with both tendencies.

Reducing psi in the therapist's communications

Relational and postmodern thinking emphasizes that the therapist remains situated within the field of inquiry, and may see truths only from his or her own perspectives (e.g., Hanly, 1999). Absolute and unambiguous truth is out of reach. To reduce the level of falsity in the clinical interaction, the therapist must attempt to see the *psi* elements in one's and other group members' thinking (Bion, 1965, p. 168).

Case example: The therapist deceives the group; a subgroup deceives the therapist

After the last of our children left for college, my wife and I considered parting with our large suburban house, wherein I maintained my professional office, and experimentally listed our home with a realtor while we explored Manhattan. Were we to move, I planned on obtaining local office space and did not intend to disturb my practice. I felt that any mention of our speculative plans would cause needless anxiety for patients, and remained silent in my group and individual practice. However, a woman in combined treatment was a professional realtor from another town, and I wondered if Amy would see the listing, and how she would respond in session.

A topic of our individual sessions (even prior to the decision to list our house) concerned how much a patient can know about the analyst. Amy liked that the sessions were about her, unlike her relationship with her intrusive and self-centered mother. She also appreciated that I was unlike her passive father, and husband—I was not one of those "uh huh" analysts, I spoke my mind and she knew where I stood. She appreciated that I was not dramatic and explosive, the way she was so often. In her view, I did my job of dealing with every group member in a fair-minded, evenhanded way, and Amy respected and hated me for it.

"I don't get to see the real you. You wouldn't be like this with your friends and family," she argued, quite reasonably.

"I hope not," I responded, "they aren't hanging out with me for therapy. But why isn't being like I am with you real, maybe even realer than what passes for social and family life?"

Amy remained unsatisfied but usually found little more to say on this topic, and we drifted to other subjects. But on one occasion, she continued: "You know, I get the real estate listings for your town."

"I figured."

"So why didn't you tell me you were moving? You better open an office out here, I'm not commuting into the City three times a week."

My explanation that no decision has been made seemed not to register, and I asked whether she believed me. "Yes, but you didn't tell me that your were *thinking* of moving, that's what I mean I don't know who you really are, not that I expect or even want you to tell me everything you are thinking."

Then, later in the session: "I hope you realize that almost everyone in group knows, we talk about it every week. I would have burst; I couldn't keep it a secret and hide it from the group, like you did. Are you mad?"

"I don't think so," I replied, feeling fairly uncomfortable, "but I am interested." Apparently, whether my house was sold remained a weekly cliffhanger to the subgroup that carried out post-session huddles in my driveway. I inquired why Amy did not bring the subject to the whole group in session.

"The 'driveway group' has lots of secrets, just the way you do. But I don't want to talk about it anymore and you can bring it up in group if you want," Amy replied.

I rejoined with a lighthearted "So can you if you want," and then Amy closed the subject with "I don't want."

My opening of the following group session did not go smoothly: "So, I hear I'm moving. At least this is the buzz."

Two members had not been privy to the rumor reacted strongly. Rose, a distinguished, elderly woman, in intensive combined therapy for many years, blanched, began to tear, and turned on me with an uncharacteristically intense anger. She felt betrayed. Dan, usually reticent and acquiescent, accused Amy of invading my privacy. Amy protested; she had innocently come across the realty listing and felt too scared to bring the news into group. "I knew it would upset Rose and I feel bad."

I reiterated that a move was uncertain, that I was not planning on disturbing the group, not even by changing the time or significantly modifying the location. I then said: "Rose is angry at me, Dan is angry at Amy, Amy is guilty over Rose, what's upsetting the rest of you?"

A sizeable subgroup of men lived or worked in Manhattan, and they were the first to speak, vocalizing their pleasure were I to relocate. Another woman, Randi, sensibly reminded them geography was not the issue, but what I did, or did not do, in terms of letting in the group on my plans. One of the commuters, Todd, said he was resigned to such behavior from therapists, and was not one of the angry ones: "I expect Richard to be sharp, not to be honest. He probably would rather be skiing."

Given my frequent winter breaks, there was no hiding my interest and enthusiasm for the sport, and I answered with an unconflicted: "For sure, but why does that make me dishonest?"

"This is your business, and how you run your business in your business," Todd answered with intensity. When another member suggested that he was probably the angriest, he had to agree, and he connected me to all the fallen idols of his life. Other group members worked with him, and with each other, as they shared their beliefs about what a therapist should share, and how I stacked up compared to their ideals. I remained a quiet witness to their varying reactions to me.

The group then turned to the ashen Rose, who spoke with her usual poise and refinement. She reviewed with the group her history: the early death of her mother, abandonment by her father, and a childhood of shuttling between aloof grandparents. And now again, from the one person she trusted!

Randi began to explain why I might find it in the group's best interest to withhold personal information. But I believed she needlessly was attempting to take care of Rose (and me) and I intervened: "You don't have to mend fences, Randi; like everyone else, Rose needs to talk about her feelings." Rose began to sob, and the group waited respectfully. At last, Rose could be unhappy publicly. She did not have to maintain the self-imposed rules of polite, that is *psi,* society. No one needed or expected her to regain composure and deny her pain.

Then, in an effort to address the subgrouping and reengage the group at large, I offered softly: "I can understand why the driveway group wanted to keep secret. You're sensitive to my right to privacy and don't want to blame me for withholding information. Now, with Rose so hurt and angry, you must feel like co-conspirators.

"Leave me out of it!" Rose interrupted with uncharacteristic edge, surprising and pleasing herself, along with the rest us. With relief, the group went on to other subjects.

Discussion

Amy's information about my real estate activities confronted, in sequence, me, the subgroup, and the whole group, with *psi*: the thorny issue of my personal candor, and by extension, of the authenticity of the psychotherapy *Establishment*. Falsity—real and perceived—is built into the very fabric of the group therapist's communications. Rarely is a question directed to the therapist's person answered frankly, and this begins with the response to a member's greeting of "How are you?" Indeed, often a considerable distance exists between how the analyst relates to the patient as a professional-at-work, and how he or she feels at a particular existential moment.

We may contain our anxiety and be quiet, or answer conventionally, with the best of conscious rationales: to maintain therapeutic space, provide a (relatively) blank screen, preserve the therapeutic alliance, and so forth. And, should we accommodate and self-disclose, we may be consciously as well as nonconsciously avoiding, and yet also inadvertently conveying other aspects of personal experience (Frank, 1997; Greenberg, 1995). Thus, neither action nor inaction removes the therapist from the ambiguous relationship to truth and falsity.

Amy had deposited into the group culture information about me that I had chosen not to share, but which had occupied my mental space, as well as Amy's. While the truth was out, its diverse meanings evolved, to the extent to which members could tolerate mental experience. Todd, for example, in sharing his cynical but not necessarily inaccurate preconceptions about the psychotherapy *Establishment*, and stimulating group interaction, amplified the group's awareness of different relational pattern with authority figures.

In talking about her traumatic childhood in the context of the group experience, Rose offered "narrative" as well as "historic" truth (Spence, 1982). She voiced what has to be among the worst of any group member's fantasies regarding clinical false-heartedness: orphaned by the good-mother therapist, cast out by the paternal-leader, and disregarded by the family-group. Certainly, it was within the range of possibility that I would disperse our group for my own interests. And in fantasy, the truth was that I had done so already.

Even more than her words, Rose's sobs and angry outburst dramatized most meaningfully what I had done. "Leave me out of it!" she cried out. In her mind, I had left her out of it, and there was no easy way to repair. I was the embodiment of the abandoning-neglectful-exiling parent, for Rose individually, and now, I felt, for the group collectively. My impulse was to offer these thoughts, to resurrect—in my eyes—the vision of the good therapist while talking of the bad one. But I decided that these interpretations would be self-serving, to relieve myself of the group's projective identifications, as articulated by Rose.

To be an authentic container for projections, the therapist must achieve the sense of "'becoming" those aspects of the patient's self to which attention has been drawn. Any interpretation has elements of falsity, since it involves a theory *about* the therapeutic experience, and evades this painful process of "becoming" (Bion, 1975).

When in the internal state of "becoming," the therapist may feel "on the verge of a breakdown, or some kind of mental disaster" (1975, p. 206). For, among the consequences of "becoming" is a painfully "high price" one has to pay for increased self/other consciousness: "becoming 'responsible' and therefore guilty" (1965, p. 164). And indeed, I felt guilty for being deceptive, propagating conspirators, and causing mental anguish, even though I knew—and believed that the group knew—that I had done the right thing and nothing wrong.

I had to be in the narrative, and with other group members, look into the painfully ambiguous gap that so often exists between the therapist's limited transparency and unqualified honesty. Interpreting group process or individual and group transferences, while professionally appropriate, easily might represent a *psi* element. While I felt personally anxious by not defending myself, I felt more real as a person relating to other persons, and more real as a professional, as I became aware of my dilemma. Said differently, in accepting myself as a real person with my own needs, interests, and insecurities in caring for other individuals, I crossed over a barrier of professionalism that to some extent was self-protective and false. Perhaps this acceptance of self-doubt and uncertainty is an aspect of "becoming," and exemplifies Bion's (1970) statement that: "the more 'real' the psychoanalyst is the more he can be at one with the reality of the patient" (p. 28).

Differentiating "falsity" from "lying"

Lying may be differentiated from the larger category of falsification, in that in falsity, the individual is unable to accept the truth, whereas in lying, the individual falsifies what they have perceived as truth (Bion, 1970). In another words, the liar knows enough truth to make sure his communication is untrue. What is particularly relevant to the group therapist is the liar's parasitic dependence on the audience, which makes the liar vulnerable should he be disbelieved.

However, without exposure, the lie severs the link between thinkers and hence, the therapist and the group itself is in danger.

Case example: Exposing lying and tolerating the consequences

Allan, a successful accountant, entered one of my long-term analytic groups. He tearfully and convincingly described to the group his tumultuous marriage to an irrational, raging wife. He was handsome, charming, and sympathetic, but also overbearingly macho and self-centered, and it did not take the group long to call attention to some of his contributions to the marital difficulties. Ella, his wife, finding Allan's new therapy encouraging, in contrast to a succession of former therapies, scheduled a series of marital consultations.

With some good humor, Ella let me know that she found me "difficult and unfair" but that since Allan seemed to feel the same way about me (and about her), she wanted to continue the marital treatment, and wanted also to pursue her own individual and group therapy with me. Also with some good humor, I reflected that the mates were difficult and unfair with each other, and I reserved the right to call attention to my viewpoint should they assent to separate therapies.

In doing marital consultation, I regularly consider supplementing or even replacing couples work with separate individual and group therapies, and therefore I had no particular reservation responding positively to Ella's request. In establishing working relationships involving both members of the couple and myself, I emphasize that while we will respect the privacy of each marital partner, a primary task is to learn to communicate openly and constructively, and this may entail sharing of data from the respective treatments.

And so, in Allan's group we heard of Ella's offenses, and in Ella's group we heard of Allan's. Each group heard only one side of the story however, and possessed a very partial, corrupt version of the truth. For a therapist treating both halves of a couple two choices exist: to remain silent, and risk colluding with each member's dishonesty and misleading the group; or to speak, and risk betraying confidences and damaging the individual's and group's trust.

I often opt for the second choice. It seems to me disingenuous for a therapist to act as if not in possession of extra-group information when one is, and a betrayal to withhold rather than to disclose such information when it could be helpful. The relational approach involves the therapist's sharing thinking, and the basis and biases of one's thinking (Aron, 1996). I will debate a member's testimony about a mate, and about the reporter's own behavior, and provide my reasoning for doing so.

Not surprisingly, my mode of addressing marital dynamics put me in harm's way in both groups. Allan and Ella turned on me with a modified version of moral outrage usually reserved for each other and which, in its unmodified form, made their conjoint marital therapy eventually unworkable. Each accused me of being influenced by the other and unfair, which gave me the opportunity to reply: "That's just what your mate said, and not in any nicer way." I suggested that it could be worthwhile to look at how I was being treated, even if I was entirely off base, as each felt the respective mate was. The exercise turned attention away from marital specifics to here-and-now group process: how members cope with disagreement and their effects on other members.

Of the two, Allan ostensibly appeared the better group citizen. He verbalized appreciation of negative feedback, and could diverge from marital preoccupations to become cooperatively involved in group life. Ella remained fixated on Allan and at times seemed illogical and unreasonable. Confronted with group feedback, she justified a need to "vent." This made her the less sympathetic figure, and even in her group, Allan's contributions could seem minor in comparison to his wife's unrelenting outbursts.

Over the next two years, however, Ella began to detail, with increasing alarm, financial and legal crises brought on by Allan's professional behavior. While she initially thought of him as having been guilty only of misjudgment, she came to apprehend that Allan treated others and not only her with arrogance and deceit. This realization, coupled with progress in her own therapy, made Ella feel less deserving of such treatment, and she initiated proceedings to end the marriage.

Allan acknowledged the reality of some of Ella's accusations but put them in a different context. His accounting firm itself was being investigated, not only him personally. Besides, his infractions, professional, marital, and otherwise, were pre-therapy, and he was a changed man, he insisted, while Ella remained jealous and confused. One minute Ella would threaten him physically, and the next enjoy their sexual contact.

Allan could not believe she would carry through with her divorce threats, and only after legal pressure did he submit to leave home. Allan vowed never to abandon his children, or desert our group that had given him so much support and guidance throughout his stormy marriage. However, once in separate residence, Allan had to readjust his budgeting, and this meant eliminating individual sessions. He then began to delay payment of group fees, with the excuse that his wife formerly had paid the bills. The pattern continued, with increasingly lengthy intervals between payments, and a mounting unpaid balance.

Not wanting to embarrass Allan, I spoke to him after the group sessions. Several small checks bounced and then a larger one. With trepidation, I alerted him that I had to discuss these developments in group. He assented, and greeted the group discussion amiably. As a professional himself, he understood the issue of settling accounts, particularly since many of his own clients were in arrears. He did not expect me to carry him indefinitely. Everyone knew of his legal hassles, complicated by divorce proceedings with the insufferable Ella, a stock market "bust," a sports car lease that he was renegotiating, and the expense of a child-friendly apartment, and "the kids come first, before me or Rich."

I found myself tangled and near a therapeutic precipice. Allan subtly was changing the focus of discussion. I found the ethical and not the financial lapses unacceptable. If I went along, as if to say, "Yes, of course, you are having financial difficulties," I would be humoring Allan in an effort to get along and not look greedy and uncaring to the group members. If I did not go along, I could be perceived as prescribing how he should live, or even worse, as calling him dishonest and a liar. Bion (1970) described my predicament: "The analyst is challenged to accept them [the patient's falsifications], at the risk of showing himself unmindful of the truth, or to reject them and assume the role of being the patient's conscience" (p. 98).

I had to cut through Allan's dissimulation without cutting him down, that is, without being judge and jury: to address and not punish Allan for his fraudulence. Allan did not make the therapeutic task easy, for he refused to consider what was transpiring within him, or between us, that endangered his group membership. He clung to the economics of our relative positions, denied the ethical significance of his financial transgressions, and promised that payments would be forthcoming.

I was surprised that not one among Allan's affectionate group members protested when—after another month of promises and nonpayment—we agreed that Allan had to take a leave of absence. He left a check that evening to cover a portion of what was now a large balance. As the reader might have predicted, it bounced.

In the session that followed, I anticipated the group's disapprobation, both for evicting Allan, and for prolonging his stay. I found instead a supportive group far more ready for therapeutic divorce than I had been. The members reviewed how each of us—me particularly—had attempted to confront Allan with his histrionics, exaggerations, and rationalizations. Apparently, none felt my sense of guilt and failure. However, we all cared for Allan, worried for him, and mourned his loss.

Discussion

Allan left our group unshaken in his "acceptance of the lie as a working principle of superior efficacy" (Bion, 1970, p. 99). Allan perpetuated psi by "gaslighting" (Calef & Weinshel, 1981), subtly changing the rules of interpersonal engagement such that he appeared as a blameless victim and not ruthless victimizer. His lying—the disarming protestations of innocence and desire to do the right thing—tended to confuse and undermine the mentality of those who would otherwise challenge his prevarications.

Allan adjusted to group by becoming one of the vocal leaders. As long as he could live undisturbed in an omnipotent mental world wherein he ruled over others, Allan could be perceptive, genuinely caring, and responsive to feedback. However he did not modify the basic defense of projecting and transferring mental conflict to others. Thus, like Ella, the members remained conflicted, unsure, and even guilty for suspecting the self-righteous Allan of malfeasance.

In a similar vein, I hesitated and questioned the validity of my doubts about Allan's sincerity regarding the bounced checks, even my right to discuss the issue of payment. Truth, particularly in the hands of the therapist, may itself become an instrument of gaslighting. I did not want to use what I knew about Allan, particularly the fact of his not paying my fees, to retaliate by unduly influencing group process and Allan's relations to other members. Yet, it would have been false to cloak myself in a therapeutic shroud of being understanding, nonjudgmental, and lenient. I would have spared others and myself the realization that Allan was making unfortunate moral choices with meaningful consequences.

Truth hurts, and its absence: Further discussion of the three case examples

Truth often hurts, as does the absence of truth. In the first case example, involving Rob's unacknowledged pursuit of his ex-wife, I felt pain for not knowing truth. In the second case, involving my real estate activities, I felt pain for concealing truth. With Allan, I felt pain for revealing truth.

In all three groups, the need for truth motivated other members to take chances in the group setting and confront an *Establishment* figure who represented aspects of *psi*. In the first group, Rob, the group elder, represented the *Establishment*, while in the second group, it was me, the therapist. In the third, Allan convincingly masqueraded as good group citizen. In the first two group situations, confronting falsity with truth was rewarding. In the third situation, quite the reverse, Allan stalemated constructive group efforts. Faced with his deception, he responded with further deceit, which was of crucial diagnostic and prognostic significance. Presented with truth that he could not undermine, Allan attempted to kill the messengers, his accounting partners, Ella, and the group. In substituting lying for the basic need for truth, Allan suffered personality and social deterioration.

In retrospect, Allan represents a treatment failure. To the extent that he came to his sessions and seemed to be working therapeutically, there was an aspect of his personality that wanted to be cured. Unfortunately, some patients present too great a challenge, or changing life circumstances may overpower their constructive efforts. Possible mistakes in my treatment decisions may have involved putting him into that group, any group at all, or in not better confronting his falsity and rationing truth more skillfully.

Ella stayed in treatment, and reported the following. Allan had amassed significant ethical lapses such that he was asked to resign his partnership at his accounting firm. His license was suspended, and he was reduced to working for other accountants. He abandoned his children for a number of years; his subsequent maneuverings in divorce court landed him in jail for nonpayment of alimony and child support. He exhibited within himself the turmoil and chaos that he had stimulated in his wife. Ella, free from the interactional dynamics, was able to establish a successful career as a teacher while holding her family together.

The 19th century American philosopher, Henry David Thoreau, offered a thought that nicely captures the group process of these three clinical examples: "As a snow-drift is formed where there is a lull in the wind, so, one would say, where there is a lull of truth, an institution springs up. But the truth blows right on over it, nevertheless, and at length blows it down" (2008, p. 67). In the three groups, a culture of openness to the exploration of truth and falsity was a decisive therapeutic factor. Thoreau's optimism was borne out. Thus, whereas the group may foster *Establishment* orthodoxy, it also may function as a normalizing "matrix," (Foulkes, 1964), a salutary culture in which members surrender their falsifying defenses. One characteristic of a dynamic, evolving group is an ability to examine and challenge its conformist tendencies. All group members have the potential to disrupt falsity and aid the group and its leader in life-affirming truth seeking. While the therapist ensures the integrity of the culture, the members, and not solely the therapist, break up old relational patterns and experiment with new ones.

Truth and falsity in group: Modifying an either/or stance

One's version of truth can be wielded as a hurtful weapon or, in a seeming paradox, falsity can facilitate the building and maintenance of constructive relationships. "Tell me what you are thinking!" a partner demands in the midst of a marital quarrel. "How do I look?" a provocatively clad adolescent asks the group and an inwardly wincing group therapist. Questions such as these do not always seek truthful answers, and even when they do, diplomacy, minimization, shadings of feeling and meaning—even white lies—lubricate and make possible social relations (see *Chapter eight*).

Straying from what is exactly true and completely honest is not necessarily malicious, self-serving, or harmful to another. A group member may be honest but merciless, and one must be careful how to ask for or volunteer truth. While becoming open and confrontational represents growth for some group members and some group therapists, for others, patience and tact is the greater achievement. An aspect of human growth and development is coming to acknowledge and understand, if not fully accept, the fictions and disguises—the self presentations (Goffman, 1972)—that, to a greater or lesser extent, each of us adopts to preserve sanity, good spirits, and interpersonal relationships.

In Aristotelian logic truth and falsity are categorically distinct, but this is not so in human relations. And in the nonconscious, nothing is false. Truth seeking and truth evading may exist simultaneously, and on different levels of awareness, and may be used for different intrapsychic and interpersonal purposes. When intentional, falsification or even lying may represent a familial, social, or cultural mode; or be adaptive, a method of coping with an indelicate, or potentially toxic situation.

There are many truths, and many ways of being truthful and searching for truth, and many ways of falsifying. The built-in ambiguity of thought and language works for and against advancing truthful intrapsychic and interpersonal relations. Communications that are true from one perspective may be false from another. When we feel we are being useful and honest—and indeed succeeding—we also may be building intrapsychic and interpersonal barriers that are not easily surmounted. Truth and falsification may be utilized to bypass and submerge psychic pain, promote communicative barriers, and make thinking and feeling more difficult. But both are modes of dealing with that which is difficult, and either may represent an appreciation of the unavoidable separation between people and between what can be known and what can be tolerated. An important truth is that so often there is no clear demarcation between what is true or false, and each points us in the other direction.

Falsification encompasses a wide range of mental activity and interpersonal behaviors, only some of which—intellectualization, rationalization, minimization, denial, dramatization, lying, and enactment—have been described in this chapter (see also, for example, Gediman & Lieberman, 1996). One may mislead by overstating, understating, or withholding or shading information and feedback to other members. Tact, putting up a brave front, maintaining a stiff upper lift, seeing the bright side and the silver lining, avoiding the evil eye, being the devil's advocate or a good group citizen, doing the right thing, maintaining a winning personality, humility, pride, arrogance—these patterns of thinking and behaving narrow the capacity to discover, tolerate, and come to feel and understand that which we would also like to avoid.

No one presents or is expected to present an unexpurgated version of oneself; no group functions with unfettered communications. In the therapy group, the pertinent factors leading to deception may be not known, and even when they are, falsity, like any psychological event, may open a path to exploration of underlying intrapsychic and interpersonal realities. When noncensorially brought to attention, the falsifying aspects of one's psychology and interpersonal relationships present an opportunity for exercising curiosity and furthering dialogue. Psychic truth, which must include understanding the efforts taken to avoid it, ultimately may become more tolerable than hiding from it, but truth is never complete.

CHAPTER THREE

The two faces of the group therapist

As leader of the group, we introduce principles and practices that normalize group relations and provide a sense of continuity and regularity. To establish cohesion, we encourage bonding among members and monitor each member's bond to us. Conforming to the group norms provides an important sense of identity, regularity, and security for the therapist as well as for other group members. Yet, we risk creating a conformist *Establishment*, becoming too comfortable in the overt and covert alliances and compromises we make with other group members our self and put off thinking about and investigating these arrangements.

There needs to be, then, dialectical tension in our functioning. In order to preserve a well-working group, or attend to the difficulties of an ineffective one, the leader must be constructive and deconstructive. As I will propose in later chapters, the leader not only responds to rebelliousness, as emphasized in traditional Freudian approaches to groups, but also, functions as rebel.

As a powerful agent of change, the clinician must disturb the very status quo that he or she works to establish. This involves anxiety, of course, provoking personal and group psychological upheaval. The leader works to dislodge group members from the state of basic assumptive "groupishness" that all group participants, including the therapist, reflexively settle into (Caper, 1999).

In other words, an essential aspect of our identity as significant leader is to disturb our identity as *Establishment* leader. And thus, we must present two faces: We encourage the group to question and challenge the very principles and practices that we assert. Additionally, we are two-faced in another sense of the term: Like all humans, the therapist may be false and insincere, and functions with *psi*.

The Freudian ideal, the Bionion ideal, and intersubjective realities

Although aware of the limitations of perceptual reality, Freud at the same time desired to create an objective science of psychoanalysis. This meant the analyst becoming, as much as possible, an analytic instrument, free of distorting subjective influence. Freud's ideal state of analytic neutrality, anonymity, and abstinence is challenged by postmodern theory, which emphasizes that the observer remains situated within the field of inquiry, and may see truth only from his or her own perspectives. The therapist plays a role in constructing and organizing what is being observed.

The analyst's technique may have unintended and unexplored consequences, facilitating the distortion of the patient's perceptions, and imposing distortions of one's own. For example, after attempting to uncover his patients' truth through hypnosis, Freud came across the talking cure and the method of free-association. But free-association may be evasive, and not all patients can or will free-associate. Further, the patient's associations are not "free," but relate to and are influenced by the therapist's psychology, theory and the very technique itself (Caper, 1997; Hoffman, 2006; Symington, 1990). To give a different example, offering genetic reconstructions, while veridical, may remove the participants from that which has immediate interactional relevance.

Bion described the effective leader as one capable of absorbing group projections of *basic assumptions* to understand the group's defenses and emotional struggles. He assumed the leader, referred to as "exceptional individual," "genius," or "messiah," could adequately contain and understand the resulting "subjective reactions" and make them, rather than the observed facts of the group, the source of the most important interpretations (1961, pp. 148–149). Yet, similarly to Freud (1912e), he acknowledged that in deciding what aspects of clinical interactions should be dealt with, and in what terms, "to a great extent the choice is already determined by the analyst's personality" (Bion, 1965, p. 166).

From the earliest writing, Bion analogized the group leader to a warrior, one who "should have the outlook, and the sort of intuitive sympathetic flair, of the good unit [military] commander" (Bion, 1943, published in 1961, p. 22). Even when Bion (1970) recast the leader's relationship to the group in terms of the container-contained, the bellicose connotation was preserved. "I use the word ['containing'] with its military implication of one force containing another" (p. 112). He did not consider that his personality and leadership style co-determined the conflictual group dynamics that he described with profound originality and depth, and more than a touch of mordant irony.

Towards being a relational group therapist: The therapist's two faces

An unavoidable dimension of *psi* exists in *all* situations involving human beings, including the therapist's clinical relationships and communications. In his groundbreaking work on transference and countertransference, Racker (1968) called attention to *psi* in psychoanalytic culture, theory, and practice, although he did not use the term, as he identified the iatrogenic "myth" of the "analyst without anxiety or anger."

Even when we think we are benefiting others with our investigatory stance, discoveries, and formulations of truth, we—as well as our patients—may come to other conclusions. "A truth that's told with bad intent/Beats all the lies you can invent" (William Blake, 1974). We must accept the inevitability of impurity in our feelings, motives, and intentions. We strive to be aware of them and sometimes it is useful to acknowledge them openly to the group.

Jacobs (2001) gave clinical examples of his self-protective use of an "analytic screen," and courageously shared his dawning self-awareness with his analysands. His term referred to "situations in which particular needs, conflicts, and biases of the analyst, not infrequently rooted in narcissistic conflicts, lie embedded within, and are concealed by, his quite proper and correct interventions … derived from well-accepted theory and long-established techniques" (p. 654). The core elements of classical psychoanalysis (and group therapy) may contribute to maintaining the static, "hierarchical arrangement of power and privilege in the psychoanalytic situation" (Gerson, 1996, p. 626). They constrain the therapist's access to the most powerful source of information (and misinformation): one's own subjective experience.

The therapist's theory and technique bring organization and directionality to the psychotherapeutic experience, which privilege and prohibit modes of patient-therapist interactions (Hoffman, 1992, 2004; McLaughlin, 1996). Who the therapist is—his or her identity in professional and societal hierarchies of status and authority—influences what the analyst says and its credibility, and thus, a significant element of what is considered truth resides in the analyst's *Establishment* position (see Foucault, 1978).

I argue that the therapist can understand and participate *authentically* only to the extent that he or she internally acknowledges and deals with one's own falsity—the compromises we make to come to terms with the unavoidable countertransference anxieties, resistances, fantasies, and affects that are in the very fabric of intersubjective experience (see *Chapter eight,* section on *Authenticity.*) The authentic therapist, rather than being the oracular translator of the nonconscious and thus the all-knowing Sphinx, tolerates doubt and uncertainty, shares aspects of his or her emotional thinking, and aids others in developing and expressing their thoughts. This view of group process and leadership gives the contemporary group therapist wide technical latitude in how to invite others into truth seeking, which is a relational process.

In my opinion, such factors as inspection, introspection, retrospection, the longevity and stability of a group, do not vouchsafe objectivity or inoculate therapists from the tendency to rationalize who we are, how we feel, and what we are doing. Recognizing our own evasiveness is not easy, as we set up screens—analytic and otherwise—to hide ourselves from ourselves, as well as to hide ourselves from our groups. Even when a therapist intentionally self discloses, one is not fully aware of or certain of one's own motivation. The therapist may be consciously as well as nonconsciously avoiding and yet also inadvertently conveying other aspects of personal experience (Aron, 1991; Frank, 1997; Greenberg, 1995). The contours of intentional and unintentional self-disclosures are ambiguous and fluctuating; they reflect truth and falsity, and in turn, both are reflected in the two faces of the therapist.

Relational theorists (Chused, 1992; Renik, 1993; Spezzano, 1996) suggest that both patient and analyst do most of their thinking nonconsciously. Derivatives from the nonconscious gradually emerge into preconsciousness or consciousness, and it often takes time for significant truth to be understood, formulated, and shared. From this point of view, we could characterize a group's evolution as dependent on the therapist's progressive understanding and working through, not only of one's transferences and countertransferences, as traditionally conceived, but also, of one's tendencies toward *psi*.

We cannot be sure if we are advancing or evading significance. One truth may hide behind, obscure, or, more positively, bring to the fore another. As one patient put it: "I'm feeling a pit in my stomach. I don't know if it is because I think I am lying to you or telling the truth." Psychological upheaval—that pit in the stomach feeling—occurs when we are getting close to *significance*; it is unavoidable for both therapist and member, as we make decisions how and if to pursue that which we anticipate as painful.

Feeling that "pit in the stomach" pain, the group therapist may take evasive action. We may act reasonably, on target and professional, and yet be inauthentic, or we may omit or modify certain truths in self-interest, while justifying such behavior as in the interests of others.

Contemporary therapists no longer rest comfortably on assumptions of clinical authority and certainty, and we are in the process of reassessing traditional oppositions, such as between word and action (Greenberg, 1996), transference and countertransference, resistance and legitimate challenge, social and true self. No therapist is "purified" and functions as a "telephone receiver," Freud's (1912e) metaphors for the well-analyzed clinician. Self-awareness remains tentative and uncertain, and is revised according to the shifting currents of present-day reality.

The therapist's reactions are idiosyncratic and specific to the intersubjective context, tested, monitored, and responded to with varying accuracy by others. We cannot rest securely in the correctness of our own perceptions, and we need to find the thread of truth in the perception of others, even if seemingly exaggerated and distorted. Surely, group members form valid insights regarding the therapist's personality and the complexities of their therapist's psychology (see Gill, 1994). Groups unify and not only project, but also protect themselves from the leader's subjective reactions, which rarely if ever are "genius," and even when inspired remain capable of challenge. An aspect of therapeutic containing is remaining curious about members' perceptions and responding respectfully to their communications.

In the following case example involving a subgroup and the therapist, communications were far from ideal. *Establishment* principles of group behavior that I valued were being threatened by covert, extra-group telephone contact between two members. I did not want to be provoked into premature action, but could not be *laissez faire* and leave it to the couple or draft the group at large to resolve the situation. Sooner or later, I would have to protect the group as well as the subgroup from a boundary violation. At the same time, I needed to invite awareness about and challenge to my *Establishment* stance. We should derive *significance* from the experience.

Previewing the 3 Rs

Case example: Maintaining the Establishment; developing significant truth

Erica had begun a combined individual-group therapy after an extramarital affair with Robert. A free spirited woman in her early fifties, popular with both sexes, she was the group's "yes, but." "Yes," she acknowledged being impulsive and inconsiderate at times, "but," she did not want to hurt anybody. She wished her husband would just let her do what she wanted since he did not seem to enjoy her company.

In an individual session, Erica teasingly revealed a budding cell phone romance with Tom, a younger member in her group, who had his own marital difficulties. "You were right when you said I would find a 'Robert' in the group. Would you kick us out if Tom and I slept together?" [*Chapter six, Rebellion, section on "exile"*]. She added playfully and not reassuringly: "Not that I am going to."

I now understood the intense bonding that formed between the two members; a coupling that had distressed several group members, in part because of its elusive vagueness. Erica's coyness, as much as her confession, troubled me and I felt angry at being duped. I believed that my anger was both Erica's wish and fear, and that both of us needed me to find an adequate way to express it

I replied to her question about sexual engagement in a casual, unreassuring tone that I realized was similar to hers: "We'll have to see if you get kicked out, but it's a strong possibility." As typical with the oppositional Erica, when I asked her to discuss the situation further in group, she refused. "That would take the fun out of it." I continued, wondering if I were maintaining sufficient equanimity and not being unduly threatening or punitive: "Then the decision to have an affair remains with you and Tom, and the decision to kick you out remains with me."

Erica smiled. She reported being surprised that I would be so conventional and conservative, but added that she liked that I responded to her immediately and unequivocally. "I was afraid you wouldn't answer me, or answer the question with a question." She mockingly imitated an imaginary therapist: "'What do you think I should do, Erica?' Yech!" She said she respected that I did not "cop out" and that I answered her forcefully. I would be willing to commit myself and make a decision regarding her continuation. I felt momentarily relieved to be perceived as sufficient, in contrast to her passive father and preoccupied husband who, according to Erica, left decisions to their mates and became resentful.

"Of course, I could have an affair and not tell you," she reminded me combatively.

"That would just magnify my importance," I retorted.

"I hate you, and maybe you're right, but I really don't want to be with Tom. But I still want to be with Robert," she answered concretely. She then reassured me that that she did not want to keep secrets, lie to me, or otherwise damage our relationship.

"Well, could we say that you do and you don't want to keep secrets, and that you are and you aren't having an affair, and we are just beginning to understand why?"

Erica responded with an equivocal "Maybe."

Taking encouragement, I again asked her to consider how her current "cell phone affair" with Tom might relate to the group, or to me specifically.

"We're not having a cell phone affair!" Erica protested. "Sometimes we talk about sex and it gets me very excited, but we talk about the group too. Tom talks to me when he can't communicate in group. He doesn't want me to tell you. That is one of the things I don't like about him. Robert would never make those demands. It isn't fair, and I told him he was putting pressure on me, putting me in the middle."

I smiled: "Mmm, you're in the middle between Tom and me. Three in the bed."

"Very funny. I know you think that's what affairs are about. You're not my husband. Why is it always about you?" Erica asked rhetorically.

Now it was my turn to be concrete. "Why is it?"

"It's not, it's not you here. I can say what I want and I know how you feel, sort of. Maybe it's you in group. I'm very aware of you in group, how you relate to everyone, what you are really thinking. I don't feel free."

"I'm different in group?" I asked.

"Not really, maybe I just believe that you are more honest with me here and don't just act therapeutic. You can't be so balanced and fair to everyone as you are in group, so I don't believe you. It's more obvious in group that you're being a therapist. I know you think this has to do with my anger at my mother, with rules, rules, rules, teaching me how to be socially appropriate and a phony like her. I never knew what she was really feeling. Tell me she's in bed with us too."

I could not do otherwise: "Yes, all of us. Your phony, rule-making mother, your unavailable husband-father, me, the worst of both. You and Tom can turn your backs on us, but you know we're there."

The individual sessions with Erica succeeded in decoding the symbolic underlay expressed in her enactment with Tom. That is, in my treating the "acting out" as *resistance*, searching for and interpreting what I believe were the symbolic roots of her behavior, we made some sense of her motives for coupling (see *Chapter five*, on *Resistance*). However, Tom did not attend individual sessions, and I had become increasingly concerned and puzzled by his sudden taciturnity. The group frequently discussed and played with sexual attractions (and repulsions), and an open acknowledgment of their flirtatious relationship hardly would be shocking. Indeed, in a recent secession, all the women had concurred with Erica that the shaggy, angular Tom was witty and sexy. But they rated him only a one-night stand, because Tom could become inaccessible and moody, as he had been lately.

Since Tom continued to engage Erica, knowing that she talked to me about their relationship and shared the content of their conversations, I assumed that he wanted me to know, but to know what? And how could I use the knowledge?

Further, I felt it my duty to call attention to their clandestine relationship (see *Chapter eight*, on therapeutic *integrity*). Left unexplored, the shared deception of Erica and Tom could have a negative impact on group process as well as on the two members themselves. "The link between one mind and another that leads to destruction of both is the lie" (Bion, 1970, p. 104). Their surreptitious coupling had to be addressed in terms of its symbolic significance, deconstructed rather than merely exposed or even banned.

I had that pit-in-the-stomach feeling. I did not want to fulfill a role as the group's primitive superego, a Cerberus, truth's monstrous guardian. I did not want to make pronouncements behind an analytic screen, a Tiresias, truth's depressingly omniscient prophet. Finally, I did not want to become the group Judas, who used truth to betray. I could become a bad object for being conscripted to hide the truth, and a bad object for being goaded to expose it. "My conscience hath a thousand several tongues/And every tongue brings in a several tale/And every tale condemns me for a villain" (Shakespeare, *Richard III, V, v*). And perhaps, the significance for Tom was in my villainy, as it had been for Erica.

In group, some members may be quiet, while others, like Tom, are obtrusively quiet. Tom was Erica's counterpart. While Erica tended to be noisily deceptive, Tom provocatively dummied up. Even in being secretive, Tom revealed in his furtive glances and coy behavior, his involvement with Erica, and a need to be attended to. I therefore could rationalize my calling attention to their interaction, since it was a secret that to some extent everyone knew.

My first interventional foray was as follows:

"What?" I inquired, looking at Tom, then at Erica, and then at Tom again, thereby calling attention to the eye play between them.

"What?" he echoed.

"The looks, back and forth with Erica, what are you saying?"

"What do you mean?" he teased, with false innocence.

"What do you mean 'what do you mean?'" I teased back.

After several more verbal volleys, Erica broke in: "I can't stand when you do this, Tom, I feel used. He knows we talk to each other, and you know he knows we talk to each other."

Tom sobered in response to Erica's annoyance, and with an air of self-righteousness, said he was not thinking of anything in particular. And then, again with humor: "So what, what?"

Several other group members encouraged Tom to speak, to let us in to what was seemed to be disturbing him. Was it about group or something else?

"It's not about group. I have subjects I just can't talk about." Tom was an executive in the securities industry, and while he assured us he was not under investigation, or likely to be caught in the current web of Wall Street scandal, he had many colleagues and friends who were. While Tom's reasonable explanation—which we had heard before—convinced no one, it succeeded in extinguishing our inquiry and the group moved on to other subjects. However, Tom seemed to appreciate the effort to connect to him, for he participated in the remainder of the session with insights useful to other members.

In the following weeks, pursuing Tom met limited success, for when and how he would talk, and what he would reveal, remained unpredictable and sometimes difficult to link up to the ongoing group dynamics. On one occasion, he brought us up to date on some of his marital difficulties: "My wife goes about her business, ignoring me. She doesn't tell me what's going on, I don't either. I give her the silent treatment."

A member volunteered: "This reminds me of how you described your parents' marriage. They went about their business giving each other the silent treatment, and your father went off and had his secret affairs."

From another member: "This reminds me of what you do in group, getting silent and keeping secrets." Tom reiterated that he had certain subjects that he could not and would not talk about. The group confirmed that everyone had these subjects; everyone had secrets. "Not like mine," he insisted with mounting annoyance.

I suggested that the issue was not his secrets, but his creating secrets here, and giving the silent treatment. (I was alluding to his stance of *refusal*, of course.) "Who are you giving the treatment to here?"

Tom looked around. "Nobody," and then, suddenly, "maybe you."

"Why me?"

He replied: "You keep secrets from me, why shouldn't I keep secrets from you?"

The group seemed dumbfounded, and I asked him to elaborate: "What secrets?"

"Everything. You don't answer any questions, you just deflect. You're doing it now. You expect me to tell you everything, and you tell us nothing. I feel manipulated. When I first came to group I trusted you, I could tell that you knew what you were doing. I've learned a lot about myself, more than I expected to, more than I even wanted to. I began to feel that is your plan, like we're puppets. Psychotherapy puppets."

Erica tried to protect me and reason with Tom. I smiled at her reassuringly, as if to say that we did not need protection from Tom's truth. I continued with Tom: "And you don't go along, you go against me because you feel I'm forcing you to do what you don't want to do," I suggested, "learn about yourself more than you want to."

"Exactly!" he replied, victoriously. "I never get a straight answer about you, and I'm not going to give one about me. I was manipulated by my parents and I don't want to be manipulated by you, even if it is for my benefit." He then reconsidered, and with an endearing self-deprecation, continued: "Sounds pretty stupid, huh!"

I sympathized: "How else can you protect yourself from my influence but to clam up here and open up when you get away from me."

Discussion: Coupling as transference resistance to the two-faced therapist

There are, of course, many ways of analyzing the extra-group coupling and the attendant group interactions. Particularly relevant are the phenomena of *resistance, rebellion* and *refusal*, which I have parenthetically referred to and will develop in the following chapters.

I now consider the behavior of the two members in relationship to this chapter's topic of the two-faced therapist. I will use the term, "coupling," to distinguish the group members' behavior from the *basic assumption, pairing,* which would involve the whole group. In my evaluation, the group at large upheld *work group* functioning. The other members asserted an exploratory attitude, while realistic about the potential dangers of the couples' behavior to themselves and to the group. They also monitored my fairness and contributed their own feelings and ideas as we dealt with the couple and the group situation.

Erica and Tom each had suffered through painful awakenings in group, as we reconstructed their childhoods utilizing their respective transferences, primarily to the therapist. In terms of their histories, both had parents who perpetuated *psi* by "gaslighting" (Calef & Weinshel, 1981), behaving as if they were irreproachable and subtly undermining their children's mentality when diverging from prescribed (i.e., *Establishment*) parental modes of thinking and feeling.

Erica's mother attempted, with some success, to be her daughter's arbiter in all matters of taste and human relations. She interrogated Erica's friends and downgraded them once they were gone, such that as an adolescent, the ambivalent Erica entered into clandestine peer relationships. She guiltily hid her affections—sexual and otherwise—from her parents, or rebelliously exposed them. Erica came to understand the origin of a formerly inexpressible sense of claustrophobic anxiety, which she had fought against by developing a lively, hyper-interactive lifestyle. In her "yes, but" transference, she protected herself from my control by monopolizing our individual sessions, and contesting me in group. Her cell phone relationship with Tom served as sanctuary, rebellion, and retaliation, but it was also a plea for attention.

While Erica's adolescence was of self-conscious, covert and overt *rebellion*, Tom's was of self-denial and acquiescence. His parents' message had been that his family was special, and he complied by being a "perfect" child, a star in the classroom and on the playing fields. In treatment, he remembered that as a trusting teenager, he consciously *refused* to respond to certain inner urgings that had to do with rebellious feelings and thoughts towards the parents, whom he had adored and obeyed. The price of Tom's mental repudiation had been intense moodiness and inexplicable angry outbursts, which he carried into his adulthood.

Tom found the group experience "mind blowing," as he came to understand his obvious and painful lack of satisfaction in all his achievements, and why he had often been sad and anxious even during his supposedly happy childhood. He accepted that he had maintained an idealized version of his family, and that actually there were prominent marital and family masquerades that he had participated in sustaining.

"You took away my heroes," he proclaimed, to me particularly, with a slightly threatening humor, "you better be careful!" Although

Tom achieved some awareness of his tendency to idealize, he still became angry and recalcitrant when others disappointed him. Now he expected everyone to be self-serving, and since he valued and depended on me, I became a focus of his mistrust. Was I really concerned for him or just doing my job? From Tom's point of view, my therapeutic methods remained oblique and unexplained, and my intentions suspect.

Like Shakespeare's Hamlet, who also suffered a prolonged adolescence, the taciturn Tom needed to find the truth about an *Establishment* leader with devious motives. "You would play upon me/you would seem to know my stops, you would pluck/out the heart of my mystery, you would sound me/from my lowest note to the top of my compass—and there is much music, excellent voice, in this/ little organ—yet cannot you make it speak' (*Hamlet, III, ii*).

And like Hamlet, the sardonic Tom put "an antic disposition on" (*I, v*), and used his words, silences, and a play within the play—his cell phone liaison with Erica—to refuse and to rebel. He could "speak daggers but use none" (III, iii). Via counter-falsification, Tom could "catch" me and I would reveal my real self: "The play's the thing/ Wherein I'll catch the conscience of the King" (*III, i*).

Discussion continued: Facing the two-faces without (undue) falsity

I had concluded that whereas Erica and Tom each valued the group and their relationship to me as significant leader, they formed intense transference resistances, coupled, and together refused and rebelled against my role as *Establishment* leader, which they equated with falsity. As a pair, they believed that my primary goal was protecting my professional interests, that is, the existence of my group, rather than being concerned about the impact of a taboo affair on them individually. And further, they did not believe I would honestly acknowledge my priorities. As Erica—often the symbolic mouthpiece of the couple—said to me in another individual session, "You don't care if we have an affair or not, except if it interferes with your group. You don't have to answer me personally, not that you would. As a professional, you can't have your patients sleeping with each other."

Erica had no reason to be optimistic. I would be gaslighting to deny the reality that, to a major extent, I determined the rules of our interpersonal engagement. According to these rules, the patient is to be "personal," while the therapist remains "professional," even when caring.

In the patient-therapist relationship, there are inherent subject-object disjunctions. While the patient has one therapist, the therapist has many patients, and additionally, the group therapist is concerned with establishing and maintaining the group itself. The patient values the therapist as a subject, a special person, and wants to be treated as a special person and not primarily as an object among many, a patient in a group. But the therapist implicitly demands to treat, and be treated, as an object, a professional, and not primarily as a subject, a special person.

We may see here that as the therapist, I could not but be personal when being professional. My reactivity to challenge and defiance, my investigative and interpretative pacing, tact, empathic gestures, and bonding efforts—all these verbal and nonverbal variables and more—represented me, and conveyed information to the group about my caring: how I approached and avoided the truth. In being professional, functioning with two faces—of *Establishment* and of *significance*—significant truth about the therapist also is revealed. Issues of the therapist's authenticity, his or her sincerity and insincerity, truth and falsity, are open to public scrutiny (*Chapter eight*).

I came to understand that a primary nonconscious motive for Erica and Tom's coupling was to test me, to discover how I would respond to their rebellious defiance of my principles and practices, how and if I could meld the two identities of group leadership without being false. In finally addressing the subgrouping and searching for its significance via questioning, confronting, clarifying, and interpreting, I was being—but also calling attention to me—as the *Establishment* professional.

In exposing the truth, I attempted to address and not punish Erica or Tom for what could be considered, symbolically, a moral as well as a group violation. Also, while I did my best to represent the *Establishment*, I attempted to convey recognition of Erica and Tom's conflict with me as *Establishment* figure, and that their predicament had personal meaning to me as well as to them, and that I felt affected by it (Pollack & Slavin, 1998). Thus, I attempted to assert moral principles without being moralistic, and therapeutic principles without being stereotypically therapeutic.

With nonconscious intent, the two members made me face the two faces of group leadership. What was of vital significance was not the merely factual truth, such as "I have no whiskey," or "Erica and Tom have a cell phone relationship." Significance emerges from how and why the therapist addresses the truth, and which truth, and the therapist's success in engaging other members in the truth-seeking process.

My interventions served to break up Erica and Tom as an illicit dyad within the group.

However, the group culture now includes cell phone subgroups of varying and shifting memberships. Tom and Erica's extra-group flirtation had destructive potential for the group. The new configurations, since they are acknowledged and open for discussion, represent a more gentle *rebellion* against my leadership. To some extent, Erica and Tom's enactment has had revolutionary impact: the group functions with expanded boundaries, yet is also more cohesive.

Therapist as conservator and challenger of group process

Ideally, empathic and truth-seeking needs of patients (and the therapist) will come to support one another. However, an aspect of human growth and development is to accept another type of "pit in the stomach" anxiety: that which arises from awareness of the inevitable element of separation between people and between what can be known and what can be tolerated. Therapists adjust and integrate different subjective self-states; these are dependent on the real and imagined roles, present and historical, and ensuing relationships with the group and its members. Among the most important roles are the two faces we present to the group: spokesperson of the *Establishment* and spokesperson of *significant* truth.

However, we risk being two-faced in another sense of the term, that is, false. The relationship between the two professional faces of the group leader is not a simple one, and *psi* may be associated with either or both therapeutic stances. To reduce the level of falsity in our leadership, we need to expose and consider with the group these dual representations. Most likely, there is an important level of social reality to the group's perceptions, which contribute to the enduring enactments involving *resistance, rebellion* and *refusal.*

In theory the therapist seeks truth and uses truth as an instrument for exploration, and not for certainty. In practice, however, the therapist often is more and less truthful, and more and less certain, than he or she should be. Exaggerated or deficient empathy, anxiety, personal blind spots, loyalty to outdated and ill-advised principles or to that which merely is current and fashionable, and inevitable ignorance, influence what the analyst perceives as the truth, and how and when the analyst approaches and evades it.

Along with other group members, we learn retrospectively as we observe process, review countertransference, and listen to the group's feedback, both symbolic and actual. For we function with our own pit-in-the stomach pain when caring for other individuals, and we cannot be sure whether that pain helps us navigate two essential directions at once: to be the conservator and challenger of group process and culture.

To foster *significance*, the therapist must attempt to identify falsity in oneself as well as in others. However, despite our expertise, we deceive ourselves, perhaps even more than we do others. Our best intentions may be clumsy and out of sync with person and group process. For example, premature, ill-timed, or experience-distant "deep" interpretations may stimulate resistance and energize defenses, and so serve to forestall or stifle meaning making. Therapist-influenced dynamics supersede the clinician's theoretical or technical orientation, and in our attempts to be both conservator and challenger, we sometimes achieve more, or less, in our practice than what we preach. Our amiable, sincere, and patient efforts to reach the group count for a lot, and we fumble and are forgiven for our fumbling, more than we know.

In my opinion, in well-working analytic groups, therapist and members mutually and regularly enlighten one another. Empathic and truth-seeking needs are not necessarily or mainly antagonistic; they often are sequential and at moments, harmoniously coexist. However, the pit-in-the-stomach anxiety cannot be fully assuaged. Even in exemplary group communications, truth remains with the small "t", uncertain, impure, and incomplete.

PART II

RESISTANCE, REBELLION AND REFUSAL

CHAPTER FOUR

Introducing the 3 Rs of relational group psychotherapy

> All men by nature desire to know.
>
> —Aristotle, *Metaphysics*

> I am met with hostility and live in such isolation that one might suppose that I had discovered the greatest truths.
>
> —Freud, from a letter of March 13, 1896; in Laplanche & Pontalis, 1973, p. 397

Configuring the 3 Rs

I was assigned an afternoon's workshop at a regional group therapy conference. The topic was "Formulating the Unformulated." I had anticipated that the attendees might want me to lead an experiential group, and then use the data to discuss ideas developed in *Relational Group Psychotherapy: From Basic Assumptions to Passion*. However, the challenges that arose and the relationships that developed within the group impacted on me and opened up a line of thought that—in calling attention to dynamics of *rebellion* and *refusal*—prompted what was for me a new understanding of *resistance*.

I describe a painful emotional juncture, not unique to me, I am sure. The situation is this: The group therapist or leader has gone too far, feels he or she has gone too far, or has been accused of going too far. The offended group member generates a network of sympathy and support, and attention turns antagonistically to the leader. Questions are raised regarding the leader's mental and emotional balance, principles and practices, personality, psychodynamics, and motivation.

Case example: A workshop on "Formulating the unformulated"

Entering my assigned room, I felt heartened by a full roster of attendees, a few recognized from previous presentations. I introduced the topic of "Formulating the Unformulated" with some remarks pertaining to Bion's ideas on the subject. Prior to such contemporary relational theorists as Bromberg (1998) or Stern (1997), Bion described in metatheory, in my opinion, not since equaled, how important aspects of intrapsychic and interpersonal communication take place on preverbal levels in which thinking and feeling remain partially undeveloped, verbally unarticulated, and segregated from each other.[1]

I invited people to determine how we should proceed. After a spirited debate and a sharing of interests, the group decided on the afternoon's format, the anticipated combination of experiential and didactic learning, with emphasis on the former. I agreed, and added that, most likely, I would be more active than if I was leading an ongoing psychotherapy group, both because of the large number (22) of participants and in order to call attention to the role of the leader.

---

[1]Bion postulated substrata of protomental contents—*premonitions* and *beta elements*—that need to be transformed so they can become thoughts. Bion called this necessary process the *"alpha-function." Alpha functioning* organizes into conscious and unconscious thoughts disparate and chaotic eruptions of "raw" or unmediated protomental experience so that they may be felt and thought about as feelings and ideas. The ongoing transformation of *beta* into *alpha elements* provides consciousness and unconsciousness with symbols, nameable affects in the form of ideas, feelings, and emotional thoughts of increasing complexity that may be expressed in fantasy, dreams, art, science, mathematics, etc. *Alpha function* serves to link individuals to themselves and others, and thus, extends relational awareness. (See *Appendix I.*)

The early give-and-take revealed many sophisticated participants, well versed in psychoanalytic theory. For example, several volunteered that they wanted to alter their "paranoid" and "schizoid" outlooks that they habitually brought to group experience. The room seemed to relax and affably settle in when I encouraged people to stick to their feelings, and for now, leave it to me to bandy about the Kleinian and Bionion formulations.

But one woman, Myra, regularly interjected herself and insisted on framing process in these terms, and asked me to comment and clarify. As to be expected, members wanted to know more about Myra, why she wanted to know, and why now. Ignoring the curiosity about her, she simply reminded the group that I had written a book on relational group psychotherapy, and therefore I was an expert. She spoke with an accent, which added to an impression that she was different, perhaps foreign to an experiential workshop. However, her questions were easy to field, and for a while I succeeded in relating them, and her, to ongoing group process. Her interruptions continued and members turned to her with alternating helpful and hostile attention.

For whatever reasons, Myra was not translating the feedback in a useful way. She seemed not to understand, and frayed members' patience. I nipped a spirited, but indirect, attack led by Kenneth, a man sitting to my right, with a sardonic aside to the group at large: "If we were concerned with scapegoating, rather than unformulated experience, I could not have written a script for a better foil." I told Myra I would try to answer her interesting questions later, and turned to engage a segment of the room which had not yet spoken.

But Kenneth protested angrily at my cutting him off. What was I saying to him? I replied that I was aware of interrupting him, and that I had assumed he would understand that it was not about him, but an effort to protect Myra, and keep the group from being mired in the easily "formulated." He said he did understand, but did not like the way I had done it. I sympathized and said I was sure that I could have done it better, and apologized for offending him. Sitting next to each other, we had turned our bodily positions, such to be literally face to face, and thus our moment of intense intimacy was observable to all.

Michael, sitting across the room, broke our brief silence by checking in with Kenneth, how did he feel about my response?

Kenneth replied that he was satisfied by my explanation and our exchange. Michael then complimented me for handling the matter straightforwardly. Kenneth clarified that he realized that I had been trying to move the group into a more feeling level, and that he had a tendency to intellectualize. Still, he did not like being interrupted and, while he agreed with Michael that he liked my directness, he was holding his judgment about me in abeyance.

Jane, a woman flanking my left, seemed to have little doubt about me. She said she was shaken by the interaction and felt I had lost control of the group. She declined to comment further. Karen introduced herself, saying that it was too bad Jane felt that way. She liked Kenneth's directness, both that he could confront me so early in the group, and that he could be reasonable and self-reflective. Michael concurred and reiterated his positive feelings about the group. "I'd like to continue," Karen interceded. Michael said, "Go ahead." She said she was not comfortable speaking in groups, and wanted to speak up and say that, before she lost courage and retreated. Now she felt uncomfortable!

Karen's acknowledgment brought out several who said that it was difficult to break the ice and speak up. Karen said that they would get much more out of the experience if they did, "See, I'm already saying more than I usually do!" Her warmth seemed to encourage others to introduce themselves, describe some of their life issues, and enter into affecting dialogue with the group at large.

As if to cool the developing emotional intensity, a person cheerfully told about herself, a hiker in the Sierras. She connected to another person with extensive camping and wilderness experience. A third spoke of fly-fishing, a fourth, a photography expedition to Africa. Conveying a sense of making an intervention almost too obvious, I suggested that the group get back to our indoor adventure. As if I had said the opposite, Jane launched into her own lengthy travelogue, which seemed not only to disappoint but also to stun the group. Despite several polite attempts to redirect her conversation, she found a cohort to continue an exchange. At some point, I interceded, and asked them if they could relate more directly to what they were feeling in the group.

While her partner voiced appreciation for my stepping in, Jane became irate, and attempted to draft Kenneth by referring to our early interaction. Kenneth supported my leadership, however, and along with others, attempted to work with Jane, explaining what she was doing, asking her to be more direct. She seemed dejected and confused, and still not a bit happy with me. In order to move things along and avoid another scapegoating, I complimented Jane for letting us know how she felt about me.

Several of the less secure participants took a chance, speaking briefly about the group experience or their personal lives, while conveying a touching vulnerability that stimulated the group's cautious curiosity. Tom, who initially had described himself as "schizoid," reported a life crisis. Married late, he and his wife had their last chance to conceive. He had lived a life without having to care for another, and could he do it? Eric shared that he had just become a father, and he began to cry when he considered how it felt. He knew he was different than his own father, who cared, but could not show it. Perhaps Tom needed to think about his relationship to his own father. Karen commented that although Tom did not say much, he conveyed a great deal of caring, and that she thought he would be a great parent. As if to prove her point, Tom thanked Eric for his insight regarding fathers and gently attended to Eric's sadness.

Michael joined in the midst of the exchange between the two men, informing the group that although he was even older than Tom, he remained ambivalent about settling down and having a child. Several women were interested, he informed us, maybe he was in love with at least one of them, but he was not sure if he was ready, or that he ever would be ready. Eric thought that would be too bad. Yes, it would be, Michael rejoined poignantly, but took the conversation no further.

Ben turned to Karen and commented how much he enjoyed her participation. Even when she was not saying anything, she had lively eyes. Karen, taken aback and quizzical, smiled in return. Michael volunteered that he too, noticed Karen, and agreed that she was contributing a lot to "process." His reference redirected attention to an abstraction, the group entity, and away from the couple. (I am using the term "couple" to differentiate two members who are working at awareness, and not operating from the *basic assumption, pairing*.)

Addressing Michael, I said that I believed he could take something from the afternoon's workshop that eventually might help him in making a decision about his life. I commented that he tended to get in the middle of exchanges between other members. And then, as an afterthought, I added that he was functioning as the group's "Oedipal child."

Michael at first seemed interested in my insight, but shortly became enraged. "You have some nerve to call me 'Oedipal,' you don't know my situation. I have been in analysis for 15 years, with several highly qualified and well-known people. You know me for a couple of hours, where do you get off analyzing me?"

Concerned by the intensity of Michael's response, several members tried without success to soothe and reason with him, to bring out what upset him so. Kenneth turned attention to my leadership. "We didn't contract for psychotherapy," he reprimanded.

Gail, a woman who had spoken only briefly, explained that I was interpreting an "enactment," something that occurred in group and in all human relationships, whether or not involving psychotherapy. She went on, "That's the beauty of group, the deepest issues may come out after a few moments. Michael calls attention to himself whenever two people start to connect."

"I feel like getting up and leaving, but I won't," Michael continued.

Ben attempted to mediate the situation. He said he hoped Michael would stay and try to work this out. He understood how Michael felt, but he believed that I made the comment in the spirit of trying to connect and be helpful. Ben suggested that Michael might be reacting to how, as much as what, I said. Ben had been in another of my workshops. He observed that mostly, I put my comments as mere ideas to be considered, or not considered. But I had spoken differently to Michael, with an air of certainty.

My use of "Oedipal" bothered several people who spoke up. It sounded "clinical." Why did I use the term? How was it helpful?

Gail said that I was a psychoanalyst and the term did not necessarily mean the same to me as it might to others. "What is so bad about the term, anyway?" Karen declared, and some others silently concurred.

I too was perplexed, for the group had begun with many members speaking in psychoanalytic shorthand, and I assumed liberty to use the vocabulary.

"It sounds like name calling," someone replied.

Ben said that he believed I meant "Oedipal" metaphorically, and not literally, but psychoanalytic terms should be avoided, because they carry with them a lot of baggage. Particularly when the leader says them, they mean more. How was Michael doing?

"Not very well. I don't need this. [to me] You don't know anything about me. I am a widower … my wife died many years ago and I still carry around unfinished business. Maybe I'm still in mourning. I haven't been able to really commit since then. I don't know if I want to build my own family." Michael continued to talk earnestly to the group. While feeling supportive and encouraging of him, I also felt clumsy for my intervention and guilty for having opened his wound.

Kenneth turned attention back to me; he wondered if I was angry with Michael, and that is why I spoke to him that way. I said that as far as I was aware, I might have had too much "desire" to connect with Michael and be helpful. Perhaps my desire is what Ben heard as certainty.

Kenneth remained unconvinced, as if I did not know my own feelings, which was, of course, a distinct possibility. I asked Michael if he felt I was angry with him.

"No, I think you like me and are interested in me. I liked you, until now. I still do. I think you were genuinely trying to be helpful. But it felt like a kick in the butt."

"I'm afraid I've heard that comment more than once regarding my technical finesse."

Michael replied: "In all fairness, I've heard more than once that *I* need a kick in the butt."

"Well, we both are getting our butt kicked this afternoon," I said, as we exchanged warm smiles.

Ben commented that he was glad that Michael stayed. Had he left, it would have been bad for him, and for the group. He was grateful that we had a chance to work on what happened. I asked him why this was personally important to him. He said it meant a lot that an authority figure could be flexible and listen, and even acknowledge mistakes and shortcomings. His own father was quite the opposite: rigid and self-righteous.

Ben responded positively when I suggested that although he knew something about his relationship to his father, he had used the group experience to formulate unformulated feelings and thoughts. While it seemed evident that, like Michael's (perhaps Jane's and Kenneth's as well), Ben's reaction to me had an "Oedipal" cast,

I chose not to share my opinion. I turned to the group, saying that I was aware of time constraints, and that the participants also might want to formulate their experience. Some members did so, while others opted to comment on the most recent interaction, pick up and continue earlier links, or merely say good-bye.

Myra did not ask any more questions; rather, she reported having been intensely involved during the session, although she was not ready to put her feelings into words. Jane said that she could: she had remained angry and disappointed in me. She turned to several of the younger participants, letting them know that their struggles reminded her of her earlier self, and of some of the choices she had made and not made. Members reflected that she was communicating differently, and touchingly, and they raised the possibility that her "formulating" had to do with the leader's influence on group process. Jane stiffened, and did not address me directly.

Kenneth remained somber, and he was one of the few who did not participate in the remaining half hour. However, as people were exiting, he revealed himself to be an editor of a forthcoming book on group therapy. To my surprise, he asked whether I would contribute a chapter.

Still, I left the workshop not convinced about the durability of the repair between Michael and myself and the meaning of the group experience for all the members. And, although the participants rated the workshop highly on their review forms, I remained vaguely rattled and in doubt regarding what people thought of it and of me. Perhaps uncertainty is a valuable, even necessary dimension of the pursuit of truth, an aspect of formulating—and reformulating—the unformulated.

Three perspectives on the group experience

In the group, challenges to my leadership seemed to arise from many psychic sources, some strictly within and some apart from (though influenced by) the arena of the nonconscious: for instance, philosophically and metapsychologically, pragmatically, politically, and willfully. I began to think about and categorize group themes, processes, and suborganizations according to three perspectives; these did not fit neatly within classical or contemporary psychoanalytic and psychoanalytic group frameworks, with their emphasis on nonconscious and "primitive" or irrational processes, transference-countertransference, and transference-countertransference resistance. The formulations regarding truth and falsity, as explained in *Chapters two* and *three*, came to provide an overarching link.

I believed I was struggling to make sense of the group experience and to present meaningful truths. But members had sharply divergent reactions and opinions regarding the significance and appropriateness of these truths, and how I evaluated the truths of others. Some members voiced approval of my methods and our achievements as a group. Others stated or implied that my truths were false, useless, irrelevant, inappropriate, or needlessly painful. I could not assume that my modes of leadership (*Chapter eight*) had beneficial impact.

Surely, if the members were "resisting," the term provides a wide theoretical umbrella. Too wide, in my opinion, and applied too colloquially to divergent clinical situations—situations calling for different types of therapeutic interactions: debate, negotiation and compromise, confrontation, exhortation, limit-setting, and of course, exploration and interpretation.

As in this case example, group members may make demands for us to reconsider our theoretical assumptions and techniques, and how we are attempting to apply them. They may close off avenues of interaction, keeping certain topics, persons, or ideas off limits. Challenges and standoffs may refer to the immediate and particular clinical situation, or represent more enduring features of relationships. They may refer to the person, manner, or method of conveying truth, and which truths, rather than truth-seeking itself. I thought that the terms *rebellion* and *refusal* bring out these crucial facets of group behavior and of psychotherapeutic treatment. Such factors referring to person and process need to be examined and negotiated, segregated from overweening preconceptions, assumptions, and clinical approaches traditionally associated with *resistance*.

In developing his clinical theory of resistance, Freud described instances when a patient stopped talking, or talking meaningfully, as in blockages in free-association or claims of having nothing to say. Dependent on the particular situation existing between participants, the clinical data first may be considered and explored as a *refusal* to mentate, or a *rebellion* against the "basic rule" to share mental contents.

I came to understand and use the concept of *resistance* in a more restricted and possibly precise sense, always involving nonconscious and symbolic processes. This hallmark of *resistance*—nonconscious symbolic activity that both veils and reveals truth—certainly occurs in *rebellion* and *refusal*. We assume the existence of nonconscious activity behind any conscious thought and action (Isaacs, 1952). But at certain junctures, *resistance*, in the narrower sense, is not the clinically most relevant or useful avenue to follow. And too, as we shall see, there are instances wherein *rebellion* and *refusal* may be best considered to function as qualitatively distinct phenomena.

The three descriptors may represent different "layers" of intrapsychic and/or interpersonal response, or divergent response modes; they may operate sequentially, co-exist, or happen at once, and their relative prominence may vary according to observer and point of view. In sum, *rebellion* and *refusal* may function as specific strategies or pathways of *resistance*, qualitatively distinct phenomena, or both, depending on the context and point of view. That which is meaningful in clinical—and perhaps all—relationships needs time and introspective and interactive experience to cohere and develop.

In the context of psychoanalytic psychotherapy, *resistance* involves, in Ferenzci's phrase, a "dialogue of unconsciousnesses." *Resistance* signifies proximity to unarticulated truth in the here-and-now therapeutic situation. Truth is developed and revealed gradually, through disguise and indirection, dream, metaphor, symptom formation, transference-countertransference, enactment, and so forth, but always involving symbolization. The therapeutic response is interpretation or, contemporarily, also sharing of one's thinking, with the goal of mutual discovery of nonconscious experience (Aron, 1996).

In contrast to *resistance*, *rebellion* opposes recourse to the nonconscious, and seeks or demands a mutual consciousness. *Rebellion* arises from conflicts of therapeutic assumptions and values, the metapsychological premises and pragmatic usefulness of particular truth, and the methodology of reaching them. Negotiating disagreements in tactics, pragmatics, and goals are essential aspects of process. The possibility exists of sociopolitical action—changing or ending the system of psychotherapeutic engagement.

Refusal expresses a negative attitude or unwillingness towards thinking about truth, or certain truths and their applications, a stance that may be contextually legitimate, and constructive. Whereas in *resistance* and *rebellion*, the participants may become immersed in conflict and process, *refusal* may engender intellectual void, without annihilating relationships.[2] Refusal, having conscious and willful intent, calls attention to itself, and therapeutically, may require explanation, confrontation, exhortation, and trust building, as well as patience and the acceptance of the inviolable.

As we shall discover in this and the following chapters, individuals—therapists and group leaders as well as patients and group members—resist, rebel, or refuse for all sorts of motives, and are typical of group situation. Further, the patterns may serve as an impetus to discovery, debate, independent thinking, and fresh modes of relating. Hence, these categories do not refer necessarily to inherently positive or negative qualities, or to a particular outcome. Indeed, an individual in *resistance* may remain relatively disaffected, while one in *rebellion* or even *refusal* may commit energetically to the therapeutic relationship and process.

I now continue the introduction to the theory and clinical utility of the *3 Rs* as I describe the workshop group dynamics according to the perspectives of *resistance, rebellion* and *refusal.*

Resistance

In the workshop's brief time span, irrational, unformulated, partially unformulated, and symbolized themes regarding genesis, growth, parenting, family, sexuality, and competition were expressed and further developed. Birth motifs were presaged by the workshop's title: "Formulating the Unformulated." The very idea of "a group" pre-formulates emotion and idea: In anticipating a workshop, each participant mentally affixes to a vague entity, a group-as-fetus. And, upon entering the workshop space, the fetus almost immediately becomes the baby born—the roomful of people becomes a "group."

---

[2]With the exception of the rebellious strategy of "*anarchy*," which has as its goal the destruction of thinking, thinkers, and thought-provoking relationships, and may involve attacks on both consciousness and unconsciousness (*Chapter six*).

The psychological DNAs of the participants combine and develop rapidly and somewhat predictably. Bion referred to this almost instantaneous process of group formation as "valency," representing a primitive or infantile mindset shared by all the members, who irrationally relate (as in "chemical bond") to the group as a human entity with a singular personality.

Perhaps the most difficult, and saddest, aspect of the leader's job is to separate sufficiently from this neonatal group to become its leader. While the group struggles with babyhood, to maintain connection and to feel secure, the leader struggles with parenthood, to separate and to feel adequate. Certainly the leader has birthing anxieties, fantasies, and wishes in proposing, preparing, and entering a workshop. I am aware of self-doubt: Will I deliver a healthy, truth-seeking group? Can I adequately nurture such a group, and challenge the group's inherent antagonism to what they need? Will the group love me?

Bion developed the influential idea that psychotherapy patients and groups attempt to control thinking, particularly the therapist's, by excessive projective identification, reinforced by gestural, paraverbal (e.g., tone and cadence), and verbal behaviors. The analyst may lose the ability to have the "moral freedom" (Racker, 1968) to think anything, and may instead feel trapped and manipulated. Likely, the analyst also feels that he or she is not functioning therapeutically. The analyst must "shake oneself out the numbing feeling," to be able to think about and make meaning out of otherwise thought-destroying interactions (Bion, 1961, p.149).

In the workshop, I quickly came to feel as if I were a good parent to some members, and a bad parent to others. My sense of "playing a part … in somebody else's phantasy" matched Bion's (1961, p. 149) description of the experience of being the object of projective identification. When Kenneth chastized me for interrupting, I felt numbed by many sets of accusatory eyes, including my own. It was possible that, despite my conscious intention to be objective and not to retaliate, I divided the room into good children/bad children in terms of how members treated me as good/bad parent. Eric's message to Tom, to think about the father-son relationship, applied to me as well.

Relational theorists have suggested that both patient and therapist do most emotional thinking nonconsciously. In the workshop situation, I had to accept that my words and actions were partially derivatives of my own irrational and nonconscious cognitive-emotional activities, and only retrospectively could I begin to become aware of the enactments that I contributed to. In our controversial interaction, Michael and I met at emotional crossroads, an intersection of our father-son psychologies. In retrospect, we came to understand that we had engaged in mutual "butt kicking"—certainly a less lethal enactment than played out between Oedipus and his father.

In his landmark book, *Transference and Countertransference*, Racker (1968) suggested that a neglected aspect of the Oedipus complex was the analyst's wish to be king, not only of other people, but also of one's own nonconscious. He described how the analyst's verbal and nonverbal behavior was variable and inconsistent, professional and personal, mature and immature, healthy and neurotic, and regulated by the emotional state of the relational matrix: "[The analyst's] internal and external dependencies, anxieties, and pathological defenses ... [respond] to every event of the analytic situation" (p. 132). So, the best I could do as leader was eradicate, as much as I could, not my own Oedipus complex, but my resistance to increasing self-awareness of it.

Bion (1965, p. 168) coined the phrase "proto-resistance" to describe a crucial feature of the analyst's subjective experience, an anticipatory anxiety regarding the antagonism of a patient to an interpretation not yet made. The question remains then, whether I was anxious enough in relating to Michael and other group members. Perhaps Ben was right, in that I was too certain, or Kenneth was right, that I was frustrated with Michael and angry. In the workshop, I myself had raised the possibility that I had too much Oedipal "desire" to connect with him and be helpful.

I took consolation from the thought that, while my conflicts, character structure, misunderstandings, and empathic failures contributed to the multileveled resistances in the group, they also provided vehicles for working them through. Another thought also consoled me, which is that my intervention with Michael was accurate, appropriate psychoanalytically, and suitable for a workshop with sophisticated professionals. Bion (1965) put it thus: "Freud stated as one of the criteria by which a psycho-analyst was to be judged was the degree of understanding allegiance he paid to the theory of the Oedipus complex.... [T]ime has done nothing to suggest that he erred by over-estimation; evidence of the Oedipus complex is never absent though it can be unobserved" (pp. 49–50).

No one said the truth was easy. Interventions often are as difficult for the leader to offer as for groups to receive, and sometimes we feel and are made to feel bad: thoughtless, destructive, and even crazy, for making them. Confronting resistance, counter-resistance, and "proto-resistance" remains an uncertain, confusing procedure, and often a mark of success is ongoing discomfort and self-doubt. The journey from unformulated to formulated is fretful and incomplete.

Rebellion

Group members feel intersubjective tensions that arise from differences in beliefs about how their group should function, and at times they rebel against the group process. There are different pathways of rebellion, differentiated by their processes and outcomes: *defiance, secession/exile, anarchy,* or *revolution* (*Chapter six*). Rebellion denotes a strategy of social action, adopted by a faction, when other avenues of influence seem futile or unattractive, a judgment that depends on the group's genuine receptivity to discussion and change, and equally, on the state of mind of the rebelling faction. While rebellion represents a mental attitude, it is useful to think of group process, and rebellion as an attempt to move the group in a different direction.

In rebellion, unlike resistance, the ideas and feelings that are expressed, and the behaviors that are planned or enacted, are not to be considered primarily as psychological phenomena, with non-conscious levels of meaning, to be brought into conscious awareness and appreciated for their symbolism. Rebellion focuses attention on the idea of the group: What kind of group is this and is it acceptable? The basic premises and values of the group are at the center of the controversy, to be acknowledged, and addressed on that level.

Thus I emphasize that the conflict of therapeutic assumptions and values leading to rebellion may exist quite apart from resistance, dynamic and character issues, or transference-countertransference per se. The conflict may represent reasonable differences in beliefs in what constitutes an effective group experience. Exposing and discussing the differences in perspectives, and what are believed to be incongruities in underlying or basic values, becomes an essential aspect of the group process. Psychodynamic issues underlying the clash also may be analyzed, in due course.

However, in human relations serious misalliances may be unavoidable. The various pathways of rebellion are not always subject to modification via negotiation, compromise, and analysis. For example, our group worked around Jane's stubborn *defiance*, which remained unresolved. Michael threatened *secession*, and if the group truly was unsafe, secession was the choice pathway. Similarly, if an individual or faction had used the group for harm of self or others, I would have *exiled* the offending membership. In *revolution*, the premises of the rebelling faction come to overpower and dominate the group, which goes on to a new phase. However, revolution may rise organically as part of the group's development, and hence, the group's transformation may not always be immediate or obvious, or result from a single or dramatic event.

As mentioned earlier, the conflict leading to the action pathways of rebellion may not involve antagonism to all forms of truth and manners of pursuing it, but to the particular group approach or to the type of truth pursued. In our group, Myra wanted didactic truth, and initially she defied adhering to the agreed-upon experiential format. Kenneth initiated rebellion against me. What was I "saying" to him by interrupting, he asked defiantly. It was not clear whether he objected in principle to a leader's interrupting, anyone interrupting, or my oblique mode of interrupting. Still, I found his reasons for defying me—as far as I understood them—sensible and possibly valid, and I apologized, and directly explained my behavior.

How did Kenneth feel about my response?, Michael asked. While I suspected Michael of kindling lingering embers of discontent, I accepted the legitimacy of his inquiry. Kenneth supported me, and the fan of rebellion passed to Jane. I had "lost control" of the group. I heard in her declaration a revolutionary clarion call for new leadership, which brought out the loyalists. As spokesperson, Karen promoted my principles: speak up, share feelings, self-reflect, and others followed. But Jane broke the intimacy with her insistent travelogue, and would not adhere to my injunction to relate her feelings to the group. She clung to her view of group process, and once again mounted an unsuccessful challenge to my leadership. I felt I had to protect her from the group's counter-insurgency.

Then, another challenge occurred, this time instigated by my "Oedipal child" remark. I could not be sure whether Michael's outrage was a rebellious ploy to oust my leadership. Kenneth's chilly assertion that I was practicing uncontracted psychotherapy amplified my threat of exile. Ben served ostensibly as the great compromiser: I could continue to lead, but avoid all psychoanalytic terms. My theory and technique of group leadership was up for debate. A revolutionary troika of men—Michael, Kenneth, and Ben—set about to decide the fate of our group.

Agazarian (1997) usefully distinguished between functional subgroups, which serve to contain differences until they can be integrated within the group as a whole, versus stereotype subgroups, which are estranged or formed in opposition to the group (or group leader), becoming extreme, inflexible, and fragmenting.

Was the rebellion phase specific, an occurrence that would be directed against any leader (Bennis & Shepard, 1956; Freud, 1912–1913; 1921c)? Were the three men jockeying for status, power, and influence? Or, was the rebellion against me specifically?

Of course, I was a rebel too. While, on the one hand, the group leader is a primary agent in fostering a sense of continuity, cohesion, and regularity, he or she is also a powerful agent of change, and therefore wears "two faces" (*Chapter three*). The leader must at times "be destructive of the laws, conventions, culture, and therefore coherence, of a group within the group, if not of the whole group" (Bion, 1970, p. 64). The group leader, symbolically, linguistically, and behaviorally, may traverse the various pathways of rebellion, taking multiple roles of defiant instigator, anarchist, exiled outcast, secessionist, and revolutionary.

The putting-into-words process is a most important act of rebellion. Ogden (1997) asserted that an analyst's words should "upset (unsettle, decenter, disturb, perturb) the given" (p. 12). In my opinion, in any situation, as analyst or group leader, to avoid sounding omniscient or oracular and to encourage feedback, one needs to interact spontaneously, and maintain a vernacular, down-to-earth, even playful manner. Still, "clinical touch" cannot be defined, and two group leaders may think alike and make similar interventions at similar moments with quite different results. It was possible, as

Ben suggested, that it was not my words, but how I used them, that needed challenge and investigation.

Group leaders have destructive as well as constructive rebellious tendencies, independent of group phase or similar behaviors from other members. We feel intersubjective tensions that relate not only to transference-countertransferences, but also, from our own conflict between needing and desiring to think, and rebelling against the painful thinking processes and against the group that activates them.

Certainly, my version and approach to truth might have contributed to the group's rebellion, and to my response to rebellion. Apparently, I had formulated an idea that the group could not yet tolerate, and to insist upon my idea would have been unnecessarily provocative and without political purpose. However personally unnerving, I thought it important to encourage and participate in the group's discussion of my normative assumptions, leadership principles, personality, and human limitations. The group faced and lived with conflict between the leader and certain members, and their clashing versions of truth. Rebellion, not entirely quashed or even resolved, to some extent enhanced the group experience.

Refusal

Certain truths, and certain modes of truth seeking, may be experienced as destructive to the self or to the other, and not potentially beneficial. In an effort to preserve sanity and equanimity, sometimes we abandon thinkers and thinking. *Refusal* thus establishes a mental boundary between what is considered appropriate and inappropriate for intrapsychic or interpersonal dialogue. Nonconscious as well as conscious processes of feeling, thinking, and meaning-making are refused entry, left undeveloped, or obstructed. Working with refusal requires appreciating how and why the mind and truth-seeking interactions are being rejected.

The refusal to feel, to think, to make meaning—to confront and search for psychic truth—is more pervasive than we recognize. Refusal may be conscious and overt, or it may be disguised via confusion, indecision, ambivalence, intellectualization, distraction, emotional withdrawal, compliance, and cliché. Refusal is a strategy that may be used in any of the three *basic assumptions*. At this level of functioning, group members refuse the instruments psychoanalytic theory uses to uncover resistances and cope with rebellions: thought, language, and those who use and respect thought and language.

While refusal is a common, obvious, and even pervasive aspect of individual and group psychology, refusal is infrequently considered as a primary relational mode (*Chapter seven*). And, perhaps because group members may refuse outright, forcefully, and persistently, the group leader may refuse to think about refusal and make it a sustained focus of inquiry.

We may review by contrasting refusal with resistance and rebellion. *Resistance* involves symbol and symptom formation, transference-countertransference, and other derivatives of nonconscious activity. *Rebellion* eventuates in challenge, debate, and the possibility of sociopolitical action. Refusal thus differs from resistance, which forestalls conscious but invites nonconscious thinking, and from rebellion, which invites conscious but not nonconscious thinking. *Refusal* remains antagonistic to nonconscious and conscious versions of truth. Whereas in resistance and rebellion, the group leader becomes immersed in conflict and process, refusal engenders stalemate and intellectual void. However, as with Michael, sudden flare-ups and impulsive threats and behaviors may occur.

In the workshop, a number of individuals besides Michael exhibited the refusal mode. Myra was the first to go against the group will, and she refused to examine her behavior or to link it to ongoing group process. Her communications remained concrete and circumstantial. For example, when questioned helpfully by other members, she responded by referring to my so-called expertise, as if that would explain her insistent intellectualizations.

Like Myra, Jane rebuffed dialogue, and concluded as self-evident that I had lost control of the group. Later, I made a procedural suggestion, to return from the outdoor to the indoor adventure, i.e., to the here-and-now. Jane stunned the group by doing the opposite, inducing another member to join her in travelogue. I directly interceded and requested that the pair relate to their feelings, which relieved Jane's cohort, but Jane became irate and refused, and attempted to induct Kenneth. He refused to partner her, but he did not function in a refusal mode, since he utilized thought and language to link to her and seek meaning.

My fateful words, "Oedipal child," ignited Michael. His dramatic protests of refusal released a dark cloud of censure that spread over my intervention and me. "Psychotherapy!" Kenneth decried. "Clinical!" echoed a chorus of the self-righteous, and they could not—or would not—think about how my use of the term possibly could be helpful and not destructive.

Gail brought up the concept of enactment, referring to Michael's repeatedly inserting himself in the middle of two-person relationships. She spoke of the "beauty" of group process, and others agreed that something important had been revealed. But for a subgroup, beauty was not truth, and truth not beauty, and they remained a congregation of the unconverted. They thought I was thoughtless, and for a while, refused to think further about the possible constructive purposes of my interventions. I thought them thoughtless. To repair the breach, I could not refuse to think about refusal and convey respect for the reasons behind it. With the group's help, I found words, an attitude, and a mode of connection that encouraged a return to formulating thought.

CHAPTER FIVE

Resistance

I have introduced my ambition in *Chapter four*: to distinguish between various clinical phenomena, usually subsumed under the umbrella term *resistance*. Freud (1900a) emphasized the wide reach of this concept: "whatever interrupts the progress of the analytic work is a resistance" (p. 517). In this broadest sense, *resistance* remains a foundation concept in psychoanalysis and psychodynamic group therapy (Rosenthal, 1994).

To some extent, psychoanalytic psychotherapists agree with Freud, who held that all progress in psychotherapeutic technique hinges on the increasingly accurate evaluation of resistance (Laplanche & Pontalis, 1973, p. 395). As our techniques have evolved, so too has our understanding of resistance and our relative comfort with its manifestations.

Freud's "mythological" model of resistance

The clinical phenomenon of resistance came to light by Freud's technical innovation in the treatment of neurosis with patients not amenable to hypnosis. Freud urged that they produce memories of what had originally occasioned their symptoms. Some patients said they knew nothing, while others produced obscure recollections that they could not pursue further.

> I became still more insistent; I told the patients to lie down and deliberately close their eyes in order to "concentrate" .... I then found that without any hypnosis new recollections emerged .... This insistence involved effort on my part and so suggested the idea that I had to overcome a resistance ... *by means of my psychical work I had to overcome a psychic force in the patients which was opposed to the pathogenic ideas becoming conscious (being remembered)* (Freud & Breuer, 1893–1895, p. 268; Freud's emphasis).

Throughout his career, Freud used archeological and energic (e.g., "psychic force") images in a literal manner, also anthropomorphic metaphors and medical analogies, to describe the mechanisms and "contents" of resistance. The effect is to concretize, personalize, and pathologize, even vilify, resistance and set up the self-image of the group leader or therapist as antagonist, warrior, surgeon, and so forth—recurring metaphors of Freud's. Working through of the resistances is "a trial of patience for the analyst" (1914d, p. 155), a "struggle" (1912b, p. 102), since "the resistance accompanies the treatment step by step. Every single association, every act of the person under treatment must reckon with the resistance" (1912b, p. 103). Resistance is "violent and tenacious ... [and] the doctor must be distrustful and remain on his guard against it" (1916–1917, pp. 286–287).

Metaphors and analogies are an integral part of every scientific theory (Billow, 1977; Wurmser, 1977), and have a profound effect on clinical practice. In his joint publication with Freud, Breuer warned against the reification of metaphor: "It is only too easy to fall into a habit of thought which assumes that every substantive has a substance behind it ... and when we have become accustomed to make use metaphorically of spatial relations ... we find as time goes on that we have actually formed an idea which has lost its metaphorical nature and which we can manipulate easily as though it was real. Our mythology is then complete" (Freud & Breuer, 1893–1895, pp. 227–228).

Resistance continues to be used as an encompassing term with the negative, and sometimes misleading, connotations that Freud first established, concerning person, process, and progress.

But *resistance* may be investigated without the boundaries placed by uncritical acceptance of certain metaphors and metapsychological assumptions.

A relational model of resistance

In this chapter, I develop a narrower, more precise concept of *resistance* and place it in a relational group context. It is my contention that in resistance there is always (nonconscious) symbolizing, and so it provides a potential for psychic unfolding and communication. Resistance involves personal agency and intentionality. Stimulated by psychosocial circumstance, it develops, emerges, and evolves—communicated and understood within relational contexts.

I present five assertions about resistance. (1) Resistance regulates the development, expression, and usefulness of emotional truth. (2) Resistance is motivated by the basic conflict between thinking and not thinking. (3) Resistance reveals interplay between truth and falsity. (4) Resistance involves multiple levels and types of intersubjective interplays, including transference. (5) Resistance is not "lifted"—it works towards truth and is continuous. First, I present a case example, which I will analyze from the vantage point of each assertion. My purpose is to demonstrate how resistance brings form and content to the group experience.

Case example: A new group attempts to digest its experience

At an international meeting of group psychotherapy, I was invited to lead an early morning process group, 70 minutes on four consecutive days. Arriving before the first meeting, I found myself in a narrow, rectangular room, with eight desk chairs arranged in a small circle. I took a middle seat, and greeted members as they appeared. Nine individuals streamed in, some arriving a few minutes late, apologetic and disoriented: It was our first day, in a foreign city, at a large conference with many meeting rooms.

We located extra seating—two folding chairs—and settled as best we could. The group had formed an elongated ellipse, my position approximately equidistant from the two ends.

Participants initiated the verbal discussion by volunteering their first names, nationalities, and professional affiliations. Intermittently, three new arrivals popped in, repeating the apologies and excuses that had become both familiar and humorous, and procuring further seating which, out of necessity, they placed towards one end of the room. The group remained welcoming and friendly, as the discussion hovered on saying "hellos," renewing cursory acquaintances from prior meetings, reminiscing about visits to each others' countries, admiring the different cultures, and even, confessing guilt and sorrow for wars committed by ancestors.

A half hour had passed, and I commented that we now knew something about "there and then," but not much about "here and now." While some people seemed confused by my intervention, others made it clear that I wanted the group to remain "in the room" and that it would be a good idea. Then followed the expectable and perhaps necessary preliminary discussion of safety: Could we trust each other? The leader? Several members reassured the group that I had a "sterling reputation" and that they knew me, or knew of me. Sally, a conference organizer and the only person from the United States besides myself, gifted us with privileged information: "That's why our group is so big—it has twice as many members as the other groups."

Sally's conferment of specialness stimulated optimism: "I think it is amazing that we have people here from almost every continent." "I like that we have four days, it will give us a chance to get to know each other." Marko, in reference to himself and a man from a neighboring country, declared, "We're Scandinavian. People [there] don't talk much about their feelings, we men particularly. I want to do something different in this country."

Benito asserted that as an Italian, he had spent his youth "thinking with his cock." Now he was 60 (he gestured to his portly stomach) and he and "it" were out of commission. Given that English was a third or even fourth language for some of the participants, Benito's slang expression had to be explained, a task that several of the other men took on with some flirtatious amusement. The topic and process of translation occupied a number of the participants. Benito asserted that he wanted to use the time to "make love" to everyone, which charmed some of the women, particularly.

But Olga, a woman seated to my far right, now a lopsided endpoint, angrily rebuffed Benito's reaffirmation of the group's good cheer and manifesto of positive intentions. The session is almost over, she declared with bitterness: "It doesn't matter where I come from. In this group, I am in the 'suburbs'. All the action is happening in the 'city'." Others surrounding Olga echoed her resentments, struggling with apt English metaphors: "Yes, I am at a border town, not quite in my own country"; "The end of an island."

Sally, near the other end of the ellipse, apologized, as did several others near her, and then Sally asked us to consider how we could rearrange the chairs. These gestures seemed only to fuel Olga's anger, and she noted, accusingly, that almost all the men were on my left. "We like city life," a male quipped, attempting humor to ease the tension enveloping the room. Sally qualified that there were many more women (10) than men (5) in our group. Another woman, Irena, interrupted, and without looking at Sally, protested that she seemed to be co-leading the group. Sally apologized yet again, for talking too much and taking too much time. Several of her "city" cohorts reassured her that it was not her fault and she did not need to apologize. Some of the self-described "suburbanites" softened to agree; but still, they felt "left out," "consigned to a woman's group."

Members to my left continued to make efforts to connect to those to my right, but the attempts at repair seemed awkward and stilted, made more so by language difficulties. My interventions made little difference. Apparently, I was serving as a geographic marker. Less apparent were my leadership skills.

The session's ending was approaching, and I reminded the group that aggression and anger occur in every group, and it does not mean that we do not like each other or remain curious as well. Olga had brought into focus a particular perspective: Some people are angry for feeling "out," others may be angry at Olga for bringing these dynamics to our attention and arousing envy and guilt. Probably I am a source of anger and disappointment as well, not living up to reputation and expectations. How are we going to live with each other for the remainder of the four days, I questioned, given the physical realities of the room, limitations of the leader, felt needs of the members, and our personalities that lead to inclusion and exclusion?

We greeted the second day with the arrival of two women who had been members of disbanded groups and asked me whether they could join ours. Without conference instructions to the contrary, I felt it proper to assent. They searched and found seating, and as we settled in, another woman and a man appeared, with a similar story, and room was made for them as well.

The newcomers revealed their names and country of origin; they wanted to be part of a group and had heard positively of ours. With some pride, members informed them that we were indeed "a group." They noted that everyone had returned, and that the men had made attempts to distribute themselves throughout the room. Conversation served to integrate the new arrivals.

On Benito's initiation, several members complimented Olga for her courage for yesterday's participation. She acknowledged but did not yield to the attention. She remained unmoved psychically and physically, nonverbally broadcasting resentment from her far right location that had not changed. Some of the women surrounding Olga reported, perhaps partially for the benefit of the new members, that they had easily settled in the female outgroup, and how it related to their psychologies. Several members who initially were, or now remained, on the left side, volunteered that they had not spoken, or did not feel "in" even when speaking. Marko restated his wish to participate, but otherwise remained silent.

Sally apologized again, explaining to the larger membership that she tended to be a helper, in her childhood as well as in her role as wife and mother and now grandmother to a large brood of children and stepchildren. When others tried to reassure her of their affection or appreciation for her involvement, she brushed them off, reiterating that she did not mean to co-lead the group. I took my turn, saying that Sally was telling us something personal, and trying to locate herself in the group, like everyone else. But again, her response served to emphasize her dislocation: "I always put my foot in my mouth and I'm probably doing it again."

"So who feels in and who feels out—how does it work in here?" I asked, attempting to address what I took as a "common group tension" (Ezriel, 1950) or "focal conflict" (Whitaker & Lieberman, 1964). My query was sufficient to widen the social network of interaction, but soon, despite my repeated interventions, the exploration of group process swerved to personal histories and life stories. Several individuals who had been inactive said that they felt accepted because of the warmth and openness of others. As the session ended, Benito declared that we had become a relaxed "United Nations."

The third morning convened with a full but silent membership. I noted that we had assumed fixed positions in our cramped space, and wondered if that extended to our mental positions, that is, were people struggling with how and if to proceed? We were then interrupted: two more individuals appeared from another disbanded group. They had heard of our group, could they join? With minimal, though positive, verbal comment, we repositioned our seats and made room. "Hellos" were passed, and then, as if to regain cohesion, a thoughtful silence returned.

Marko said that he liked the active, "relational" approach of the leader, and said that he had made a resolve to speak. As if on cue, Benito interrupted, declaiming what "relational," meant to him, in terms of current existential philosophy and his own "awakening." I said that Benito might attend to the awakening of some of the members, like Marko, who had not participated and might need some assistance. But Benito ignored Marko and turned to Nadia, a woman who had not spoken the first two days.

She had begun to cry. In halting speech, only partially related to difficulties with the English language, Nadia related a dream: "It's the story of my life. I hadn't realized. My mother and sisters took my father, I couldn't. I didn't do anything about it."

Sally responded with what seemed a sense of guilt, as if the dream was about her: "Now you are doing something about it." Benito offered that she had his full interest and attention. Nadia was quiet. After a pause, a surprise: "My mother could get angry like Olga. It terrified me. I've been afraid in here."

Olga shook her head: "Sorry, sorry," as if to reassure Nadia, but remained isolated at the end of the ellipse. After several failed attempts to connect to her, I said that Olga is signaling that she is not ready to speak with us, and that other members might want our help, and mentioned Marko and Nadia. Marko responded first to my attention, telling us of his life's struggles to "relate." He felt he was taking a big step in our group, and other members agreed. I said I thought the "big step" applied to Nadia as well, and she replied that she was glad to be with us and felt better for speaking.

Later in the session I returned to Olga, and asked if she was ready to talk to us. She reproached herself for being "angry, scary." Her head remained bowed, and she spoke almost in a whisper, and in halting English. When I expressed some difficulty hearing, she seemed infuriated, as if I had criticized her. Was she angry at me?, I asked. She ignored the question (and the questioner) and continued to talk of her unhappiness. I gathered that she lived with undeserved guilt (such as within our group) and I made some reference to a "punitive superego," which I soon regretted, for she mocked my intervention as "psychoanalytic." She seemed to connect better to several of the women sitting beside her, eventually thanking them and indicating that she had participated enough.

I asked Keigo, a Japanese man sitting near Olga, who had rudimentary English and had not spoken the first two days, whether he understood the group process. He said that our group was very different from his country in that people were honest with their feelings. He wanted to let us know that he felt deeply and was affected by what he was experiencing, but did not have the words. Others expressed appreciation for his presence and participation. I said that I also was affected by what I was experiencing and often did not have the words. Sometimes, like Nadia, the words come to us in a dream.

Session three soon ended. Session four began with acknowledgment and regret about the group's ending. I emphasized that time remained for mutual growth, and at several intervals, encouraged members to ask for and offer feedback. Olga, Sally, and Benito kept a low profile; Nadia, Marko, and many other members took meaningful opportunities. When the session ended, it seemed difficult for all of us to leave the room.

Resistance: Five assertions

In revising a working concept of resistance, I extrapolate from Freud's (1915–1917) dynamic model: "We seek … to understand … [phenomena] as signs of an interplay of forces in the mind, as manifestations of purposeful intentions working concurrently or in mutual opposition" (p. 67).

Resistance regulates the development, expression, and usefulness of emotional truth

For Freud, aversive nonconscious truth set resistance into play—the archeological, buried, "repressed impulses." The goal of psychoanalytic treatment was to bring such truth to self-conscious emotional awareness: "to bring to the patient knowledge of unconscious, repressed impulses existing in him, and, for that purpose, to uncover the resistances that oppose this extension of his knowledge about himself" (Freud, 1919a, p.159).

To some degree, psychoanalysis continues to link resistance to the existence of finite, pre-existing unconscious truth, "truth" with a capital "T," e.g., repressed impulses, memories, structured fantasies (involving good/bad breast, penis, etc.). In my view, resistance is an aspect of the struggle to process and integrate shifting versions of emotional truth, from whatever perspective truth arises: rational, pre-rational and irrational, affective (the "impulses"), conscious, nonconscious, environmental, sociopolitical, interpersonal, or intrapsychic. We make "truth"—always with a small "t"—by grounding and transforming experience through different, evolving but finite perspectives.

As described in *Chapter two*, Bion (1965) replaced the polarity unconscious-conscious with infinite-finite (Symington & Symington, 1996). "Truth" is unbound, has no form, no categories, and remains unknown, as if we were in Plato's cave (hence, Bion's notation: "*0*"). The patient and the analyst bring an infinite potential into the room, but the truth that is developed and realized is bounded by their psychologies. In group, truth becomes bounded by all the vectors between and among every possible subgroup.

"Truth" refers to its own pursuit, development, and transformations that lead to the growth of the individual and group. Resistance protects against the unavoidable "growing pains," such that truth does not become too significant, too quickly, unduly affecting how we feel, think, and behave. However needed and even welcomed, truth often hurts, bringing to the fore formidable realities of ambivalence, impermanence, and uncertainty, and the necessity for change. In my view, resistance is an aspect of the struggle to process and integrate emotional truth, from whatever perspective it arises: rational, irrational, conscious, affective (the "repressed impulses"), preconscious and nonconscious, interpersonal, environmental, or sociopolitical.

The poet, Emily Dickinson (1960), wrote "The truth must dazzle gradually/Or every man be blind." Resistance allies with our current and habitual modes of "seeing," that is, of being in the world. It disguises and delays learning about and coming to "know" emotional truth. The "purposeful" intent—to make reference to the Freud quote preceding this subsection—is to modify or forestall such knowledge when it is feared as "blinding," that is, turbulent, too painful or too disturbing. A group becomes vital as fresh truths are discovered, integrated, and reconfigured in the members' intrapsychic and interpersonal relationships, and in the structure and process of the group itself.

Freud (1920g) posited the analyst as expert and arbiter of truth; the therapeutic task was to "discover the unconscious material that was concealed from the patient, put it together, and, at the right moment, communicate it to him" (p. 18). In this manner, resistance is "lifted."

But we no longer assume that the therapist has a privileged view of truth; rather, the therapist is expert in leading a search for truth. In group psychotherapy, the therapist has the special role of evaluating and responding to the truth needs of the various individuals and the group itself. It is among the therapist's primary tasks to offer protection from too much truth, or too little.

While Freud linked the analyst's *role* as stimulus for transference resistance (e.g., for the re-emergence of an unconscious Oedipal idea), we now include the analyst's *actual behaviors* as influencing factors. The therapist feels intersubjective tensions, activated by social participation, that represent the currency and history of his or her own intrapsychic and interpersonal struggles to seek and tolerate truth. These struggles, often registering on the psyches of group members, affect the therapist's credibility and ability to carry out the essential twofold task: pursuing that which is painfully immediate and most meaningful, at the same time shielding others from that which is immediate, but too painful to become meaningful. As the case example illustrates, varying confidence in the authority and safety of the therapist as one who pursues truth affects each member's and the group's resistances.

Case discussion: Can we become a group?

The initial phase found members sharing the historical and geographical, while forestalling the psychological. Resistance is immediate, a response to those aspects of present reality that are feared as painful. Whereas the danger may be anticipatory and of unknown content and origin—in self or other—it feel real. Bion (1965) commented that "There is no resistance to anything because it is believed to be false. Resistance operates because it is feared that the reality of the object is imminent" (p. 147).

When confronted with my request to locate ourselves in the present and in the room, the members redoubled protective maneuvers: reassuring each other of the "sterling" quality of the leader and professing desire to "know each other," to "make love," and "reveal and do something different." Manifest resistance, the uniformity of thought, feelings, and interactional behavior, continued with the enthusiasm greeting the translation of Benito's "thinking with his cock" trope. If we all could speak one language and understand each other and ourselves, truth could be easily obtained, and the problem of growth would be solved without pain, conflict or danger.

Olga's dramatic outburst released a torrent of divergent fantasy, feeling, and thought. We had to wait to see if and how we could transform her truths into a tolerable experience that was meaningful for her and the other participants.

I left the room and remained for that day and night in a not entirely uncomfortable state of suspension, as if a segment of my brain remained full with undigested experience. In resistance, material may be revealed slowly and amorphously. I had brief flashbacks—emotional snapshots of people and interactions—and even with urgent intention, had little success in organizing these feelings and images, much less translating them into words.

I anticipated the next morning with a need to understand where I had been, and with whom, and to discover the mental and interpersonal consequences of our interactions. Yet a nebulous sense of fullness and expectation evaporated upon my reentry into the vacant group space, and I waited with some relief as individuals streamed in.

The members' initial declaration that we were "a group" and Benito's ending summation that we were a relaxed "United Nations" were the symbolic bookends of our second meeting. Despite the return of all participants and the addition of new individuals, I remained unconvinced of both assessments. The tendency of the individuals to revert to personal stories and histories seemed to be impelled both by genuine desire to connect and to understand, and also, to dissolve the displeasure released by Olga's perspective on our experience. "There is no doubt that the resistance … operates under the sway of the pleasure principle" (Freud, 1920 g, p. 20).

In retrospect, my comment to Sally seems apt, applicable to Olga and to all who spoke and encouraged others to speak: In telling us something personal, she was trying to locate herself in the group. My interventional efforts were similarly motivated: I was trying to locate myself mentally in the group, and after the second session, was unsure I had succeeded.

The tension and suspense—even dread—that greeted the third morning's initial silence often typifies productive resistance, and indeed we were rewarded with deeply felt truth, for example, Nadia and Marko's revelations. And for that and the concluding day, I operated with greater confidence that a "group" did exist and I was its leader.

Resistance produces derivatives: Motivated by the conflict between thinking and not thinking

Resistances—"purposeful intentions working concurrently or in mutual opposition" (Freud, 1915–1917, p. 67) —are motivated to reveal and to conceal, to develop and to limit meaning. Resistance compromises by producing derivatives, allowing the individual to think, but with minimal conscious knowing.[1] Without reflection, emotional truth can be left partially or fully undeveloped and its impact seemingly muted. Still, it is common for others, such as group cohorts, to interpret that which is broadcast without conscious awareness or intention, and they make decisions how, and if to respond.

Freud linked resistance to defense mechanisms[2] and its prototype of repression. He stressed that repression did not interfere with

---

[1]Compare to a traditional view: "[Resistance represents] a compromise formation between defenses, drive derivates, painful affects, the need for punishment, and considerations of reality" (Boesky, 1988, p. 309).

[2]The relationship of resistance to defense remains ambiguous and the terms fold within each other (Lowental, 2000). Compare: "The concept of defense is broader than that of resistance since resistance is a treatment function" (Blum, 1985) with "[Resistance is] a much broader concept than defense" (Boesky, 1988, p. 309). Also, Freud (1937c): "defensive mechanisms directed against former danger recur in the treatment as *resistance* against recovery" (p. 238; his emphasis).

the unconscious, which remained active, "organizing itself further, putting out derivatives and establishing connections" (1915e, p. 149). Derivatives may reach consciousness to the extent to which they are sufficiently removed from the underlying representation, inserted with "intermediate links," or "distorted." Derivatives are coded, stored, and expressed in inchoate as well as tangible bodily sensations and movements; feelings; awake and dream images; pre-, para-, and linguistic expressions, and interpersonal enactments. Derivatives express unformulated as well as unacknowledged truth; they also may misdirect or couch falsity (*see next subsection*).

Each individual has a unique personality, distinguishable in part by those qualities that Reich (1933) first described as contributing to characteristic modes of resistance. Derivatives are "revealed in the formal aspects of the general behavior, the manner of talking, of the gait, facial expression and typical attitudes" (Reich, 1933, p. 65). Similarly, each group is unique in its "personality." Derivatives materialize in the group's characteristic modes of "being," woven into culture, process, and infrastructure. Derivatives give shape and persistence to *basic assumptions* and ensuing enactments, and of course, to the symbolic thought and language of the *work group*.

Progressive and deepening understanding of individual and group derivatives—the "hermeneutic spiral" (Gayle, 2009)—defines psychodynamic groups. In my opinion, the therapist operates best when working with derivatives in an experience-near, friendly, down-to-earth manner (in contrast to Bion's "Olympian" interpretative style). Harnessed in the service of the task, then, the derivatives of resistance function as royal roads to emotional truth and to a group's evolution.

Case discussion: Manifestations of basic assumption resistances and derivatives

Resistance accumulates internally and interpersonally, often preceded by unspecific and unpredictable sources of arousal. We assume that character and culture influence our perceptions, and additionally, that fantasy, impulse, and the irrational operate behind any thought, feeling, or action (Isaacs, 1952). If we attend to them, the derivatives of resistance are everywhere, in the fabric of human relations, in feeling, thinking, communicating and non-communicating.

Utilizing metaphor, symbols, myth, dream, condensations and displacements, and participating in nonverbal and paraverbal communication (including silence) and an evolving series of enactments, each member of our group broadcast derivatives of truth and its evasions. Some derivatives were immediate and obvious, and many more were not. They appeared in our group's "hellos"—in the contact hunger the greetings represented and in the fear and distrust they disguised and denied—in each member's particular and characteristic manner of group entry, self-presentation, and self-omission.

Sally's invitation for the participants to relax under the canopy of my and our group's special status, helped organize the group's evasiveness, one goal being to deny or minimize any thoughtful anticipation of frustration or pain. Oral provisions would prevail: The cross-cultural opportunities were "amazing"; four days would give the large group a chance for "everyone to know each other." The sexually decommissioned Benito signed on, proffering himself (rather than me) as leader of this early-structured *dependency assumption* group: He would supply "love" effortlessly, safely, and collectively.

Olga revealed a basic truth of human life that had resisted verbal expression but was symbolized by the seating arrangement: Not everyone is loved, accepted, and treated equitably. Olga's presentation was piercing, perhaps intentionally "blinding," to hurt us for hurting her. She exposed derivatives of the group's *fight/flight* dynamics, but rambunctiously propagated her own. The imagery, metaphors, and line of reasoning derived from her experience, personal and group level, conscious, pre- and nonconscious. Something deeply personal and unpredictable was embedded in her anger towards me and the men and women sharing my physical proximity. Still, the truth she revealed about the group was powerful, convincing, and resonant.

We would have to deal with the split she exposed: an "in" subgroup and an "out" subgroup, a typical process derivative of the *fight/flight assumption*. Groups are ambivalent towards messengers of truth—those who make known the "signs and manifestations"—the meanings contained in the derivatives. Like Sally, being too close (physically and professionally) to the leader of the *dependency* group (me), Olga could become a *fight/flight* scapegoat. I attempted to protect and re-integrate Olga by speaking to the *work* mentality (Bion, 1961), that aspect of group and individual functioning that wants to know and can tolerate attendant feelings of love, hate, and curiosity towards truth-bearers.

To some extent, session two was preoccupied with reconciliation—signs and manifestations of wishes to return to the imagined safety of *dependency.* The derivatives include: behavioral accommodation (particularly by the men who rearranged their seating); apologies (by Sally, first and foremost), gratitude (members to Olga), and rationalizations and explanations (by the leader, especially, who spoke about "common group tensions"). Here then, was another derivative of *dependency,* a collective fantasy that to function as a "group," we had to be of one mind, a "United Nations." Despite group reparative efforts, Olga remained unmoved and truculently "out." For as yet unknown reasons, she continued to propagate *fight/flight* dynamics.

Or it seemed, until session three.

Nadia's dream functioned as a "selected fact" (Bion, 1970), reorganizing conscious awareness of the group experience, past and present. Olga's persistent anger at the group—certainly the most dramatic derivative of sessions one and two—now could be understood as disguised bids for attention, sexual and otherwise. She was not only fighting *with* me, but primarily, fighting *for* me. Olga unleashed the female voices of those deprived of "all the [sexual] action." In resonance, Irena challenged Sally for "co-leading;" for in being the "helper," Sally was helping herself to me.

Positioning himself as the safe love object, and being the most prominent male voice after mine, Benito spoke for those wanting to usurp me. I suspected that included in his definition of "relational" was enjoyment of leadership prerogatives, which included taking all the women (Freud, 1912–1913). Certainly, his charm, empathy, and encouragement towards Olga, Nadia, and the other women did not extend across gender lines. He interrupted and silenced Marko on several occasions, and declined my invitation to aid any of his male colleagues' "awakenings."

Nadia's dream derivatives revealed *pairing assumptions*: a group preoccupied with sexual competition for the men, and we may extrapolate, between the men. From this credible perspective, Benito's trope "thinking with his cock" represented that element of individual and collective mentality that "thinks" with sexual urges and constructs a group on that basis. Olga, Sally, Nadia, and Benito had done their work in the first three sessions, expressing and enacting personal and group *dependency*, *fight/flight*, and *pairing* derivatives, and in session four, the task fell to others.

Resistance involves interplay between truth and falsity

Bion (1970) argued convincingly that, because of our limited mental, emotional, and linguistic capacities to approach the "infinite" (i.e., the unknown, "O") and to represent truth, an unavoidable and ineliminable "falsifying" dimension exists in all human relations—intrapsychic and interpersonal—in dyadic and group psychotherapy, organizations, and societies (*Chapter two*). Falsification signals anxiety, the existence of human frailty when we anticipate or are confronted with painful truth. Truth and falsity structure a group, falsity may lead to truth, and both may facilitate the building of constructive relationships.

From the perspective of "primary process" mental experience, anything felt, thought, or imagined is true, even if false at the same time. (For example, dreams may embody contradictory aspects, or represent perceptual or temporal impossibilities.) This mode of nonconscious or prerational and irrational mentation relates to the hegemony of the paranoid-schizoid position and of part-objects that constitute "truths" of psychic reality (Grotstein, 2000). A second tier of experience involves the use of logic and secondary process thinking, establishes the connection to outer reality, and re-evaluates and re-situates the realizations emanating from inner reality.

In the nonconscious, truth and falsity can exist without tension. In the second tier, the tension propels further thought. A group progresses and matures as members come to tolerate such tension, as they grapple with and partially work through tendencies toward falsity. Rather than the "sharp cleavages" that Freud (1915b, p.147) at times described, a functional mind (and a functional group) possesses a permeable boundary between systems consciousness-nonconciousness, and between experienced truth and falsity. The recognition of derivatives presents an opportunity to understand and partially integrate conscious-nonconscious, truth-falsity, in the two tiers.

Case discussion: Falsity lubricates social relations, hides and misguides, but also reveals truth

Session one commenced as a collection of strangers, communicating with masks of friendliness and behavioral niceties. I served as "host," arriving first to arrange furniture and welcome arrivals, and listening politely to the introductory back-and-forths. No one presented or was expected to present an unexpurgated version of oneself; no group begins or ever functions with unfettered communications. Conventional "presentations of self" (Goffman, 1972) lubricate human relations and make progress possible; they deform into a collusive *Establishment* when persistent and left unattended.

As time passed, I felt increasing pressure to make something happen. I could justify my impulse as reality-based and hence "true," given the conference's schedule. In terms of my inner-reality, less true, and I kept in check my desire to be "sterling," such as by being clever, confrontational, or making portentous, "deep" interpretations. Derivatives of resistance exist in all communications, and consequently, interpretations and other interventions derive from the clinician's struggle with truth: They are tentative, incomplete, and contain falsity. Calling attention to the group's artificiality or the presumable underlying paranoid anxieties would have been facile and supercilious—maneuvers to establish unearned leadership.

I was encouraged that the participants responded to my suggestion to relocate themselves "here and now." The derivatives revolved around the question that preoccupies entry to every new social situation: Am I among friends or foes? (Grotstein, 2000). Then the conversation turned to stilted encomiums about our special group and leader. I was grateful for Olga for piercing the protective cover of mutual reassurance, although alarmed by her manner of doing it.

From her position in the room, our group was rife with falsity. Olga viewed a fascistic *Establishment*: an in-group of merger-hungry members "massified" around an exalted leader, casting aside an out-group of "aggregated," disconnected women (Hopper's (2003b) terms). Olga brought to focus this painful truth: Without consensus and with questionable validity, a group quickly shapes its structure, boundaries, and hierarchies of status.

Session two represented genuine efforts at addressing our organizational problems—physical and psychological. The geometric properties of the room remained constant, of course, and despite many accommodative efforts towards her, Olga's attitudes as well. Even though anointed by the group as to my allure, I felt hostage to Olga's aggrieved silence and constrained in what I could say. I became fearful of truth, as I understood it, and cautious and unsure of my success in its presentation.

Freud (1916–1917) counseled that "If the patient is to fight his way through the normal conflict with the resistances ... he is in need of a powerful stimulus ... what turns the scale is ... simply and solely his relationship to the doctor" (p. 445). Olga refused to relate to me, or to the relationship-building efforts of other members. In being a "United Nations," did we all feel like Sally (and me), fearful and ashamed of our own realities, apologetic for putting our foot in our mouths?

In a productive group, the "interplay" of resistance, while always bidirectional, moves from thoughts, feelings, and interactions that are less conscious to more conscious, and from less true to more true. Session three revealed the registry of this process on a seemingly quiescent member. In rendering the truth of the adage, "Hell hath no fury like a woman scorned," Nadia's dream exposed Olga's subterfuge. Murmuring "Sorry" and keeping her head bowed, Olga seemed shamed and embarrassed by the "truth" of her libido as much as by her devious tactics in expressing it.

Bion believed that the effective leader has to use truth as an "explosive force" (1966, p. 37) on the *Establishment*, destroying "the laws, conventions, culture, and therefore coherence, of a group within the group, if not of the whole group" (1970, p. 64). However, all group members have the potential to disrupt falsity and aid the group and its leader in reparative truth-seeking. While to some extent the leader ensures the integrity of the group culture, other members also break up old relational patterns and experiment with new ones.

The revelation and analysis of falsity is central to this process. From the very first session, with Olga's impetus, our group confronted issues of falsity—the subgroupings, role of certain members, interpersonal and gender maneuverings, my debatable leadership. But at the same time that Olga exposed falsity, her self-presentation also promulgated it. The intensity of her emotions blocked her own self-exploration and inhibited the creative work of others.

It is expectable in human relations that truth-seeking and falsification occurs in chorus, in different degrees of awareness, and with conflicting intrapsychic and interpersonal purpose. Elements of falsification participate in the methods by which truth is attempted, and the uses to which it is put. With the benefit of hindsight and new experience, that which seemed true (or false) in an earlier session becomes subject to reevaluation and transformation.

Under the protective cover of dream, the tremulous Nadia stimulated the interpretative, truth-reparative work of session three. We moved forward to consider the group as a *pairing* organization, that is, preoccupied with derivatives of sexuality and "breeding." Inevitably, a new, if unexplored, *Establishment* was evolving in session four, as we structured an orderly leave-taking and made our conventional goodbyes.

Resistance is intersubjective, involving multiple levels and types of mental interplay, including transference

Bion was prescient about the coming relational zeitgeist, and its deflection away from one-person psychologies. His conception of optimal psychological functioning involved cognitive and affective linkages, within one's own mind, but also between one's mind and others'. And it is not necessary for the other minds to be physically or temporally present. We link to Shakespeare's or Beethoven's mind when we creatively appreciate their art. Bloom (1997) persuasively argued that every writer who sits, alone, before his blank page (or today, blank screen), relates and responds to all the minds of his or her literary ancestors, so that we must consider personal creativity a social phenomenon.

Likewise, resistances are social phenomena. They involve interactive mental relationships, intrapsychic, interpersonal and immediate, and also historic, cultural, and political. Multiple and diverse transferences are woven into the fabric of resistance, and vice-versa. The "situational genesis" (Thoma & Kachele, 1994b, p. 140) of resistance involves member-to-member transferences (including the therapist's), the symbolic and actual qualities of the group, and the larger socio-political setting in which the group is embedded (Ettin & Cohen, 2003; Hopper, 2003a,b).

Freud (1916–1917) wrote ambivalently about resistances specifically related to the therapeutic relationship, which he differentiated from other types, putting them into a special category referred to as "transference resistances." "[They] should not be one-sidedly condemned. They include so much of the most important material from the patient's past and bring it back in so convincing a fashion that they become some of the best supports of the analysis" (p. 291).

But in a sense, all resistances are transference resistances. If they differ, it is because in the therapeutic relationship, resistance serves as a psychoanalytic object, that is, subject of investigation. In this vein, Caruso (1972; in Thoma & Kachele, 1994a, p. 112) referred to resistance as an "exchange mechanism rather than defense mechanism in the interpersonal sphere." The signs and manifestations of transference resistance partially derive from and inform about group relationships—although they arise from and are generalizable to other individual and group situations as well.

It takes time to understand human experience, and truth emerges on many levels and from many perspectives. Derivatives of resistances are received, evaluated, and responded to by others, often without conscious awareness, or intent. They gradually emerge into preconsciousness and consciousness and into the group's structure, process, and content. We understand slowly and incompletely, and in this process words and actions produce *enactments*, co-creations that are learned about with the benefit of hindsight and mutual feedback.

We may appreciate how no clear delineation exists between insight and enactment—and this includes that which the therapist or leader "decides" to think about, and present or withhold as interventions. The leader's transferences and other derivatives of irrational and nonconscious (and conscious) experience are communicated by and also between and under the leader's words. Reactivity to challenge and defiance, investigative and interpretative pacing, tact, empathic gestures—all these verbal and nonverbal variables and more—represent the leader-in-action and convey information to the group: how he or she approaches and avoids the truth. In such enactments, truths about the leader are revealed. Other members feel, think, and fantasize about the leader's feelings, thoughts, object relations, and fantasies. Issues of his or her realness, sincerity and insincerity, truth and falsity, are conveyed in his or her modes of leadership (*Chapter eight*), which open to public scrutiny.

Gerson (2004) described a relational unconscious, which refers to "processes through which individuals communicate with each other without awareness about their wishes and fears, and in so doing, structure the relational unconscious according to both mutually regulated concealments and searches for recognition and expression of their individual subjectivities" (p. 81). Enactments are the "derivatives in action of the relational unconscious (p. 85).

Groups enact "transpositions" (De Mare, Piper, & Thompson, 1991) or "equivalences" (Hopper, 2003a,b)—revealing collective transferences (transformations) of a nonconsciously perceived situation from its social to its present context. Actions, fantasies, object relations, and affects that have occurred "there and then," at another time and space, are brought to the present group situation, via a process of projective and introjective identifications.

Equivalences may arise from traumatogenic experiences involving personal and social helplessness and powerlessness. They serve multiple and competing goals: to expel, attack, achieve control and mastery; above all, they are attempts to communicate (Hopper, 2003b). The group becomes a microcosm of the larger social context in which it is embedded.

The mutually stimulating effect of intersecting minds drives toward expression and translation of equivalences and other forms of enactments, allowing for that which otherwise could or would not be consciously known. Truth emerges "unbidden" (Stern, 1990), to be reworked—deepened and compounded and made yet more lucid—in the course of intrapsychic and interpersonal experience.

Case discussion: The "situational genesis" of our group structure and process

Supplementing the typical paranoid/depressive dreads and excitements accompanying group formation, our group was subject to specific determining influences: a collective, traumatized "social nonconscious" (see Hopper, 2003a,b). Almost all of us had just completed an arduous international journey spanning two or more continents. Contemporary air travel assaulted body and spirit with flight delays and cancellations, confined seating and nourishment, and at departure and arrival, human corrals, security searches, formidable presentations of identity documentation, and the sanction to travel.

Crossing international datelines dislocated time, space, and sleep/awake cycles.

Struggling with an unfamiliar foreign language to find our respective lodgings, we encountered a gritty city with a reputation for high crime, and sharp and obvious divisions between rich and poor. Our host country recently had lived through a military dictatorship wherein many people had "disappeared." Armed security forces guarded the airport, the hotels, and all public facilities.

The next morning we bussed and taxied to an unlikely conference site, a complex of municipal buildings containing a secondary school on winter's recess. A thousand of us passed through the security checkpoint, and then, registered and name-tagged, we traversed the maze of public and private offices, meeting halls, and classrooms to our respective early morning placements.

We were a collection of the unsettled, geographically, culturally, linguistically, and emotionally thrown into confusion. Somewhere in mind (and among our minds) was each person's history, distant, recent, and in formation. Existential anxieties—fears, fantasies, and thoughts concerning survival, identity, affiliation, and exile—could not be quelled or avoided. The sequelae of our traumatogenic encounters appeared immediately: The structure, process, and content of our cohering group formed the equivalences, as we contextualized, symbolized, and reenacted individual and collective transferences—including the very traumas from which we sought protection and succor.

We met in jeopardy of disappearing; as social beings, we needed each other to "be." Then perhaps we could think more abstractly and form a truth-bearing group. The "factoids" of lives: nationality, profession, previous travel, and so forth—both revealing and screening the "there and then"—were collective efforts to put some solid ground under immediate experience.

In identifying ourselves in terms of countries of origin, members declared a bond of émigré status. Perhaps in these early moments, we established our culture and goal: We would become a group that provided harbor, succoring latecomers and the displaced from other groups. As Freud (1915e) observed, "It is a very remarkable thing that the Unconscious of one human being can react upon that of another, without passing through the Conscious" (p. 194). Without conscious intent or awareness, but with implicit group and conference approval, I became the *de facto* host-protector and also, *de jure* commander of rescue operations. Symbolically (and enactively), in expanding the group boundaries to allow for new arrivals, I attempted to bring democracy and open borders to the émigrés from totalitarian and failed states.

However, a traumatized collection of individuals such as ours could not become a true *work group* without some mindful attention to social reality. To function authentically as a democracy would require tolerating further disorder and disruption. Olga was the messenger, carrying truth about our disowned experience, the equivalences between *Establishments* "there and then" and "here and now" (Hopper, 2003b). From her point of view, our group had created its own borders that were difficult to cross.

Olga made us feel the helpless vulnerability involved in our country / city / group entry, the apprehension of social and geographic isolation, and the consequences of rejection: fear and hatred of totalitarian authority and those who collude with it. Perhaps she spoke for all those conference participants who were angry "citizens," their own proposals for leadership rejected, and now subjected to envious reactions to individuals such as me.

By the end of session two, we had on some level of consciousness-nonconsciousness dealt with socio-political reality, and thus, there was some truth in Benito's declaration of our being a "United Nations." The "hermeneutic spiral"—the interactional group process that co-creates multiple and ever-deepening levels of transference meaning (Gayle, 2009)—led us to Oedipal revelations in session three. Nadia served as messenger. In describing the equivalences between her role in her family of origin and our group, she also inaugurated the process of personal revelation and mutual feedback that continued in session four.

Resistance is not "lifted"—It works toward truth and is continuous

As truth is infinite, so is resistance. Individuals and groups work toward truths as they work through resistance. Resistance determines the finite shape of the infinite: which truths become the focuses of inquiry, and how, when, and to what extent. Resistance binds a group's truths and makes them tolerable, and it is through the derivatives of resistance that truths make themselves known. Yet, reaching new realizations—to the extent they contain "blinding" elements of the "infinite"—necessarily exceed the grasp of the member and group's mental and emotional capacities. The need for truth propels the group's continuity and stimulates, shapes, and reshapes resistances.

I have described, in *Relational Group Psychotherapy,* how anxiety-ridden truths that arise from the most basic or "primitive" affects of love, hate, and curiosity (*L*, *H*, and *K*) structure the fundamental group resistances: *dependency, fight/flight,* and *pairing*. As intrapsychic and interpersonal dimensions and dynamics of the varying *basic assumption* resistances are clarified, the group works toward truth.

Truth and resistance situate in dynamic relationship, described in the tripartite model of the *"container-contained."*[3] Force is exerted in both directions, and each strongly influences the other (*Appendix I*). Truth stimulates resistance and to some (limited) extent, is contained within it.

Ongoing and shifting self-other-group evaluations influence the expression of derivatives through *anti-linking* (signaling fear of truth), *bonding* (on which more abstract linkages depend), and *symbolic* (reliance on verbal thought and language) communications. Given the need and fear of truth, all three modes likely play out in any extended human interaction. Individuals engage on many relational levels at once, and the same communication may be utilized to reach conflicting goals. Such are the manifestations of resistance—"purposeful intentions working concurrently or in mutual opposition" (Freud, 1916–1917, p. 67).

Concluding case discussion: Truth feared, resistance suffered and enjoyed

Clinicians live with the knowledge that all therapies and therapeutic interactions remain incomplete, that is, doing therapy requires accepting a level of failure. I believe it is never appropriate to say, "The patient was too resistant," or "The resistance was too strong." Resistance, as I use it, involves symbolizing, and in a relational

---

[3]"The psycho-analytic problem is the problem of growth and its harmonious resolution in the relationship between the container and the contained, repeated in individual, pair, and finally group (intra and extra psychically)" (Bion, 1970, pp. 15–16).

context, it always presents an opportunity for generating meaning and growth. To some extent then, the failure is ours, in that we have not been creative enough, or, since truth often hurts, courageous enough to bear necessary pain.

The group experience has haunted my consciousness as well as less-accessible areas of my mind. In re-examining the group experience, I have struggled to think, rather than continue to ruminate or re-live memories, themselves less productive forms of resistance. The process has been arduous, relieving, and fulfilling; my report remains unfinished and approximate, with an unavoidable fictive dimension.

Truth is infinite; but human truths are tentative, limited by personal perspective, and in constant need of revision. Were other participants assigned this task of review, their reports would differ and likely—and beneficially—contradict mine. I have discovered "thoughts unknown" (Bollas, 1999), that is, formulations within range of my own mentality—conscious-nonconscious—that I had resisted and that waited to be developed. I have also profited from thoughts residing in other minds, some not present. For instance, only in re-reading Hopper (2003 a; b) have I been able to comprehend the group structure and process as derivatives of an interlocking series of socio-psychological matrices in which we were, to some extent, traumatically immersed.

I entered our room with the presumption that the prospective members sought an experience that would involve unfolding of resistances, to embrace in self and other that which could be safely discovered and developed in the group. To some extent, our awkward and uncomfortable room became a center of learning: anchor, sanctuary, and beacon.

However, given its internal dynamics, and its respective nestings within the conference *Establishment*, a crime-ridden city, and a host country with resonances of its totalitarian past, the safety *in* and also, *of* the group remained central in individual and communal mentality. Our room marked the boundaries of a state—political and of mind—permeable to overpowering effects of competition, segregation, sexism, and imminent exile and disintegration. At varying times and according to varying perspectives I, as leader, tantalized, satisfied, and defied expectations to protect, equalize, and foster cohesion and understanding.

We were to engage, submit, rebel, falsify; to help, hinder, halt process and development. A collection of people became a group that was desired and feared, loved and hated, stimulated by curiosity about itself, and motivated by the need to bring consciousness to its emotional experience. A bidirectional revealing-concealing process emerged through which derivatives of emotional truths were captured in culture and process, in thought, language, symbols, feelings, bodily sensations, falsifications, and enactments.

Sally, Olga, Benito, Nadia, and Marko were, along with the leader, the prominent players and spokespersons, giving form and shape to the psychodynamic, organizational, and socio-political derivatives—the group in which we were all contained. To unidentified degrees, other members were also involved, responding to those aspects of group life to which attention was drawn, and identifying with the subject of focus—person, subgroup, and whole group.

The clinician's own level of self-awareness and self-understanding is at the heart of the group process. I have reconsidered my behavior—respecting limits in my capacity to know truth and reduce falsity. In striving to be an "exceptional individual" (Bion's term), the group leader participates as one of the contained and as a containing force.

Like Sally, I made sincere efforts to take care of the group, based on my own experiences as leader, parent, child, and so forth. I fostered *bonding* interactions by having members relate to each other—and to me—directly. I could easily fend off Benito's falsifying maneuvers, which I took as attempts to replace my potential leadership. My calling attention to "the room"—the potential for the untried and the unknown—were efforts to nip budding *dependency* enactments and move us forward.

To contain anger and to prevent *antilinking* forces to prevail, I drew verbal attention to my probable role in stirring up *fight/flight dynamics.* I did not rush the truth-revealing process, and when I felt it necessary, such as at the end of the first session, I kept *symbolic*-level interventions conceptually simple and linguistically down-to-earth.

While my efforts at containing in session one may have sufficed for other members, they did not work for me. Olga's protest—an amalgamation of hurt, anger, and powerlessness—had an *antilinking* effect on my mentality, such that I had difficulty thinking about the group, organizing my mixed feelings, or retrieving my day and night dreams. This is not to suggest that Olga's behaviors were inappropriate, illegitimate, or pathognomonic. Would her communications have been as sincerely truth-bearing—and effective—any other way?

In session three, Nadia made known that I served *symbolically* as a sexual object, but I was also a sexual subject. Freud (1916–1917) recognized an aspect of the interactive dimension to the working through process: "In so far as his [the patient's] transference bears a 'plus' sign, it clothes the doctor with authority and is transformed into belief in his communications and explanations" (p. 445). But to be trusted and believed, the therapist or leader—that is, his or her countertransference—must also function in the realm of "plus."

Freud (1921c) attributed the formation groups to a biological need to love and to be in harmony with others: "A group is clearly held together by a power of some kind: and to what power could this feat be better ascribed than to Eros, which holds together everything in the world" (p. 92). Writing on the analyst's stance toward the patient, Racker (1968) concluded, "To understand, to unite with another, and hence, also to love, prove to be basically one and the same" (p. 174). I was unable to *bond* with Olga sufficiently, or effectively, and hence, my attempts at *symbolic* communication fell flat.

Perhaps this explains my still-embarrassing interpretation regarding Olga's "punitive superego." This intervention was, as Olga recognized, "psychoanalytic," but also false, a clichéd derivative of my own de-linked mentality—a desperate attempt to screen myself (Jacobs, 2001) and "cure" her. I had pursued Olga, but for her mind and her felt *bonding* needs, I contained her too little and too late. She refused to favor me with her attention, and was scornful of mine.

The leader plays a role—the "leading" role—in constructing and organizing whatever is being observed. Different leaders respond to different derivatives, and some are easier to process than others. Perhaps if the circumstances of this newly forming group had been different—without the hardships and recency of journey and the mutual unfamiliarity with persons and places—I could have responded more effectively to Olga, and she to me, and we would have moved on to other enactments.

The group process was painful at times—not always revealing sterling qualities in myself or any other member. Still, it provided consolation; sharing, understanding; in translating pain into meaning, the group fulfilled deep needs, lessened pain and also, made pain more bearable.

Resistance brings form and content to the group

Freud believed that to effect cure, advance development, and assure mental health, the therapist must "expose and get rid of [resistance]" (1916–1917, p. 451). By "lifting internal resistances ... the patient's mental life is permanently changed, is raised to a high level of development and remains protected against fresh possibilities of falling ill" (1916–1917, p. 451).

Our view is that psychoanalytic psychotherapy is not about cure, but rather, about developing the capacity to suffer—and enjoy—the creative use of truth, in its interpersonal milieu. *Resistance* signifies proximity to unarticulated truths in the here-and-now therapeutic situation., Presumptions, attitudes, and beliefs that are guiding and regulating internal, interpersonal, and socio-political relationships are threatened with exposure, re-examination, and unpredictable transformation. When "mental life is permanently changed," loss occurs, as well as gain.

A cautionary fear of truth propels resistance, but an everlasting hunger for truth propels its derivatives, its publication, and its evolving exploration. To the extent to which truth is perceived as absent, grossly deficient, or overwhelming, and the containing medium precarious or treacherous, *rebellion* or outright *refusal* to participate may be viable forms of opposition to the therapist and his or her agenda (*Chapters six* and *seven*). Resistance is not to be judged on the dimension of illness, then, but on its legitimacy, given the relational context in which truth presents itself.

Resistance cannot be cured, overcome, or resolved. According to perspective and existential moment, one type and level of resistance seems prominent, and then another. Shifts in consciousness-nonconsciousness, truth and falsity, and from lower to higher levels of mental and group organization—from not thinking to thinking, from *antilinking* and *bonding* to *symbolic* manifestations of resistance—operate quickly, subtly, and recurrently. Truth is infinite and its draw and fear persistent—continuity exists although it is not always detectable, as we make, unmake, and remake our experiences meaningful. Resistance is continuous: pointing us to underlying truths, and so, resistance defines and redefines personal and group experience.

CHAPTER SIX

Rebellion

We turn to the topic of rebellion—when a faction rebels, how the group and leader respond to the conflict, and how the conflict is resolved. I presented the essence of my ideas in *Chapter eight* of *Relational Group Psychotherapy,* and I rely, with some modifications, on that text. The illustrative clinical examples and accompanying discussions are new. I also clarify and emphasize the distinctions between *anarchy* and the other pathways of rebellion: *defiance, secession/exile,* and *revolution.*

Groups are not tranquil, as they are composed of individuals with different needs, wants, and goals. Disagreement over principles and values, the direction of the group, and the modus operandi of the leader, are to be expected, and these dynamics—among others that relate more specifically to the intra- and inter-psychic relationships among individuals—structure the group's formation, motivate its membership, and drive its process.

I describe different pathways of rebellion, differentiated by their processes and outcomes: *defiance, secession/exile, anarchy,* or *revolution.* Rebellion denotes a strategy adopted by a faction, when other avenues of influence seem unappealing, or even futile—a judgment that depends on the state of mind of the rebel as well as on the group's *authenticity* (see *Chapter eight, this volume*): its genuine receptivity to discussion and change. The rebelling faction feels that to participate in the principles and practices of the current or proposed direction of group interaction would require unacceptable submission. The values represented by rebellion may be presented as intellectually, morally, emotionally, or pragmatically unassailable—absolute—not subject to extended disagreement, negotiation, or repudiation. As rebellion arises, there may seem no route available for successful compromise.

Although not always apparent, rebellions are against the leader, who determines many if not all of the group's principles and practices. For instance, a rebelling member may become a scapegoat, representing a repository of the group's displaced feelings of disappointment and betrayal by the leader who does not live up to their group's expectations. Or, at times a dissident member may usurp and become the temporary leader.

While rebellion represents a mental attitude, it impacts group process in its attempts to move the group in a different direction. Rebellion thus serves as a strategy of social action: to modify, transform, or even overthrow the group's status quo, or adamantly to oppose its revision.

Merely expressing a vexing self, or deviating from the existing group culture does not necessarily constitute rebellion. Certain individuals may spend years challenging the opinions of the group therapist or other members, while regularly attending and finding benefit in the treatment. Others may feel bonded, yet disobey the task, frame, or rules, and even may dodge treatment. Neither situation necessarily represents a true rebellion, since the members are not motivated to address or influence the group's principles or mode of operation. Quite the contrary, they may enjoy the group as constituted and have no wish for change, despite their protests and difficulties in living within it.

In contradistinction to *resistance*, as defined in *Chapter five*, when *rebellion* takes place in the psychotherapy group, the ideas and feelings that are expressed, and the behaviors that are enacted, are not presented as psychological phenomena to be studied, interpreted, and possibly modified and worked through. Rebellion focuses attention on the idea of the group: What kind of group is this and is it acceptable to me? The basic premises and values of the group are at the center of the controversy—first and foremost to be addressed on that level. Psychodynamic issues underlying the clash may be analyzed in due course, if the group successfully contains the rebellion to the extent that this level of thought and dialogue is valued.

Greenson (1967) maintained that the concept of resistance implies a rebellion against psychoanalytic principles and procedures thereby linking rebellion to dynamics of transference and pathology. Others have written of the negative therapeutic reaction and its relationship to overwhelming envy—patients who are "difficult," in large part, because of their rebellious enactments (Roth, Stone, & Kibel, 1990).

In my opinion, these suppositions are based on too facile, therapist-centric presumptions. To reiterate: A conflict of therapeutic assumptions and values leading to rebellion may exist quite apart from nonconscious processes or transference and countertransference per se, and may represent legitimate differences in points of view. In wearing the "two faces" of leadership and both preserving and deconstructing the *Establishment* (*Chapter three*) and accustomed modes of thinking, feeling, and functioning, the therapist also, and necessarily, functions as a rebel.

In rebellion, what one individual or faction feels as indispensable for proper group functioning may feel antagonistic to another's sense of security, well-being, or purpose. Exposing and discussing the difference in perspectives, and what are believed to be incongruities in underlying or basic values, may sometimes relieve impasses and forestall crises and premature terminations. Rebellions are inevitable and not always resolvable, however, and not every outcome is or can be a positive experience for the participants.

Rebellion and group process: Brief review of major theories

Since I consider rebellion as representing a possibly valid challenge, and not necessarily (or solely) a *resistance* and merely a stage of group life, my conceptualization is at some variance with the idea of rebellion as it has figured in the major theories of group formation and process. To give a most well-known example, Freud (1912–1913; 1921c) postulated that rebellion against the leader is necessary for group formation and process. He utilized myth to describe how groups, in the aftermath of a murderous rebellion against the primal father (who took all the women for himself), guiltily massed under a new father figure, and established principles and practices to normalize interpersonal relations. In Freudian group theory, group members must work through nonconscious resistance to feel and verbalize their wishes to overthrow the leader and indulge their sexual and aggressive fantasies.

Group theorists have expanded on Freudian theory by calling attention to the therapist as symbolic mother as well as father (Durkin, 1964; Foulkes, 1964; Scheidlinger, 1974; Slater, 1966) and the attendant tension between the members' adaptive compliance and constructive rebellion. Dependence on the authority of the leader and on the group normative status quo provides a sense of identity and security from belonging in shared identifications and ideals. However, submissive groups and compliant individuals lack creativity, which is stimulated by independent thought and freedom of expression.

As parent figure of either or combined gender, the therapist must balance closeness and distance in relating to the members, since rebellion against the leader is a significant factor in group formation and process. If the therapist is too remote, aggressive feelings, or defenses against such feelings, become disproportionate, and the members and group remains undeveloped. If the therapist is too friendly, "then no rebellion is necessary and, consequently, any banding together within the group takes longer and feels somewhat incomplete. Independence cannot be granted by Authority, but must be wrested from it" (Vella, 1999, p.17).

Widening his attention from the role of the leader to consider Freud's (1921c) formulation regarding the role of instincts, Bion posited an inherent conflict in the individual between narcissism and groupishness. "This bi-polarity of the instincts refers to their operation as elements in the fulfillment of the individual's life as an individual, and as elements in his life as a social or, as Aristotle would describe it, as a 'political animal'" (Bion, 1992, p.105). The individual needs groups for a sense of vitality, and one cannot develop fully without group participation. Yet the individual remains "at war" with oneself for one's very groupishness, for there are narcissistic needs that one wishes to express and satisfy anonymously via the *basic assumptions*.

Group process is characterized by submission and rebellion. However, the object of antagonism may be the group entity, or other members, the therapist, or even the self—with its contradictory motivations to be narcissistic or cooperative. The member must come to appreciate this existential situation, without believing he or she can fully resolve it.

Dialectical opposition of the developmentally early and mature, of narcissism and socialism, of primitive and sophisticated thinking, of *basic assumption* and *work group* activity, provides harmony as well as disharmony, the opportunity for growth and development as well as for chaos and destruction. In the individual and in the group, while each mode of being may rebel against the other, each needs the other for a creative, full life.

Bion's thinking has influenced subsequent writing on group theory. Agazarian (1997) described phases of group life that include inevitable rebellions. In the first phase, a group may be defensively dependent, stereotypic and conforming, or actively defiant; in either variation, the members coalesce around creating deviant roles to serve as containers for projectively identified aggression. After the group has survived a "barometric event" (Bennis & Shepard, 1956), which involves seduction, devaluation, or a symbolic coup d'etat, and when defenses are sufficiently undone and frustration is contained, the group may move away from authority and dependency preoccupations, to phases involved with intimacy and self-affirmation.

Nitsun (1996) defined an "anti-group" construct, describing conscious and nonconscious destructive attitudes and impulses manifest in most, if not all groups. He lists three sources: underlying fear, anxiety, and distrust of group process; frustration of narcissistic needs, such that the group is experienced as neglectful, depriving, and humiliating; and overabundance of aggression among members, expressed directly in hostile confrontation or indirectly in envy and rivalry, such that the group is experienced as unsafe.

When recognized and contained satisfactorily, the conflict between group and anti-group forces is generative and strengthening, a dialectical aspect of the "dynamic matrix." Foulkes' term refers to the potential of group process to correct each member's disruptive, antisocial, and destructively rebellious characteristics. In a constructive group, members "reinforce each other's normal reactions and wear down each other's neurotic reactions ... collectively they constitute the very norm from which, individually, they deviate" (Foulkes, 1983, p. 29).

Pathways of rebellion

The discussion now turns to the pathways of rebellion. When antagonists cannot resolve or live comfortably with dissent, rebellion takes various action pathways: *defiance, secession/exile, anarchy,* or *revolution.*

Defiance

Defiance represents a type of palpable and continual or phasic pressure exerted against ongoing group process and content. The group has become issue focused, and progressive development is problematic without frank acknowledgment and some attempt at resolution. Defiance would seem to be the initial mode of rebellion, from which other pathways branch out. But defiance is a pathway in itself, since dissension may be sufficiently resolved such to circumvent traversing rebellion's more radical pathways.

In terms of established group theory, as summarized above, defiance represents an organic feature of group formation and development. One constructive aspect is to test the safety of protest, and hence, defiance may actually represent increasing trust in the therapist and faith in group process. A defiant member communicates important feelings, although they may be acted out rather than verbally expressed. Defiance signals the group of distress, and the need for attention and dialogue. It alerts the therapist to possible changes in the group system and in the emotional lives of individual members.

In a destructive vein, by rigidly and repetitively demarcating what is acceptable and not acceptable, a defiant member or faction may produce static and repetitive group process, leading to impasse. Further, defiance may reach toxic proportions and may threaten the well-being of individuals members and therefore, of the group itself.

For, as defiance intensifies, a danger exists of polarization between points of view, as one or both sides substitute a coercive moral attitude for the democratic discussion of ideas. Members talk not to negotiate their differences, but to discharge anger, mete out punishment, and extinguish dissension. Loud silences, indignant facial expressions, condescending sighs, and other forms of exasperated paraverbal and nonverbal behavior are as effective as words in arousing members and determining group process. Argumentation shifts to incitement, recruitment, and subterfuge, from discourse to attack. The group risks emotional warfare—dissolution rather than revolution—and its members are exposed to traumatic injury, even symbolic murder.

Defiance may be friendly as well as hostile, overt as well as subtle and not easily or quickly identifiable. When defiance is covert, the therapist must decode its signs and identify its subterranean effects before escalation, or a counterproductive choice of another action pathway. In any conflict, negotiation is more likely, and deleterious consequences avoided when underlying issues are brought openly into the group.

Secession/exile

In this pathway of rebellion, a rupture between one or more individuals and the main group threatens reciprocal allegiances and attachments. When the contentious faction withdraws or is ejected from membership, the rebellion is suspended or quelled. Controversial issues may remain unresolved and continue to impact the group. But now, with the absence of opposing viewpoints, there are fewer occasions of open debate and exchange.

Dynamics of projection and scapegoating may be prominent. When a defiant member secedes, the possibility remains that the group nonconsciously maneuvered the individual into exile. The excluded, like the repressed, may haunt the group's consciousness with guilt and painful memories, and impede its future.

Secession or *exile* represents failure on all sides—a breakdown in communication has occurred. Dissention has not been expressed in an acceptable manner, or the leader or entire group has not been able to address and accommodate the conflict. However, in human relations, including psychotherapy groups, serious misalliances may be unavoidable, and failure should not be a surprise. The political history of psychoanalysis also may be described partially in terms of secession/exile, as endemic schisms lead to break-away groups. However, so often the new institutions, like the old, tend to be organized hierarchically around iconic figures, and enforce allegiance with the threat or actuality of excommunication.

In some situations, deselection from membership may be the most workable solution. It solves otherwise irreconcilable differences, as when factions represent two opposing ideas of the group task, and each side refuses compromise (see *Chapter seven, Refusal*), thus allowing the group to move on to other issues and to accomplish its goals.

If a group truly is unsafe or evaluated as promulgating an unethical or immoral agenda, and not capable of significant modification, secession is the choice pathway. Similarly, when an individual or faction uses the group to harm self or other, leadership requires temporarily or permanently segregating the offending membership.

Of course, there are situations when separation is a beneficial outcome of growth and development. The interests of certain members and of the main group simply may come to diverge, and bridging an increasing gulf may not be the best use of available resources. A group may have served and outlived its purpose for certain individuals, and termination may represent a constructive choice, more painful than continued membership, but opening up possibilities for needs and wishes to be better met in other settings. A group also benefits from the individual's termination process, mourning its graduates, and initiating new members.

Anarchy

We expect negativity in group: anger, nihilism, hopelessness, and contempt; intervals of confrontation and subtle and overt noncompliance. Indeed, as group leaders, we should welcome these expressions; when such data of human experience are processed and contextualized, the group and its members learn and grow in complexity and sophistication. In a psychotherapy or any dynamic, process-oriented group, challenge, rebellion against the status quo, temporary states of disintegration and confusion are necessary aspects of the creative process, leading to new directions and ideas.

In group processes of anarchy and for those individuals anarchy-inclined, disruption and disintegration are tactics, endpoints, and triumphant victories. Negative forces—spurred by a prevalence of unmitigated envy and hatred—overwhelm or threaten to overwhelm the capacities of the group to make meaning and preserve cohesiveness and trust. The Greek root of anarchy is "without a ruler." On the macro or social level, anarchy seeks to render the leader powerless and without authority, such that a group devolves into disorder and confusion, without cohesive principles and constructive purposes. On the micro or intrapsychic level, anarchy attacks the internal ruler—the mind—to attack and render useless each member's capacity to order emotional experience and think.

When anarchy predominates, excessive and violent projective identification disrupts the capacity for dialogue and thought, inducing states of disorientation, confusion, and paralysis. Empathy, thinking, language—and the social boundaries of time and space—may be applied deceitfully to undermine and invalidate truth and truth seeking. Anarchic members, who may include leaders, promote crises of miscommunication, misunderstanding, and distrust; they often bring on themselves the very anarchy they fearfully and unsuccessfully defend against.

To withstand assaults on all that the therapist believes, the therapist must maintain faith in the goodness of his or her intentions and of the group endeavor. The therapist's inner security and emotional clarity, coupled with technical craft and skill (see Part III, *Chapter eight, Modes of Therapeutic Interaction*), serve to counter and protect the group from the invalidating effects of *anarchy*, preserving the capacity for therapeutic relationships.

Revolution

In *revolution*, the premises of the rebelling faction come to overpower and dominate the group, propelling a new phase. Revolutionary transformation may not always be immediate or obvious, or result from a single or dramatic event. Only in retrospect might the speed and significance of cultural change become apparent. For example, the introduction of the computer is said to have revolutionized communication. Freud is asserted to have had a revolutionary influence on 20th century thought, and relational thinking, a similar impact on psychoanalysis (Mitchell , 1988), although not every psychoanalyst would concur.

At its prospect, revolution is frightening, and so provokes opposition. Individuals, psychotherapy and other small groups, as well as large groups such as psychoanalytic, political, or religious organizations, may regress to psychotic-like levels when presented with genuinely new and radical ideas (Bion, 1970; Jaques, 1955; Kernberg, 2000). The disruption and disorganization may feel or appear to be catastrophic, and the group may rigidify paranoiagenic defenses, or seem to fall apart in *anarchy*. Indeed, temporary or more permanent loss of familiar mental boundaries and established interpersonal alliances may be part of the growth process.

Revolution may arise organically, as part of the group's development, or be imported into the group, such as by new membership. Some members may decline to participate in the revolution, choosing instead another action pathway, *defiance*, *secession* or self-*exile*, or counter-*revolution*. The effect of Melanie Klein's ideas in London was to divide the group of psychoanalysts into rigid schisms, characterized in large measure by totalitarianism. Each subgroup was intellectually creative but exclusionary and personally wounding to members of other factions. Thus, revolutions may have elements that are reactionary as well as progressive, fascistic as well as democratic. Revolution may muffle as well as stimulate spontaneity and variety. In its extreme negative form, revolution leads to group dissolution or *anarchy*.

The therapist as revolutionary. From (1963) described a "revolutionary character," which involves open-mindedness and a high level of personal development. This brings us to the therapeutic ideal of "two faces" described in *Chapter three*, which also represents an aspect of the therapist's *integrity* (*Chapter eight*). While, on the one hand, the therapist is a primary agent in fostering a sense of continuity, cohesion, and regularity, he or she also strives to function as a powerful agent of change.

To restate the essential point, the effective group leader—symbolically, linguistically, and behaviorally—traverses each action pathway of rebellion, at various times taking the role of defiant questioner, exiled outcast, secessionist, and revolutionary. To the extent to which the leader challenges and "explodes" the group framework, he or she may function as an anarchist. But to accomplish this successfully, and avoid degeneration, a group must experience the leader's anarchy as benevolent and symbolic, but not actual.

Case example: Traversing the pathways of rebellion

I summarize the movements of a long-term psychotherapy group that relate to our topic (presented in Gotta, 2005). The therapist described her clinical population as consisting of individuals with histories of severe emotional/physical abuse and abandonment issues. Almost all members lived alone.

A group breaks the therapist's rules and regulations

It had been Gotta's practice to introduce prospective members to what was expected of them when they joined her psychotherapy group. She informed them of a few "ground rules," which included confidentiality, responsibility for payment, a three-month termination period, and prohibition from eating or drinking in sessions and from socializing out of sessions.

One of the veteran members, Steve, complained that because of Gotta's stated policies, the group could not meet outside the scheduled appointments. The sessions were too "clinical" and "dry." It would be more fun to go out with the members, and bring people closer together. Steve's proposal garnered little discussion or support. Other members wanted to keep group relationships separate from social relationships, which they recognized often caused irresolvable problems. Socializing could inhibit their reactions to each other in group; or instance, how could they feel free to get angry at each other?

Steve occasionally returned to the topic, frustrated and irritated that only one member supported him, the usually quiet Don. However, unbeknown to the therapist, once, when a core subgroup of the more independent members was absent, the remaining participants casually got together after the session.

Opening the next session with some trepidation concerning their therapist's reaction, these members confessed having gone to a local bar. They felt "strange" being together outside the office but welcomed the relaxed atmosphere. Steve, apparently the instigator, reiterated how the sessions in the office felt too artificial. "It's not like real life. When we were in the bar it felt like we were more real, we could kid around with each other and have fun." They agreed that Don was more relaxed outside the group setting: "He was really funny, so different from how he is in group."

Joan, a lonely woman who had a tendency to flirt, said she was a little uncomfortable because Hank, another member, had pursued her in the bar. He put his arm around her and she felt anxious not knowing what that meant, especially since Hank often seemed angry with her in the group. Yet, in telling her story, Joan seemed pleased, more upbeat than usual.

Gotta felt anxious, angry, and puzzled, and wondered what it meant about her person and leadership that the members had broken the no-socializing rule. She maintained equilibrium sufficiently to comment that, while many feelings had come up around this experience and it was profitable to talk about them, she did not want the group to continue meeting outside of session. She explained and offered convincing rationales for her viewpoint.

But the members took Gotta's encouragement to talk about the extra-group experience as permission to act. They devoted session time to discuss if, and then plan how and when they next would meet. Several sessions were devoted to developing and revising rules. All members were to be invited to outside activities in order to prevent feelings of exclusion; group matters should be respected and no discussion of group members or events should take place after session.

Planning and executing extra-group events did not satisfy the members. While first established to expedite arrangements, e-mail became an additional mode of after-group socializing. There was not enough time in the group to catch up with each other. If "deep work" was to occur, the group time would have to be used wisely and talking about their daily lives could be a distraction. While aware of their therapist's disapproval, the members were pleased that she could accept their feelings and cooperate in the discussion.

In truth, Gotta felt helpless, unable to change the tide of events or even limit the after-session activities. She felt she was losing control of the group, and anticipated grave consequences: *anarchy*. What if two members had an affair, or other intimate pairings and sub-groups developed and then dissolved in anger and disappointment? She worried that the members preferred "partying" together to attending sessions and submitting to the rigors of psychotherapy. The group, pulled into the vortex of mindless pleasure, would become meaningless, and the members would blame and turn against her.

Gotta offered a compromise: The members could schedule a regular after-group. She would leave her consulting room and members would decide how to continue the group discussion or bring up other topics. The entire group responded positively, and immediately and regularly began to meet. However, the therapist-sponsored after-group meetings did not succeed in pre-empting the unsanctioned after-group meetings.

The therapist's psychology contributes to the revolution

Alarmed and believing that the group's behavior might be an outcome of her own psychology as much as the collective membership's, Gotta sought supervision (with this author). She discovered that, in her own mind, and perhaps in the minds of the members, two groups existed: the therapy group, and a leaderless "party" group.

While I believed that the members preferred the therapeutic group, Gotta did not trust that she was important, and played out these beliefs by keeping a low profile. With these realizations, Gotta tentatively took assertive steps, such as inviting the group to discuss what it would be like to have her present at their outside meetings. Some thought it would be a great idea, and taking her literally, extended an invitation. Steve thought she would be inhibited and no fun, while others thought they would be "uptight" and feel judged.

Despite Gotta's success in enlivening group sessions by her more active presence, the members continued to gather, primarily at the singles' bar. Sometimes a contingent went to weekend singles' events. On one occasion, the member, Mary, hosted the group at her house. She reported feeling uncomfortable around men and only wanted to ask the women. But the men came, and she had a "good time."

Gotta did not feel reassured by the group's description of their extra-group activities, and remained concerned about the members *seceding*. But no one, save for the therapist, seemed unhappy or in conflict with the *rebellion*.

She intensified her efforts to explore *resistances*: the dynamic underpinnings of the enactments—the interaction between the members' psychologies and her own. Certainly, a pervasive and underlying group conflict existed between the members' longing for and fear of interpersonal contact. Gotta realized that she shared these conflicts: She wanted to be connected but feared being swamped by the members' needs and overwhelmed by the force of group process.

She came to appreciate that the members' anxiety and feelings of emotional disconnection in the group sessions were not based solely on experiences with and transferences from their families of origin, but also, on their actual experience of the therapist. Gotta realized how differently she functioned in the group from the individual treatments, where she was more expressive and self-revealing. For example, when Hank announced to the group that he would be going on a sailing trip for six to eight weeks during the summer, Gotta maintained a "poker face," and asked others for their reactions. In the individual session, she let Hank know that she would miss him; and Hank, touched by the therapist's self-disclosure, declared that he had not realized his importance to her.

The combined treatment of Joan provides another example. Joan often was depressed, and during intervals lasting for weeks, she would talk of her despair, saying that she did not deserve to live and that she felt like a horrible person. The group would tell Joan that her feelings were based on a horrible distortion, e.g., "You [Joan] are a beautiful person inside and out and it hurts and scares us to see you in such pain."

While Gotta tended in group to echo other members, she could be direct, even confrontational, in individual sessions. When Joan reported feeling persecuted in her family, Gotta offered that she also persecuted herself, the group, and the therapist. Gotta realized that in her own transference to the group (from her family of origin), she felt anxious that members would label her as insensitive should she speak her mind. In the individual sessions, Gotta trusted the empathic *bonding* (Billow, 2003c; 2003d) that existed between each patient and herself.

To understand and, eventually, to address interpretatively the psychodynamic underpinnings of the group's rebellion, Gotta needed to have greater access to the *therapeutic mode of sincerity (Chapter eight)*. This required trusting and showing her warm and loving feelings in the group setting, and allowing herself to receive and trust these feelings from its members (see *Relational Group Psychotherapy, Chapter five,* on *bonding* and the *container-contained;* also, *Appendix I*).

This is not to suggest that Gotta could have succeeded in heading off the *rebellion*—even if she had been able to achieve an ideal bonding posture. In my opinion—debatable and controversial—such an outcome might not have been preferable.

Discussion: Differences in values and needs spur the revolution

In Gotta's group, the members began to discuss and then, without the therapist's authorization, realized certain wishes for extra-group contact. The therapist, although alarmed, remained professional. She presented appropriate objections, based on sensible, predictable, and prevailing theoretical constructs. The group countered with intentions of its own, and took action. From Gotta's viewpoint, the rebellion signified acting-out: a violation of group boundaries, concrete thinking, and *basic assumption, fight/flight*.

Salient and painful to the therapist was the thought that the rebellion signified a challenge to her authority, and previewed the disintegration of her group. Gotta had established that activity exists within the formal group setting. But the members had decided rebelliously to establish additional meetings, where and when they wanted them.

Gotta was faced with a limited range of options in which to negotiate the members' wishes versus her own. Certainly, she could have reasserted prohibitions and stressed her role as authority figure, thereby potentiating certain transference configurations. Were members to disobey her injunctions—a likely possibility—Gotta would then have to decide whether to *exile:* discharging certain members from the group, and set up a fearsome precedent. In quashing the rebellion, the therapist could have created a suppressive, counter-revolutionary group culture.

Gotta needed to avert a situation in which members would be pressured to comply, or forced to *secede* from the group, or be *exiled* from it. She prudently opted to take time to assess the group's direction, maintaining an exploratory stance without excessive confrontation or interpretation. In supervisory dialogue, she worked on her own dynamic and characterological issues, and reconsidered certain premises of her theory and technique. This required reviewing her normative presumptions, therapeutic principles, and technical manner: how her own version and approach to truth might have contributed to her group's rebellion, and to her response to rebellion.

The rebellion seemed superficially against the leader, and to some extent it likely was spurred on and directed towards circumventing the therapist's own defenses. But by and large, and in contrast to the traditional Freudian formulation, the members were not out to *resist* Gotta, as a transference object, and to test and challenge her authority. That is, they were not staging a radical insurrection by (symbolically) overthrowing their leader, significantly altering the structure of the group session, or *refusing* the shared therapeutic goal of increased understanding. While the location and overt communicative mode of some of the meetings had changed, not so the group's purpose, organization, or preferred mode of interaction. The therapist retained her position in the hierarchy of status, power, and influence. Her values—psychoanalytic and otherwise—predominated.

The members wished to establish certain modifications, all of which involved extra-group contact among the members. The members had their own beliefs about how the group should best be run, and this involved challenging certain prevailing rules and practices of our profession. To a significant degree, the group's wishes—really demands—were non-negotiable. But were they necessarily illegitimate? Given the state of mind of the members, their emotional development, and their needs, their rebellion made sense, and might even have been in the service of accomplishing defensible modifications of treatment. Rather than primarily directed to violating and weakening the boundaries, the group's goal was to expand and strengthen them.

If the members had not moved unilaterally to action, and waited and negotiated their demands, they unlikely would have influenced the therapist's opinions and modified the group's structure. And, among its constructive outcomes, the members' rebellion fostered the therapist's growth as well as their own. She reported being more relaxed and open with invitations to prospective members, exploring their reactions and anticipations without prescribing or proscribing a code of behavior.

How the therapist introduces a group affects the way novice members respond, and influences group culture and development. Also, rules—permissions and prohibitions—may take on different meanings, according to the group's development and the here-and-now process (see *Chapter eight*, on *Integrity*). As Gotta concluded, her attempt to establish and maintain a proper "frame" (Langs, 1978), deadened her own mindset, rigidified therapist-member and member-member boundaries, and possibly contributed to rebellion. The members, motivated to increase bonding—the sense of warmth, liveliness, and interconnectedness—succeeded in satisfying this aspiration.

Interest in and the practice of leaderless or alternate meetings have waned, and few articles on the subject have appeared in the recent literature. Yalom (1995), informally surveying his colleagues, concluded that only a small number regularly schedule leaderless meetings in their practice. Although some practitioners have spoken out vociferously against the leaderless meeting, predicting *anarchy*, that is, chaotic disruption and destructive sexual acting out (e.g., Rutan, 1984), the general clinical consensus remains that such fears are unfounded (Desmond & Seligman, 1977).

Gotta has reported no evidence of "contamination" or other untoward effects of the member-initiated after-groups. Rather, supporting their claim of becoming more deeply connected to each other after a get-together, the members return to the group with heightened enthusiasm for the work. The geographically expanded alternate group has not impeded cohesion, inclusion of new members, process, or progress. Even when not physically present, the therapist remains the leader. The group has faced and now lives with conflict between therapist and members, and their clashing versions—not of truth, but of the best therapeutic methods of reaching truth. Rebellion, not quashed or even resolved, has enhanced the group experience.

Anarchy

Anarchy differentiates from other group processes of rebellion, wherein members challenge or defy the therapist, other members, or the group at large, and which are common and even considered as necessary for the foundation of the individual and group, and their development (Agazarian, 1997; Bennis & Shepard, 1956; Freud, 1913, 1921). In other pathways of rebellion, *defiance*, *secession/exile*, and *revolution*, members may dispute truth, and/or the methods to reach it, such that a group may segment, dissolve, or transform.

Ambivalent feelings and antithetical ideas create intrapsychic and social conflict. Truth-seeking entails unsettling interludes of breakdown of core defenses and established modes of feeling and thinking; the truths that are discovered likewise may be painful and disquieting. If the experiences are contained sufficiently within the group, and they provide the impetus for thought, then constructive group process and individual growth and development ensue. The group remains safe and adequate to meet truth-seeking needs, or it does not. Even if the group disbands or a member secedes, the idea—if not the particular entity—of group is preserved. The integrity of the individuals and their former links remain intact.

When *anarchy* prevails, mental and emotional links within and among individuals are grossly disturbed. Ambivalence and antithesis are not contained adequately to provide the impetus for constructive thought and action. Anarchically inclined groups and group members cannot or will not tolerate painful states of not-knowing/knowing, and oppose creative, disintegration-reintegration processes, which are both intrapsychic and interpersonal. Only one feeling and one idea may come to flourish: The group is unsafe, inadequate, and "bad." The goal—at times willfully conscious as well as nonconscious—becomes to destroy the particular group, and also, the very idea of group, which on some basic level is envied and despised.

In *Experiences in Groups*, Bion (1961) developed the seminal idea that all individuals resist tolerating and thinking about painful aspects of psychic reality, and band with others to defend against this type of experience, via *basic assumption* defenses. His later writings (1962; 1963; 1970) described how nonconscious urges to hate and destroy that which stimulates painful psychic awareness ("*truth*") may predominate over constructive motives to think. Interrelated concepts of "*anti-thinking*," or "*minus K*," "*attacks on links*," and "*parasitic*" *container-contained* relationships all involve using one's mind to invalidate emotional and mental relationships, intrapsychic and interpersonal (see *Relational Group Psychotherapy, Chapters three, five,* and *nine*; also, this volume, *Appendix I*).

Bion introduced the notion of *basic assumptions* to describe pervasive *resistances* against group growth. But at times, *basic assumptions* may eventuate in *rebellions* and *refusals*. In particular, anarchists may become extremely destructive representatives of the *fight-flight assumption* and the "*anti-group*" (Nitsun, 1996), and do not function as committed members of a "loyal opposition." Attempts at *resistance* analysis may further aggravate the situation.

Anarchy represents a playing out of destructive forces, and all individuals and all groups are capable of anarchy. The emergence of anarchy represents a challenge to leadership. The leader has to provide the positive, countervailing force, ideally, to make the individual and the group safe, but at the very least, to keep the group safe. In each of the following three clinical examples or anecdotes, members (including the leaders) had their confidence and faith in groups disturbed to the extent to which they were not protected from the effects of *anarchy*.

Case example 1: Defending against the anarchic vortex

The format of the three-day annual conference of a regional group organization consisted of lectures and demonstrations by the invited speaker (this author), along with a sequence of small experiential groups comprising prospective and current candidates. These groups were led by the senior faculty, which also met in a peer supervisory group, to which I served as consultant.

After a brief introductory go-round during our first luncheon supervisory meeting, Darlene volunteered to present her group of eight members. She felt disturbed and needed our feedback after having led two sessions. An experienced group psychotherapist in her early sixties, Darlene had a chance interaction with Vic, one of the participants in her group, on the street at the end of the conference's first day. "Take a taste," the handsome young man said, offering her a spoonful of his gelato. Taken aback, she hesitated, and then accepted.

The next morning's session began with Vic's addressing Darlene: "I guess we should talk about what happened." He spiritedly informed the group of the chance meeting, even including the ice cream's flavor. To break the group's uncomfortable pause, Darlene inquired: "So what was that interaction like for you?"

"Just playful. I don't know why I did it. I draw cats that are playful, to describe how I am. How did it feel to you?"

"Well," she smiled, "I guess I'm not 'over the hill!' I was surprised and pleased."

The man continued: "Oh, I didn't say the rest of it and I don't know why I did this with you yesterday, but a few minutes later I found you again and told you that it reminded me of how I am with my girlfriend. We like to smear whip cream on our faces and kiss."

Darlene felt herself blushing and temporarily lost composure. She retained some of these feelings in reporting to our supervisory group, confessing embarrassment and difficulty in remembering group process. "Still, I need to understand my feelings, although I recovered and the rest of the session went okay." She described how she had attempted to repair the situation by making references to Vic's self-described "playfulness." However, these interventions failed to draw Vic in, who participated minimally.

The conversation of our supportive group revolved around techniques of handling extra-group contacts—what Darlene might have said to circumvent the fateful "taste." I found myself distracted from the discussion, realized that I felt alarmed for her and by Vic, and inquired if others did. I commented that as group leaders we all make mistakes and can fall or be pushed into traps, and it is important to consider who among the membership help or, like Vic, make more difficult our release. Darlene reflected that she believed her group cared for her, but perhaps they were bewildered by or even afraid of what they had heard.

Darlene reported that the afternoon's group session was "quite intense," focused on three members who had suffered childhood abuse. She wondered if the morning's interaction with Vic had stirred up recollections, or even if the members were expressing symbolically the group's feeling of having been abused by her. Darlene felt relieved when our supervisory group reassuringly concluded that she was "holding" the guilt and anxiety for the whole group, and attempted to shift our discussion to another leader's group.

But still alarmed by what I had heard about the earlier meeting, I broke in and asked Darlene to describe Vic's behavior in the afternoon. A different picture emerged. Several individuals revealed painfully that they had been adopted, and some members began to cry when Vic spoke up: "My parents said I was adopted." He smiled, which seemed like an invitation for further dialogue.

"So you too were adopted, how did it feel to you?" a member inquired.

"No, I said they *said* I was adopted." He continued to smile, without further comment. The "joke" his parents played on him he now played on the group.

No one responded immediately, but later in the session a courageous individual initiated a gentle confrontation: "Vic, I can't tell what you feel when you smile and get quiet. It makes me anxious." A second member continued: "I agree, I get confused about you." A third: "I don't know what you mean when you talk. You seem sincere and then I feel tricked."

Vic responded: "I guess you don't really know me when I smile all the time. I need to think about that, because I want you to." He was quiet for the rest of the afternoon.

Darlene had concluded that Vic had heard the group and that the interactions were mutually beneficial. Our supervisory group concluded that Vic enacted his need to be "adopted," and that her group complied with warmth and constructive feedback.

Risking being perceived as a negativistic "visitor," and endangering my own "adoption" as uber-supervisor to our group of experienced professionals, I again expressed apprehension. Vic's group gave him—and us—quite a bit more to emotionally process and to think about than a self-protective smile. Like his gelato offering to Darlene, Vic's joke felt jarring, undermining, even violent; and in both situations, his subsequent behaviors did nothing to lessen my sense of danger.

I could not tell how receptive Darlene and our group were to my thoughts, and Darlene admitted that perhaps she was experiencing me, rather than Vic, as "throwing her off her game." We waited to see what would develop the next morning, her group's final meeting.

Darlene reported the following: Upon entering the now-familiar room, the members were jarred by an elaborate object, a vaguely Oriental shrine, placed in the group's center. It took awhile for people to acknowledge its existence, at which point Vic took ownership. "I wanted you to get to know who I am," he explained. He then asked if anyone would mind the smell of incense. An observant member reminded him of the existence of smoke detectors and water sprinklers, and Vic disappointedly agreed to leave the creation unlit. He briefly explained some of its mystical qualities: openness, oneness, and communication. Several members thanked Vic for sharing, but did not inquire further, and the group went on to other subjects.

Vic remained quiet for the rest of the session, and at several moments Darlene had the impression that he had fallen asleep, or put himself in a trance. Nevertheless, as the members began to disperse at the group's conclusion, Vic called out: "Would anyone want me to explain this before I take it apart?" Along with the others, Darlene departed hurriedly.

Discussion

Intimations of Shakespeare's *Richard III* appear in the first supervisory session, as we hear from the group leader about Vic's effects on her mental composure. Richard III, acting out "archaic, narcissistic destructive" strivings (Jacobson, 1959, p. 137), took particular pleasure in the interactional process of taking over Anne's mind, not in seducing Anne herself, whom he promptly discarded upon marrying. He wreaks havoc on the kingdom until he is destroyed.

Vic's seemingly friendly offer of gelato takes on sado-masochistic sexual overtones. He "associates" to mutual smearing and licking with his girlfriend—retold by him in his group and now, by his embarrassed group leader in the supervisory session. The chance meeting became an opportunity to assail ("smear") the boundaries of the member-leader professional relationship.

"So what was that interaction like for you?" he asked enticingly in the group meeting that followed the incident. Darlene responded *sincerely* (*Chapter eight)* to Vic's invitation, which she experienced as friendly and empathic, to the detriment of her emotional and mental balance. The seduction/destruction situation repeats on the whole group level during a later session, wherein Vic, falsely confessing to being adopted, first attracts other group members, who become confused and anxious.

Darlene had difficulty thinking usefully about the situation with Vic, yet could not get him out of her mind. She unwittingly became Vic's messenger of deceit, in reporting to our supervisory group that he made reparative gestures: "I guess you don't really know me when I smile all the time. I need to think about that, because I want you to." Darlene and the other group leaders seem reassured by his professing to take time to think, naïvely so in my opinion, which

I offered at risk of *exile*. In parallel process to Darlene's group, Vic's influence threatened to overwhelm the truth-seeking qualities of our supervisory group, and hence, to destroy its meaning.

Similarly to Darlene, I could not get Vic out of my mind. Remaining alarmed by Vic's *falsities* (*Chapters two* and *three*), I attempted to focus Darlene on *anarchy*, such that she could anticipate possible action sequences, and take protective measures.

Vic's shrine in the concluding session, like the beguiling Sphinx-like Vic himself, threatened to undermine the group's very survival. The group is spared fortuitously, by a group member who retained the mentality to detect and prevent the havoc behind Vic's invitation: smoke, noise, water, violation of space, obstruction of group time, dispersal of the membership, and destruction of the group.

Both the leader and members shun Vic's concluding invitation to explain the shrine, and they exit quickly while he speaks. His final words echo, jamming mental space—the containing medium that allows members to preserve this particular group, and the idea of group—as a benevolent, meaningful process.

Case example 2: An anarchist sinks the group

In the third session of a newly formed group, Elizabeth, on job leave while raising her two children, was questioned about her reserve. After many probes, she revealed a deep depression in the past two months, with thoughts of suicide. Unwilling to take anti-depressants because of breast-feeding her six-month-old, she had been hiding her depression from her husband. The group offered support, advice, pressure to seek individual therapy and psychopharmacology. Expressing guilt for the attention, Elizabeth insisted the group move on.

The following weeks' sessions began with members checking in: Elizabeth reported no change in her mental state and otherwise did not participate. Fearing to contribute to Elizabeth's feelings of being an unworthy burden, the therapist did not comment on the group's frustration. After several more meetings, the requests ceased for updates, and the group essentially behaved as though Elizabeth were not present. However, group vitality, as expressed though humor and sharing of successes, was muted.

The therapist felt hostage to Elizabeth's depression and reasoned that the group must feel this way as well. Still, she remained inhibited, concerned that Elizabeth would flee or deteriorate.

During the next month, one member announced termination for scheduling reasons, followed in the subsequent session by a similar announcement for financial difficulties. The therapist interpreted without positive impact these decisions as flight from exposure to painful experiences of "other group members" and one's own. Elizabeth said nothing.

Two other members expressed dissatisfaction with the group's impending contraction; they too decided leave. Elizabeth and the other remaining member agreed that people needed to do what they felt was best for them.

The therapist put the group on hiatus while she attempted to collect new members. She encouraged Elizabeth to contact an individual therapist. Elizabeth reported in a follow-up call only that she was "fine" (example from Motherwell & Shay, 2005).

Discussion

The group embraced the noncomunicative Elizabeth; she *refused* (*Chapters four* and *seven*) to link up to their concern, support, and attempts to supply meaning. Was she suicidal, a lethal or depressed character, postpartumly depressed, or merely overwhelmed with two young children and without the verbal resources and trust to make herself known? Tellingly, she rejected discussing the idea of combined or conjoined individual-group therapy, or of a psychiatric consultation, repelling even potential therapeutic alliances.

Elizabeth fitted the profile described by Freud (1916d), as lacking in interest and love. These are two of the three basic emotions that link human beings to each other and from which meaning may accrue. I am referring to Bion's trilogy of "passion:" an integration of *LHK*, urges for love, hate, and knowledge (*Chapter eight; Appendix I*). Elizabeth exhibited a surfeit of disavowed hatred, however, holding the group hostage, scaring all members into silence, retreat, and flight.

Like Shakespeare's Richard III, and Vic in the above case example, Elizabeth proceeded from "a mental constellation of revolt," feeling justified taking revenge and tormenting others (Freud, 1916d,

p. 248). While professing guilt and gratitude, the *anarchically*-inclined Elizabeth transmitted instead a subtle satisfaction in her purposeful mindlessness, unconcerned with her aversive effects on others and "fine" after the group disbands.

Members of a newly formed group, particularly, are not equipped conceptually or emotionally to deal with the rebellious machinations of a resolutely *anarchic* individual. They are not able to balance an instinctive interest and concern (*K* and *L*) in a patient they do not know, with a constructive anger (*H*) towards the same patient who will not be known. Left unchallenged and uncontained, Elizabeth dispersed the members' budding reciprocal allegiances and attachments, and the group process moved from *exile* (of Elizabeth), to *secession*, and the group destructed.

From this example we may understand that whenever *anarchy* is prominent, there is disowned, but pressing aggression against self and other. To reach and relieve the anarchic individual, and integrate her into the group, the therapist must link up the patient's dissociated aggression to the here-and-now treatment situation. This first requires recognizing and linking up one's own aggressive feelings and thoughts. Like other group members, the therapist, frustrated in the urge to care and be curious, may become overstimulated and possibly frightened by an urge to hate and be hateful.

Maltsberger & Buie (1973) suggested a reciprocal relationship between the therapist's incapacity to tolerate conscious sadistic wishes and the intensity of the therapist's aversive avoidance of such a patient. Thus, when the aggressive urge is disavowed in the therapist, as it is in the patient, the group member remains not understood and unreached. Indeed, I believe Elizabeth felt "guilty" when receiving caring attention because of her contempt for the group's *falsity*, their avoidance of her need for hating attention.

The primary object link Elizabeth seemed capable or willing to make was through the emotion of hatred. Some anarchic individuals feel relieved of their nonconscious guilt and begin to interest themselves in the group when it becomes apparent that the leader will not tolerate treatment-destructive behaviors, but at the same time is not frightened, wounded, or killed by criticism, disapproval, or direct attack. When such individuals are dealt with firmly, fairly, and not treated as fragile or fearsome objects, they sometimes reveal social dimensions of their personalities—humor, flirtatiousness, irony, curiosity. They may be recruited as allies against anarchic elements in their own personalities.

However, such individuals as Elizabeth may insist on making others responsible for their survival and that of the group itself. They may act as if they are dead already, and fight therapeutic efforts to be brought back to life (Hendin, 1981). Any patient can defeat any therapist, and the therapist must accept one's own limits in motivation, skill, and strength (Billow, 1999a). If the patient's continued presence threatens the survival of the group and cannot be redirected, the therapist must remove (*exile*) the individual from the group setting.

In addressing the treatment-destructive, *anarchic* group member, the therapist must be relatively comfortable feeling sadistic, ineffectual, worthless and useless; guilty for being sadistic, ineffectual, worthless and useless; and guilty for hating the patient for provoking these feelings. The group therapist's first goal is to preserve oneself, which means preserving a functional, interactional relational consciousness and nonconsciousness. If the therapist's mentality is sinking, then the anarchic member drowns, often taking the group along.

Case example 3: The group leaders induce anarchy

The custom of our graduate school in clinical psychology was to run interview groups of prospective candidates. The groups were three hours in duration, with ten or even 12 individuals, and led by a professor with an advanced graduate student in attendance. Many years ago, I served as the latter, and as we entered the room, the youthful assistant professor declared: "Hello, welcome, let's get real!" and fell still. As you might expect, the circle stiffened, and we leaders spent our time attempting to deal with what we labeled as "*resistance*."

Some candidates simply *refused* to participate, sacrificing their chances to enter our program. A subgroup, ostensibly making the best of the situation, decided that the best policy was to introduce oneself and explain reasons for wanting to become a clinical psychologist. An insufferably dull first hour followed, and then, another seemingly impenetrable silence.

The professor warned that he would end the group in 20 minutes. The implicit threat was clear: None of the candidates would be considered for acceptance. The room remained immobile, the silence unbroken, the session soon over.

Discussion

As quoted earlier in this volume, Bion (1966, p. 37) challenged the therapist to function with "the impact of an explosive force on a preexisting framework." But to accomplish this successfully, and avoid degeneration, a group must experience the leader's anarchy as benevolent and symbolic, but not actual, and certainly, not final. When a leader introduces anarchy, he or she is attacking a previous group model of structure and leadership, with the goal of achieving a creative reintegration.

Our anarchic leadership provides an object lesson of how not to initiate a group. Interventions in the opening stages need to modify—not unduly stimulate—persecutory and other *basic assumption* anxieties and fantasies. Most likely, the naïve professor's conscious intention was to reveal these underlying dynamics, which represent one aspect of "getting real," the "dark side" (Brown, 2003) of every situation wherein people cluster. However, the professor's explosive opener scared people already anxious by the interview process, such that the assemblage was experienced as perverse and unsafe. We leaders failed to explicitly mention or prepare the group for such feelings—indeed, the professor's forceful intervention seemed to forbid their expression, potentiating the terror.

The subgroup's robotic efforts to introduce themselves were intellectually "real," but evasive and false, impoverished in basic emotions. Green (2000, p. 20) proposed "speech addressed to another person is based on a cycle of established, mutual excitations … instinctual excitation recathects the circuit of speech, enriching its flow, preventing it from drying up." "Excitations" were withdrawn, leaving each individual isolated, without a speakeable consciousness. Individuals could not, or would not, broadcast the truth about the actuality of the competition among the candidates, the provocative leadership, and one's feelings about this difficult, aggressively-tinged situation. After awhile, the candidates sunk into a hopeless and fearful refusal, no matter the negative consequences to themselves.

The leaders lacked sufficient skills to readdress the *anarchy* we had unwittingly created. Judging from my own feelings at the time, and extrapolating to the professor's, I surmise that he was frightened at the dimensions of the responsibility of the task—hated the feelings and the newly-forming group for "causing" them—and attempted to rid himself of unsavory feelings by means of projective identification into the members, who then became paralyzed by fear, both induced by the leaders and their own.

Further discussion of the three case examples

Anarchically prone individuals induce anarchy into the group process. Likewise, group anarchy, such as induced by the leaders in the interview group, induces anarchy in the participants. In the first example, the effects of Vic's anarchy on Darlene's group are equivocal. The members likely derived some benefit, but the experience was damaged, at least partially, by Vic's behavior, which overwhelmed the leader. In the second and third examples, respectively involving Elizabeth and the clinical psychology applicants, leadership was in disarray, and the groups disintegrated nonproductively, with some likely injury to the participants.

In each of the case examples, members (including the leader) had their confidence and faith in groups disturbed to the extent to which they were not protected from *anarchy's* treacherous vortex. In the first two examples, the leader or other members made attempts to be pro-thought, and put into words what they believed was happening or should happen. Still, their words had unintended consequences, misapplied or misinterpreted—projectively utilized to disrupt dialogue and destroy thought-based relationships.

The leader must identify and call attention to the seriousness and destructive potential of anarchy early enough, and needs to be sufficiently skillful and powerful to turn the situation into one wherein constructive thinking is possible. Action strategies—identifying and protecting members from anarchic behaviors—serve to maintain or restore leadership and the functional group (*Chapter eight, Diplomacy*). If these fail, and the group matrix (Foulkes, 1983) cannot fulfill a reparative function, then the group is in trouble.

Rebellion: Leadership variables remain central

To some extent, rebellions are always against the leader. And, leadership variables influence and may even determine the extent, the form, and the outcome of rebellions. The leader mainly is responsible for introducing, maintaining, and preserving the group's principles and practices; ideally, and at the same time, he or she also questions and even challenges them, aiding the group in breaking out of the familiar (the *Establishment*) and generating new thought (*Chapter three*). If we lead properly, our groups take us to unknown and unpredictable places. Rebellions are part of that process.

To foster creative, democratic evolution of a group, and avoid unproductive, contentious rebellions, the leader must provide "oversight," asserting influence regarding dynamic currents and conflicts such that they do not derail or polarize, identifying current themes and motifs, establishing common reference points, and producing bonding or unifying interventions (Ettin, 2003). A "pro-group" manner of leadership (Wilke, 2003), interactive, analytical, philosophical, and humane, does not shield the group from rebellions, however, but makes them more likely to be understood, negotiated successfully, and put to constructive goals.

CHAPTER SEVEN

Refusal

As explained in earlier chapters, all efforts to delay, modify, or counter forward movement of psychotherapeutic work traditionally have been captured under the umbrella term of *resistance*. In distinguishing a category of *refusal*, I aim to signify divergent processes and strategies of reaching, sharing, or rejecting mental content in the social setting. More narrowly defined, *resistance* refers to the dynamics and defenses that block nonconscious-to-conscious processing, and there is always symbolization. As explained in *Chapter five*, working through of resistance entails embracing vague and partially unformulated aspects of internal experience and gradually articulating these elements, to make them comprehensible to self and other.

Refusal, in contrast, involves a willful nonparticipation in discovering or learning about psychic material, with a goal often of suspending or blocking some mental activity. It is predicated on the sense or anticipation that something is or might go awry. The phenomenology of *refusal* manifests by opposition, noncompliance, and emotional, mental, or social withdrawal. What I am identifying as *refusal* most often has been understood as a specific, intense form or strategy of resistance, blocking psychotherapeutic process and progress. However, as we shall see, there are instances and domains where *refusal* may be adaptive.

Differentiating resistance from refusal

Resistance

Resistance regulates emotional awareness. It defends and protects against emotional truths becoming too significant, too quickly, unduly affecting how we feel, think, and behave (Grotstein, 2000, 2004). While resistance opposes consciousness (Freud, 1923b), it pervades and reveals nonconscious thinking. What is resisted may be thought about and communicated without immediate awareness, via metaphor, symbols, myth, dream, associations, affect discharges, and participation in enactments. In group therapy, each member broadcasts such derivatives—resisted versions of emotional experience—which are received, evaluated, and responded to by others. With the aid of the therapist's interventions and interpretations, multiple meanings of individual, subgroup, and whole group experience gradually and often indirectly reveal themselves and become integrated into consciousness and affective life. We see then how resistance potentially functions as a "royal road" to emotional awareness.

Subjectively, the elaboration of resistance invokes tension, anxiety, suspense, and surprise. The group becomes immersed in emotional thinking via interactive cognitive-emotional processes involving introspection, sharing feeling and thought, transference-countertransference revelation, interpretation, experimental (inter) actions and so forth. Working with and on resistance intensifies interpersonal intimacy and group cohesion.

Refusal

In *refusal*, the individual, subgroup, or group detours, blocks access to, or invalidates the communicative instruments—thinking, empathy, and language—used to explore resistances and its derivatives. Refusal thus establishes a mental boundary between what is considered appropriate and inappropriate for intrapsychic or interpersonal dialogue.

As a psychological event, refusal occurs on preverbal and nonverbal in addition to verbal levels—we may refuse sensations and images—and introspectively and enactively, as well as dialogically. Whereas it involves and affects the entire group, refusal may manifest primarily intrapsychically, such as in the mind of a group member, or be expressed via a spokesperson, or in dyadic and subgroup formations. Similarly in this respect to *resistance*, others intuitively recognize and become informed by refusal, and individuals vary in response to its impact.

Refusal may be explicit, as in "I don't want to talk about it." Refusal is also subtle, disguised as conformity or pseudocompliance, wherein what is said or felt adds little weight to the unfolding of potential meaning, and may serve as a distraction or obstruction. In actuality, refusal is pervasive. All discourse has major and minor elements of refusal, since we are continuously making decisions to pursue certain mental directions and not others. In the clinical situation, internal or interpersonal dialogue, free association, affect display, insight, confrontation, or interpretation—each is more or less relevant, authentic, or well timed, and so represents a compromise between advancing and averting emotional thinking.

In *resistance* material is mentalized pre- and nonconsciously, but may be revealed to consciousness slowly, indirectly, and even stubbornly. In *refusal*, the mentation process may be stalled, or kept hidden and walled off from the interpersonal world, often without explanation. While refusal may be dramatic and provoke curiosity, it eventuates into irritation, boredom, and psychic "deadness." Identifying refusal and elaborating, when possible, its rationales in terms of the here-and-now group context informs the group and is advantageous. Now one can think about and come to understand something about the refusing individual or subgroup and the situation stimulating the behavior. Working with and through refusal may also require reassuring bonding efforts (Billow, 2003c; d), confrontation, exhortation, and negotiation.

In creating a temporary impasse or resilient stalemate, refusal affirms separateness, without necessarily annihilating relationships.

Indeed, not all refusals may be resolved, and an aspect of being with others is abiding differences that cannot be negotiated.

Clinical example: A shifting balance between resistance and refusal

As per our contract, I began a workshop at a regional group psychotherapy conference with a brief lecture on the topic of "resistance and refusal," and then our group of 20 shifted into an experiential mode. Several members broke the ice by sharing their pleasure and expectations regarding our time together. But after some light banter, the room became anxiously silent. A woman exclaimed: "I have to speak up or else I will remain preoccupied. My husband called right before we started saying our 20-month old bit him on the arm and wouldn't let go. I feel so guilty attending the conference and leaving him with our two little kids. I can't help thinking I'm doing something very wrong in being here, and that's why my son has become a biter."

A number of members comforted the young mother, declaring that her husband was a "big boy" and could handle the situation, expressing annoyance that he would call and worry her, and sharing their own experiences with children who go through a biting stage. After a discussion lasting several minutes, in which the group functioned on a practical if concrete level, the woman thanked and assured us that she had no intention of leaving.

The metaphor of "biting" clicked in to our clinician-filled room and wove itself into a variety of introductory contributions: "I heard you [the leader] could be a biter. I'm going to wait and see if you are." "I'm afraid that I could be a biter." "I don't think you [the leader] could protect me from other biters." "I have been bitten in groups and it really hurt and took a lot of time to repair." "I've been a biter and have hurt people and I don't want to do that anymore."

The symbolizing process provided access to resisted expressions of wish and fear, both conscious and nonconscious. Via metaphor usage, the members took hesitant first-steps at relating to the group and volunteering personal information. Soon however, the "biting" trope wore itself out by repetition and overuse—we now seemed to have moved from a resistance to a refusal mode.

Typical in new therapeutic groups, and even more so in quasi-therapeutic workshops, members (including leaders) may "do" group yet refuse to "be" in it. I could not feel "passion" in others or in myself, the partially pre- and irrational and unformulated impulses of curiosity, love, and hate that need to be experienced and expressed, but with "intensity and warmth though without any suggestion of violence" (Bion, 1963, pp. 12–13; see also, *Chapter eight; Appendix I*). While often resisted as "not nice," passion energizes and informs our nonconsciousness and consciousness and stimulates group process (Billow, 2000a, b; 2003c). From this point of view, "biting" had lost its semantic vitality and became an impediment, an instrument of refusal, rather than its former function as a vehicle to discover, express, and explore resisted emotional meaning.

However, I understood the continued use of the "biting" metaphor also as a symbol of hunger for the type of experience I have just referred to as "passion." To move forward and expand the boundaries of what could be felt, thought, and talked about, I needed to find words, an attitude, and a mode of authentic connection that would lessen the anticipation of psychic pain and the likelihood of harm ("violence") should affective truth be pursued.

I attempted to communicate simply without being clever or self-consciously symbolic, which could continue refusal, the group process of talking "at" rather than "with." I said that it was understandable that people were afraid and could be hurt in an experiential group, but "come on already—you must have been willing to be hurt 'a little' since you wanted to be here." This unpolished exhortation seemed to work sufficiently to nudge some members out of the refusal mode to relate and respond more directly to each other. Via the "bridging" technique (Ormont, 1992), I expanded the number of active participants and interactions. My participation allowed the room to get a firmer impression how I worked with individuals, subgroups, and the group at large.

Some of the members circled back to me, offering their own first impressions—tentative emotional awareness—what they liked and did not like about my personality and leadership, and the safety and danger I provided in response to their curiosity. While I encouraged these interactions, I did not always directly or immediately respond, and made no effort to self-reveal.

Still, I was not primarily in a refusal mode, for I could feel a variety of rational and irrational feelings and thoughts, some pleasant and many less so, and I must assume that I communicated something about them. Participating, and not merely observing, deepened my engagement in the projective-introjective processes that hypothetically gird (inter) subjectivity, stimulate transference-countertransference and its resistances, and guide behavior, both symbolic and real.

At a later point in the workshop, I again felt emotionally and intellectually blank, which I assumed reflected an inhibitory drift of refusal among the participants, myself included. I pushed forward once more with an exhortation: "We have about an hour left, you'll have to 'pump it up' a bit if you want anything to happen here."

I took my own advice and searched out the silent members and cast for emotional information about their experience. Some spoke quite movingly, referring to their fear of group, their frustration with themselves, and their desire to reveal and become "known." The contrast with their previous stance of overt refusal had powerful effects on the other members. One participant described the process of her expanding emotional awareness: "I hadn't realized I had a negative reaction to you when you were silent. I hated you for withholding. When you spoke, even about not being willing or able to speak, I could see who you were. My feelings changed, but I also felt guilty for having wanted to 'bite' you." For a moment, "biting" again became a symbolic vehicle expressing "not nice" aggressive feeling, and so part of the unfolding process of exploring resistance. Individuals expressed and contextualized a variety of ambivalent feelings and attendant thoughts and the guilt associated with them.

Some of these elements of emotional experience had been felt but remained "frozen" and undeveloped, the consequence of refused entry either into public dialogue or even consciousness. Other feelings and thoughts emerged and developed linguistically as group members relaxed sufficiently to take chances with themselves and each other. At this interval the group had reached "passion," as members expressed, with sufficient warmth, intensity, and self-control, derivatives of love, hate, and curiosity (*LHK*, see *Appendix I*).

During the debriefing period of the workshop, we talked of the difference between *resistance* (narrowly defined) and *refusal*. Many members continued to confuse the terms. Whereas I could clarify matters conceptually, I asked the participants to consider how the group shifted between more and less "alive" modes of functioning. To what extent did individuals allow themselves to suffer and enjoy the struggle to think and feel—to actualize their experience and their awareness of it, and to put it into words? Or, were they aware of "tuning out," "closing down," withholding, or censoring, and might they make other choices in meeting again?

Discussion: Resistance and/or refusal

Obviously, nonconscious processes operate at all times, and we assume the existence of nonconscious fantasy and thought behind any thought and action (Isaacs, 1952). In the clinical moment it may not be clear what predominates, resistance or refusal, or the balance between them. The situation must be experienced as it develops. If the feeling is of lifelessness and dead-ends, most likely refusal is prominent, and after a suitable interval, needs to be addressed vigorously by the therapist. In contrast, if the sense of possibility of struggle remains active, this is more properly thought of as resistance, and the therapist may wait, inquire, explore nonconscious derivatives, and finally, interpret.

Resistance and refusal both may happen at once, and be expressed to varying degrees in the same interaction. As exemplified by the subsequent verbal contributions of silent members, that which is refused initially may await instantiation in a safer context. As a group progresses, refusal may evolve into resistance or even cathartic revelation, yet provide impetus for a new cycle of refusal.

"Refusal" situated in and removed from the Freudian lexicon

In the psychoanalytic lexis, *refusal* rarely has been considered per se, differentiated from other clinical phenomena. While many of Freud's important metapsychological papers involved the concept of refusal, his writings and their translations reveal semantic overlap, inconsistency, and ambiguity. For example, in a single paper, Freud (1924b) used "refuse" interchangeably with "repress," "suppress," "withdraw," "flight," "turn away," "consign to amnesia," "instantly forget," "rationalize," and "disavow."

Freud early (1894) linked the mechanism of refusal to projection, which he understood as repression "into the outside world" (Laplanche & Pontalis, 1973, p. 353). The individual refuses to recognize or repudiates something in him or herself, and projects it outside, where it resides uncomfortably. "What was abolished internally returns from without" (Freud, 1911c, p. 71). The content of the refused returns, although it may return in an altered state—hence the repressive process of symbolization—only to be reprojected once more. Schreber (Freud, 1911) unconsciously transformed an intolerable feeling (homosexual love) into its opposite and (re)projected it outward. Thus the transformation: "I don't love him, he hates me." The cycle of projection-introjection-projection may continue, bypassing resistance and the subsequent discovery and working through processes.

Even when the contents of the repressed are not projected but impinge on consciousness, the individual may continue to refuse recognition. In discussing hysteria, Freud (Freud & Breuer, 1895d) wrote of emerging "memories which the patient disavows even in reproducing them" (p. 289). The "no" of negation may mark the bringing to consciousness of repressed material (Freud, 1909d, p. 183), but as with any symbol, the individual may continue to disown affective significance (Freud, 1925h, p. 236).

In his late period, Freud developed the concept of "disavowal," perhaps in an attempt to differentiate the repression-based mechanisms of neurosis from psychosis, without relying so heavily on the concept of projection to describe the latter. Whereas in neurosis, the goal is to avoid awareness of internal reality, i.e., to keep an instinct under repression, in the latter, it is to avoid awareness of "a portion of the real external world" (Freud, 1940, p. 204). He labeled as psychotic, "amentia," in which the individual withdraws cathexis (interest). "Not only is the acceptance of new perceptions refused, but the internal world, too … loses it significance" (Freud, 1924a, pp. 150–151).

Freud (1927e) also introduced the metapsychological concept of "splitting," in which repudiation and affirmation exists "side by side" (p. 156), as in the fetishist who both disavows and recognizes the perception of the woman's lack of penis. Freud came to see splitting, which thus involves refusal, as "a universal characteristic of neuroses" (1940a, p. 204). Freud never resolved whether refusal represented primarily neurotic or psychotic phenomena. But it is not resolvable, since refusals occur in neurosis and psychosis, indeed, across clinical and, as I will argue in a later section, across non-clinical domains.

In the psychoanalytic lexis, refusal, when referred to or implied, represents a marker of pathology. To varying degrees, psychoanalytic theorists give special status to verbal linguistic symbols: A person can know something and can think about it when he or she can formulate it in words. Consider Freud (1915e): "The conscious presentation comprises the presentation of the thing plus the presentation of the word belonging to it, while the unconscious presentation is the presentation of the thing alone" (p. 201).

Green (1999), to give a prominent recent example, organized the various psychoanalytic terms related to pathological negativity along the lines of increasing failure to utilize linguistically unconscious experience: repression-negation, disavowal-splitting, and foreclosure-rejection. He invoked Lacan, who defined foreclosure as "a function of the unconscious that is distinct from the repressed" (Lacan, 1977, p. 200) and posited it as the mechanism initiating psychosis. Symbolization is rejected ("symbolic abolition"), such that a potentially abstract idea is left without the benefit of primary process thinking and remains concrete, even when put into words.

By refusing to adequately formulate a threatening experience, the individual avoids feeling and thinking in a realistic manner about whatever is dangerous. Of course, a strategy of dissociation, rejection, and denial of nonconscious experience is not limited to incipient or actual psychosis. Donnel Stern (1999), for example, described aspects of the process of leaving nonconscious experience "unformulated" that are common and relate to refusal. "Disturbing glimmers of meaning are terminated before they reach the level of articulation at which they would be explicitly meaningful. The corresponding conscious experience may be vagueness, confusion, boredom or complacency, and the absence of curiosity about the other … or a conviction of one's rightness" (p.12).

All individuals are capable of mental avoidance. We use words without thinking about their possible meanings, and insist upon the prosaic and superficial. Refusal may be added to the list of psychopathologies of everyday life.

And finally, not all silences or manifestly literal communications represent refusal. Aspects of the human experience remain ineffable, intuitive, and we may feel, think, and communicate without recourse to fully developed verbal discourse, which is not always necessary or even possible.

Three categories of refusal in the clinical situation

In reviewing psychoanalytic concepts involving refusal, three categories of mental and social experience are salient: (a) refusal to perceive external experience; (b) refusal to think about what one knows; (c) refusal to think about what one does not know. These categories are not exclusive of each other; a clinical scenario may entail elements of all. It is useful in deciding clinical focus to understand in which of the domains the impasse resides.

Refusal to perceive external experience

Refusal to perceive external reality appears clinically in distortion, narrowing of affective interest or cognitive focus, hysterical and fetishistic "'not seeing,'" negative hallucination, and in physical withdrawal (e.g., phobia). Perceptual refusal is prominent in psychosis as well as characterological disturbances, and as a reaction to trauma and other high stress situations.

Case example: Refusing presence: Perceptual, social, mental

Astute and caring toward others, Susan blocked receiving such ministration. She functioned in group therapy as her own diagnostician and interpreter, describing the mechanics and psychological origins of her many symptoms and interpersonal problems. "I know, I think all of you are like my mother, and I'm being a good girl and doing the mothering," she recited. For years, she claimed to see me as her cruel father. She could not perceive me as interested in her or even in doing my job well. I was "difficult" when I interrupted one of her forays into didactic helpfulness, and encouraged her to think emotionally rather than intellectually—as in asking her "What are you feeling?"—and "punishing" when I expressed alarm at her self-destructive behaviors that had demonstrable effects on her health.

Several years passed before she could look at me without making a face, or perceive that I was making one at her. Eventually she stopped bemoaning my treatment, acknowledged gratefully that life had significantly improved, and no longer withheld from me the warmth and humor she offered to other members.

But Susan habitually appeared 15 minutes late to our sessions, and although she conveyed remorse, neither group pressure nor analysis had influence, and we came to accept Susan with her own schedule.

She sporadically made efforts to be on time, and no sooner had we celebrated six weeks of punctuality, then she initiated intervals of missed sessions that could last four or more weeks. Was she letting us know that she had accomplished her goals and wished to leave group? Not at all, she insisted, and came up with a variety of excuses and explanations that she nonetheless understood as irrational: "I sometimes set out, but stop at a local yogurt bar and binge for the length of the session. I feel glued and disgusted with myself." "I just lose the energy to come. I want to, but I suddenly feel painfully tired." "It's the same as when I signed up for a ceramics class. I was dying to attend, but I managed to go on the wrong day and was mad at myself. The next week I had a cold."

In the midst of the latest series of extended absences, a group member suggested "voting her out." Others protested that it was not fair to talk about Susan when not present, and besides, it was my job to make such a decision. I said that I was unsure as to how to proceed, and that I wondered if I was doing Susan or anyone else a favor by allowing the mutually hurtful situation to continue. We agreed that it would be better to await Susan's return.

Susan appeared late for the next session, amid a group discussion on leisure reading. "I feel so good when I do, but I never seem to have the time." "I have the time, but I can't stand being comfortable for long. I'm sitting in a great chair, but get anxious and then get busy doing nothing." "I love airplanes. I'm 'trapped,' I have to be good to myself and read my books." The conversation ended abruptly and all eyes turned to Susan, the message being "explain your absences!" But we had suspended a group theme of refusal that could relate to Susan without making her the "patient" or pariah, two roles which she too easily absorbed. I asked: "Could we tell Susan what we are talking about?"

Rather than focusing on Susan's "acting out" and grilling her about her negativity, members elaborated their own: "I can't stand really taking for myself. Or I can, but only up to some point. I can't stay involved in a good book, even though I love it. Like here, after awhile, I need to turn the conversation away from myself." "It can't get too good—when I'm centered on me I get jittery." "I can feel good and enjoy being myself when I'm in certain special situations, like in the airplane, or here, but only during the session."

Susan joined in, linking her psychology to other group members: "Group is hard to take, all the love and attention. I can't stand the contrast with my childhood. I still would rather think of you [therapist] as harsh, rather than really interested in me. You might have saved my life. But I'd rather avoid the whole thing, even though I suffer when I don't come and feel bad all week."

I wondered whether Susan meant by "avoid the whole thing" our group, or life itself. And then, in resonance with the group theme, I continued to introspect: To what extent do I block out perceptions of being loved and appreciated? How might this be affecting my own life, as well as our group?

Case discussion: Emotional misperception in the group

Certain individuals—and all of us at certain times—emotionally misperceive feedback as unfriendly and unhelpful, no matter how benevolently offered or appreciated rationally. Interpreting resistances was counterproductive, for while Susan presented herself for help, she then rejected it. She could agree intellectually with my dynamic formulations yet perceive them as "one-upping" her. She readily felt humiliated when members expressed concern, or when I attempted to reason with her, or set limits. Although she claimed to "know better than to think this way," she felt that we were not being caring, but "losing patience," "angry," or "rubbing her nose" in disapproved behavior.

She could be sensitive and affectionate to others, or sarcastic and hostile, mainly to herself or to me. She was "here" in body as well as in spirit and then, by maintaining a closed mind, holding on to her painful misperceptions, or inexplicitly disappearing, she refused to be with us. Who was the real Susan and should one respond to her with relaxed empathy or with alarm? In caring for Susan, one had also to dislike Susan for how she treated herself. She induced ambivalence and easily felt persecuted when her refusals were not accepted unconditionally. In effect, she set up ("co-created") a sado-masochistic therapeutic situation in which to misperceive and feel misperceived.

I came to understand the importance of protecting Susan from interpretation, confrontation, or challenge. Still, it would not have been helpful to simply accommodate Susan and ignore her behavior, which would have been inauthentic and perceived by her as such. Whenever possible, I identified Susan's refusals as a problem common to others in the group, rather than as a problem she had with others. Gradually, Susan has become less overtly antagonistic, and sees her persistent refusals as based on conflicts within herself, rather than with the group and its leader.

Although fortified with enhanced feelings of attachment and intellectual understanding of the dynamics linked to her refusals and the underlying resistances, Susan has not overcome her pattern of absence and lateness. We may hypothesize that her refusals have at their roots nonconscious and very entrenched components connected to other nonconscious mechanisms such as pernicious sado-masochism. Quite likely, Susan's refusals, in the form of lateness and absences, served to disguise and discharge her underlying, mostly nonconscious rage at the therapy, therapist, and group for intruding into carefully guarded psychic arenas involving childhood ill-treatment. To be helpful and not validate her misperceptions, our group had to avoid being provoked from entering into "new editions" (Freud, 1912b) of abuse scenarios.

Refusal to think about what one knows

Refusal to think about relevant "facts," memories, attitudes, and behaviors appears clinically in conjunction with defenses of splitting and encapsulation, and also in post-traumatic syndromes, other dissociative phenomena, and the "repetition compulsion." Painful scenarios may be remembered, felt and dreamt about, and enacted, but remain, in effect, mentally "frozen." Their significance may be discounted, or treated as insurmountable and a rationale for escapist thought and behavior.

For instance, in one group, when a member expressed appreciation for my telephoning and inquiring after a missed session, another exclaimed: "I would hate it if you called. I like that no one questions me when I miss. I would have quit a long time ago. You know that I play hooky sometimes. I had to 'fess up' to my parents and I won't do it for you." In effect, the group's incuriosity represented our empathic response to the member's adamant refusal to re-examine an obvious, seemingly well-known aspect of his psychology. He had no wish to re-experience unpleasant childhood feelings and attach them to the group or to me, although that is what therapeutic movement would have required.

In the following example, the individual came to re-experience and link feelings to parents and therapeutically, to parent figures (her husband, the therapist, and the group-as-a-whole); however, reaching emotional understanding did not change her pattern of refusal.

Case example: Refusal in the "working through"

Ruth began missing group sessions with a variety of excuses; the most plausible being that she had relocated geographically and travels to my office were now lengthy. As a partial accommodation, I agreed to reschedule her bi-weekly marital sessions to just before the group time.

"Tell him, Ruth," her husband began. With some trepidation, Ruth revealed that she felt "forced" to stay in group by her husband, who monitored her attendance. She wanted to "take a break." Did I, too, have a role in forcing her? She assented apologetically. I acknowledged wanting her to remain, but not if she felt coerced. I did not like how that made me feel about myself; her husband appreciated my adding that I was sure that he felt the same way.

At some later point in the session I identified what I believed to be the enactment (i.e., the *resistance* being played out interactionally). I reviewed how she grew up trapped, prematurely exposed to her parents' divorce drama, first captive to her mother's depression, and then shuttled to her father, where as an adolescent she was an overstimulated witness to his free-wheeling bachelorhood.

The couple felt the retrospective analysis helpful in explaining Ruth's inconsistent behavior that contributed to their marital difficulties. Ruth could be warm to her husband and abruptly turn cold;

she could be sexually involved, then unexpectedly feel degraded and "needing space." We discovered that in both of these situations, her mood changed to a variant of refusal once she felt pressure (Bion's concept of "violence")—imagined or real—to conform to her husband's will.

I suggested that before leaving group, Ruth might want to consider saying good-bye, even discussing feeling coerced. However, she should not return if she heard my suggestion as forcing her to do something she did not want to do. In the marital session we had made links to nonconscious and symbolic issues, i.e., to the underlying resistances that motivated her refusals. Still, the issue of refusal had to remain front and center. Interpretations, in which her traumatic past was related to her present marital and group situations, could not be expected immediately to dissolve or override her powerful wish to refuse.

Perhaps she took encouragement from our validation, for she returned, and conveyed to the group members the gist of the marital session. They did not object when Ruth offered to continue on an every other session basis. "That feels right to me, I won't feel pressured, or that I have to be here. Maybe my feelings will change later." I agreed to this unorthodox arrangement with an experimental, "Let's see how it goes" attitude.

Discussion: Resistance analyzed without working through refusal

Ruth's refusals—and the traumas that instigated them—often get revisited in her intrapsychic and interpersonal work and partake in our group process and culture. While we did and continue to analyze productively (the derivatives of) her resistance, Ruth's basic attitude has not changed, and she continues on the bi-weekly basis. Similarly to the group with Susan as a member, the psychology of refusal remains in the immediacy of the group, whether she is present or not.

Thus, however beneficial to understand and analyze the nonconscious or irrational substrate of refusal, the impasse may yet stand, the interpersonal problems unresolved. We may consider refusal as the tip of the iceberg. Even when the iceberg of resistance seemingly is exposed and explored, the obstacle may remain.

The depth and breadth of re-experienced or anticipated mental and/or interactional scenarios—of desire, fear, and rage—may be felt as unbearable. When one cannot rely on repression, suppression, and dissociation—and a sufficiently nonviolent process of emotional unfolding—refusal feels safest, and remains the preferred option.

Refusal to think about what one does not know

Refusal to think about and develop incipient feelings and thoughts—a muted receptivity to "fresh" internal and external experience—appears clinically in depressive syndromes, so-called "rigid" characters (including schizoid and obsessive compulsive disorders), and in concrete, immature, or inadequate personalities. Additionally, all of us have limited capacity to tolerate the unfamiliar and the unknown.

Case example: "Premature giveupitus"

Jack appeared for consultation on the suggestion of his new psychiatrist, the latest in a succession of therapists whose methods and medicines had not "helped me with my problems." The 35-year-old man explained wearily: "I'm depressed. I had severe learning disabilities, and my parents were told I would never go to college. But I made it. My mother worked with me every night, my father made sure I had the best tutors. He was also my basketball coach. I got so good I was scouted. I quit after I saw how much better the other guys were. I also have a sexual problem. I usually back away. Sometimes I have performance issues."

I offered that Jack had another problem that could affect his membership in group: "premature giveupitus." He laughed, but insisted: "I've done individual, I don't know why but I think a group could help and I could help other people too." I eventually agreed, and was encouraged by the mutual affection that quickly developed with the veteran members. They were more successful than I in countering Jack's interludes of benumbing depression, such as by challenging his "pity parties" and encouraging his dating.

Finally: "I met this woman, Helene. She's really interesting, we've been talking on the phone." Jack casually added: "She's married."

Several people at once: "Married!" "Doesn't that bother you?" "Does she have kids?" Jack smiled: "She has kids. No, it doesn't bother me. I like it. I find it kind of exciting." Other members interrupted: "You better be careful. You don't know what you are getting yourself into. She could be a user." "Her husband could get 'goons' to beat the crap out of you." Throughout, Jack maintained, "Helene isn't like that."

At some point I broke into the go-round of prudent if frenzied counsel: "A married woman is 'lifting' Jack's spirits!" Our playful group did not ignore the Oedipal allusion ("lifting" referring to an erection), which generated a discussion about the appeal of unavailable partners. Then, jarringly, one member, Tom, irately turned on me: "I can't believe that you are promoting Jack dating someone married."

The group objected: "We're not even talking about Jack, now." "Richard wasn't encouraging or discouraging Jack, he was just exploring." "I hate it when you get so moralistic."

I believed that Tom's concreteness and ensuing diatribe had the purpose to extinguish an increasingly uncomfortable exploration, by redirecting the topic either to my behavior or his. At an earlier time in our group, Tom painfully came to acknowledge the possibility that his idolized father had an outside relationship throughout his marriage. His mother, through depression, anger, and innuendo conveyed her vague suspicions, but they were never openly discussed with the children or brought to meaning. Each family member suffered from refusal, deprived of collaborative and mutual understanding. The price of Tom's allegiance to the family style of denial and falsification had been a history of intense moodiness and impenetrable angry outbursts.

The session was nearing its end, and I reintroduced the Oedipal theme related to refusal, to Jack's "problems" and to Tom's disruptive tactics. I surprised Tom by commenting that I appreciated his willingness not to refuse dialogue, but to openly take issue with me, something no one did with his own father. Although I took a risk in reinserting an (Oedipal) idea he wished to avoid elaborating, he seemed pleased and calmed by my attention. I then reminded the group of another aspect of this topic that we had insufficiently developed and hence refused: "All of us have lusted after a married person. Jack was just beginning to tell us about his lust." We had time only for an abbreviated discussion of attractions to mothers and fathers and their group representatives. Still, I trusted that the theme would be thought and dreamt about, and revisited in future sessions.

Indeed, Jack began the next session with an Oedipal denial: "I'm sorry to have caused such a commotion last time we met. I went out with Helene, 'the married woman.' She was nothing like she was on the phone. It was a horrendous 30 minutes. But I'm not trying to date my mother. [laughs] I was thinking how all of you are so into yourselves, trying to figure yourselves out. I'm not really into myself. Maybe because you've been doing it so long and you are all so smart."

Jack's denial of trying to date his mother contained a promising "avowal of the signifier itself that it annuls" (Lacan, 1977, p. 201). Lacan reminds us that the nonconscious may betray its work while at the same time the speaker consciously refuses to develop further what is signified. I interrupted the group's reassuring responses and pushed Jack further: "You're not into getting into why you're not into yourself." Jack responded with an affirmative negative: "That's right. I don't know why." I continued: "Well, who got into you?"

Jack: "I can't think of anybody, maybe just my parents, but I don't let them in. I know they're unhappy when I'm negative—maybe I'm punishing them because I'm not happy."

"Maybe you're unhappy because you want to punish them," I rejoined, and then, catching Tom's eye, added to the hypothesis, "for how they got into you." Although no words passed directly between us, Tom seemed sobered by the interaction, and for the first time, he expanded on his parents' indoctrination of refusal: "My parents taught me not to do my own thinking, and were they into me!" Jack thanked us without letting us know how and if we affected him.

A few months later, Jack began a session reporting that he had been rained out of a golf outing and chose a surprise visit home. His mother greeted him with a hug and a comment: "Poor Jack, you don't have any mazel [Yiddish for "luck"]."

"You got 'slimed'!" Tom responded insightfully, no longer partnering Jack in refusing. Jack continued: "I felt really bad, and then I realized that she does that to me all the time, making me 'poor Jack'!" Tom: "Your father doesn't say anything? Doesn't that make you mad?" Other members joined in: "Your parents needed you to be the 'problem child'." Jack receded as the group did his work as well as their own.

After another interval of several months, Jack introduced his first dream with an apologetic disclaimer: "I hardly ever dream, and this doesn't make any sense to me. I was with my entire family, at the airport, maybe in Florida. Their luggage had arrived and everyone was waiting for mine. My father got very angry and went after me, and it was very scary. He's not like that. It was slippery and every time he took a swing he fell. I didn't want him to get hurt but I was glad that he didn't get me. Then the dream shifted and I was in a pool and everyone was around me and I couldn't get out."

The members played with certain images from the dream. The "family" and the "pool" stood for the group, and they reviewed some of our recent work and turned to Jack for clarification. Who is Jack's father in our group, and who is angry at whom? Jack became puzzled and did not take their questions further. Like the father in the dream, I felt tempted to "go after" him, but he was "slippery" and I could get frustrated and "scary" in pursuing him. Surrounded by the "pool" of the members' associations, Jack wanted egress from his own mind.

Unlike Tom, who showed that he tolerated and benefited from mental pursuit and the introduction of fresh ideas, Jack could take mental challenge just so far before quitting. I commented that Jack did not feel quite ready to deal with his own "baggage" but that it was coming his way soon. The group seemed to have no choice but to go on to other subjects.

Discussion: Refusal "trumps" resistance

Jack's dream supplied the symbolic elements for thinking, and the group attempted to fulfill its containing function (by developing ideas), but not enough, as Jack's refusal was stronger. In seeming to abandon symbolization, Jack also deprived other members of reaching deeper into a shared psychological experience.

In the immediacy of the psychotherapeutic situation, refusal may "trump" resistance, such to block or curtail formulating new ideas. However, the nonconscious still has cards to play. For, behind the closed gates of refusal resides resistance, and what is foreclosed consciously may be worked over nonconsciously (Freud, 1940a, p. 203) and co-[non]consciously. While Jack manifestly disengaged from the dream work, others were able to receive and unpack some of the Oedipal "baggage" from his nonconscious and supply material, which Jack and the group built on in further work.

A person such as Jack may limit participation in the group setting for a host of reasons—insecurity and anxiety about pursuing derivatives of repression, but also, social embarrassment, such as fear of exposure and humiliation, and finally, apprehension about changing one's role in the group and in life. Thus, refusal has elements that relate to the "social unconscious" (Hopper, 2003a), and specifically, to the immediate social setting and one's role in it. To renounce resolutely "premature giveupitus," i.e., his characterological stance of mental and social refusal, and think consciously and persistently about the nonconscious, Jack must change radically his view of himself and renegotiate his group as well as primary relationships. At present, Jack's stultifying refusal has shifted gradually but not entirely into a workable resistance. Refusal remains both Jack's front line defense and his fallback position.

Not all refusals are examples of resistance

Refusal may not signify maladjustment or antagonism to all forms of mentation and manners of pursuing it, but rather, to the particular approach or purpose of the endeavor. The assumptions, methods, and goals of certain types of meaning making may be challenged metapsychologically, philosophically, ethically, pragmatically, and politically. As with each of the *3 Rs*, *refusal* sits in an interpersonal context and its locus and legitimacy must be judged by psychosocial circumstance and viewpoint.

For instance, until 1973, homosexuality was considered a category of mental disorder. The patient who wished to be accepted for pursuing an alternative lifestyle was understood by the psychoanalytic establishment as refusing to explore underlying (Oedipal and pre-Oedipal) dynamics. The certainty in this truth has shifted due to political action as well as by the importation of new ideas from related fields of biology and child development. The rules of discourse have changed, and promulgating any remnant of the prior view often is *refused*, now labeled "heterocentric" or unscientific.

To give further examples, dependent on one's values and the political climate, rejection of the role of the fighting soldier may be classified as "neurotic" and cause for group treatment (as in Bion, 1961, treating World War II servicemen), or heroic and stimulus for social protest, (as with the draftees who evaded the Vietnam War). As a society, we debate whether certain explorations in the realm of nuclear physics or genetic biology represent a search for truth that far exceeds our moral capabilities of using it. The philosopher of science, Nicholas Rescher (1987), questioned whether "there are things we ought not to know on moral grounds. ... Here, inappropriateness lies only in the mode of acquisition or in the prospect of misuse" (p. 9). In certain instances, then, *refusal* may be also an act of *rebellion* (*Chapter six*), an attempt to move social dialogue, process, and organization in a different direction.

Certain forms of refusals—declinations, omissions, and commissions—may embody a familial, social, or cultural mode. They may represent an adaptive means of coping with an indelicate, feared, or potentially destructive interpersonal situation. Also, refusal may guard against over- or improper stimulation, social or mental. Regarding the latter, efforts to control intrusive feelings and thoughts, intellectualization, and rumination often are in the service of expanding emotional awareness, and are different from shutting down or overly concretizing thought and feeling.

A strategy of refusal may partake in any of Bion's three *basic assumptions*. Refusal may signify an inability to symbolize in connection with overwhelming anxieties. Yet, refusal may calm anxieties and appropriately address it causes. Refusal remains a valid option for the *work group*, as in establishing or maintaining boundaries, limit setting, protecting privacy, or defying unrealistic or unethical requests or expectations, whether promulgated by group members or leader. Thus, while refusal may represent a failure of mentation, it may also signify a conscious and well thought-out decision, for instance, the avoidance of arrogant curiosity (Bion, 1967), or of a pursuit that is deemed misdirected, ill-timed, unhealthy, immoral, or merely worthless.

There are then social and clinical situations wherein refusal may be considered appropriate, a legitimate response in thought and behavior, and not a strategy of evasion. A stance of refusal to think about, develop, and actualize certain ideas may be deemed pathological, cowardly, stubborn, or ignorant, or life affirming, courageous, discretionary, or wise.

The therapist's refusals: Interactive effects

As we considered in *Chapters two* and *three*, truth may hurt, as does its absence, and group therapists must protect their groups from too much or too little emotional awareness. We monitor what we pursue with others, and what we share about ourselves. Certain subjects and modes of interactions remain "off limits," for instance, advancing a political or religious point of view, socializing, and physical manipulation

It could be argued that therapists refuse more than other group members, with the best of professional intentions. Refusal begins nonverbally, with a therapist's warm smile and a professional countenance obscuring more complex feelings. It often continues with "Fine," the response to the patient's, "Hello, how are you?" More than one individual has asked: "Would you tell me if you weren't 'fine'?"

Our various rationales for refusal have historic contexts but they are not immutable. For instance, during its first five decades, psychoanalysis refused to consider the data of countertransference as a heuristic approach to expanding emotional awareness. Countertransference analysis has since entered the hallowed "common ground" of mainstream psychoanalytic thinking, writing, and technique (Gabbard, 1995). Still, to an extent far greater than our patients, we exercise restraint and do not share many aspects of our persona.

Favoring a classical psychoanalytic stance, Green (1999) maintained that "it is not as an individual that he [the analyst] expresses himself but as an image 'created' by the situation" (p. 99). Fundamental to the meaning-making process are the effects of the analyst's "non-presence and the attribute which the human psyche has of responding to this absence by means of representation (hallucinatory, fantasmatic, cognitive, etc.,)" (pp. 99–100).

Hoffman (1992; 1996) has proposed that ultimately, it is the analyst's refusal of the ritualized role that Green described that establishes the conditions for the analysand's self-understanding. The therapist's *sincerity* (*Chapter eight*), that is, genuine interest and concern, becomes an emotional reference point, grounding the patient (and clinician) such that interpretations can be emotionally and not merely intellectually meaningful.

However, given that both the motivation for and the act of refusal may exist without awareness, we may discover that we refuse to be sincere and forthcoming when we ought to assent, and assent when we need to refuse. Recognizing our own limitations in pursuing and tolerating emotional awareness is not easy, for we hide ourselves from ourselves, as well from others. The tendency exists to conceal ignorance, and to omit or modify certain truths in self-interest, while justifying such behavior as in the interests of others. Refusal or failure to refuse—each may indicate underlying counter-resistance and a need for self (and group) examination.

Case example: A therapist's multiple refusals

A therapist reported that the introduction of a new member brought several lively weeks to group sessions, but there ensued a phase marked by lengthy opening silences and intervals of communicative gaps. Most distressing to the therapist, the members remained mute to his various interventions: "Do we have unfinished business?" "What is the silence telling us?" "Are the members uncomfortable with the new member, and angry with me for his presence?" "So what gives?" he demanded finally. "You don't have any trouble talking in the waiting room?"

A veteran explained, addressing the novice member: "See, in the waiting room we have small talk. We don't have small talk in here. [Referring gently to the therapist:] He doesn't allow it." The therapist understood the spokesperson's communication as confirmation of group resistance to him as "bad mother," "forbidding father," "controlling parent," and so forth. He continued to hunt for symbolic derivatives of negative transference, which he found and interpreted to no avail.

In supervision, I asked the therapist to consider that the group was abiding by an unspoken communication from him: "We must be meaningful." This actually represented a powerful refusal by the therapist, his implicit stricture against "small talk." Certainly, this experienced and talented therapist fully understood that small talk does not necessarily remain small, and may serve a pragmatic purpose, e.g., fostering inclusion of the new member and solidifying member-to-member bonding. Despite this knowledge, he remained allied to so-called "deep work and interpretations," a la Bion and his idealized fantasy of my work and me.

We agreed that he needed to "get real," which meant to sit back for awhile, enjoy the group, and let the group enjoy his enjoyment, no matter the ostensible level of dialogue. Still, he had difficulty tolerating a group phase of apparent "no meaning" (i.e., "small talk"). He remained convinced that I would find a way to have my cake and eat it too, i.e., "being real" while also pursuing deep truths and being profound, as he felt I was now.

Discussion: Therapists exhibit the range of refusal

In supervision, we attempted to work through the therapist's personal struggle by identifying how the various subtypes of clinical refusal impeded his constructing a more accurate view of the group and group-leader dynamics. Because this was supervision, and not psychotherapy, the dynamic *resistances* were less the topic of our meetings, and so I was inclined to push less hard against his refusals.

a. *Refusal to perceive external experience.* The therapist remained unconvinced that he was misperceiving the group's silence as indicating negative feelings towards him. He "wanted to believe" but could not share my perception of the group as appreciative and struggling to work within his constraints.
b. *Refusal to think about what one knows.* Even after coming to understand the effects of his own presumptions and behavior—his clinical orientation and nonverbal communications—on what he initially perceived as the group's refusal, he had difficulty utilizing his knowledge to modify his felt commitment to "deep work."
c. *Refusal to think about what one does not know.* The flow of seemingly insignificant dialogue, the "small talk," continued to stimulate his anxiety. The temptation to offer preformulated hypotheses interfered with his capacity to listen for latent themes, so to help develop new meaning and awareness. As well, his idealization of clinical psychoanalysis represented a refusal to see me as real, off

a pedestal. Hence, he could not believe, much less identify with, an image of me as enduring interludes of ignorance, doubt, and uncertainty.

Refusal as interpersonal impasse

We may appreciate from the clinical examples how refusal eventuates as interpersonal impasse: the behavioral outcome of two (or more) opposing points of view. An element of antagonistic mutuality exists, for the circumstances in which one individual refuses, the refuser is not acceding to the pressure the other exerts to participate. Each attempts to define or redefine the parameters of the clinical situation. When faced with refusal, the other must reconsider his or her position; else, by rejecting the legitimacy of the refuser, one risks becoming a refuser as well.

Resolving, modifying, or working around refusal may stretch the limits of the group therapist's creativity, flexibility, and willingness to negotiate in dealing with a difficult clinical situation. For the clinician will find little therapeutic traction in insisting to treat refusal as resistance per se, such as by reintroducing themes, metaphorizing, playing with, or interpreting symbolic communications and nonconscious derivatives. When the therapist can understand his or her own role in the refusal, he or she is more likely to participate in a clinically and personally illuminating experience.

Conclusion: Refusal legitimized

I have defined the concept of *refusal*, as distinguished from an overarching term, *resistance*, to capture and organize disparate ways the work of group psychotherapy is challenged and opposed. Studying refusal helps us explore areas of intersubjectivity, ambivalence, and conflict. While for some individuals, refusal lies at the core of character, for all of us there are core areas of refusal, seemingly inviolable areas of experience that we wish to preserve, despite the personal and interpersonal costs. While we attempt to understand and overcome refusal, we also are confined to work within and around its boundaries.

Refusal may be identified on whole group, subgroup, and individual levels, as a mode of influence and control, character style, defense mechanism, couple or family dynamic, protective device, weapon, stance, and also, as an appropriate choice. Refusal supports the maintenance of taboo (as in the Oedipal situation), and relates to specific and cumulative traumas. While serving a protective function by shielding from real and anticipated pain, refusal may also perpetuate the relationship to psychological pain by forestalling efforts to deal with it.

In exploring conceptual parameters of the term, fresh opportunities are created for the therapist to meet group and group member without premature interpretation or limiting meaning to interpretation of defense and underlying resistance. When one cannot rely on repression-based defenses and processes to release painful emotions and attendant thoughts and fantasy in a nonviolent fashion, or trust how they will be received, refusal becomes a preferred option. As a strategy or pathway of resistance, refusal may be understood as a front line defense, as well as a fallback position.

At times, *refusal* transforms into *resistance*, as members put into words, action, and/or dream imagery the motives for characteristic patterns of refusal. At other times, refusal leads to *rebellion* and a renegotiation of the therapeutic contract, stated and/or enacted. Some refusals persist; refusal remains an option for therapist and all group members at various degrees of legitimacy. While signifying a negative stance towards certain emotional truths and/or their development, refusal also functions as an intrapsychic and interpersonal regulator. Refusal may be legitimatized and used constructively in understanding, organizing, and building meaning in the group setting.

PART III

MODES OF THERAPEUTIC INTERACTION

CHAPTER EIGHT

The four modes of therapeutic interaction

Managing truth

I refer again to Emily Dickinson's poem: "Tell the truth, but tell it slant .... The truth must dazzle gradually, or every man be blind," which expresses our limited capacity to tolerate truth and its effects. As emphasized throughout the *3 Rs*: individuals and groups of all sizes need and long for truth, which is necessary for security and growth. But, significant truth is often anxiety arousing, and not easy to reach, contain, and communicate. And, even when benevolently offered and welcomed, truth may hurt, mislead, or obstruct.

Freud (1920g) considered the analyst the arbiter of truth. The therapeutic task was to reveal the repressed: "discover the unconscious material that was concealed from the patient, put it together, and, at the right moment, communicate it to him" (1920, p. 18). I have suggested that, to the extent to which the therapist is expert, it is in pursuing a search for emotionally meaningful truth: evaluating and responding to the truth needs of the various individuals and the group itself and detecting and minimizing the impact of falsity.

The group therapist has the special role of managing truth: evaluating and responding to the truth needs of the various individuals and the group itself. He or she maintains the belief that interest in truth remains basic, and that group members think about the ongoing group experience when *resisting*, *rebelling* against, or *refusing* certain emotional links to understanding it. Our primary task is twofold: pursuing that which is painfully immediate and most meaningful; and the same time shielding others from that which is immediate, but too painful to become meaningful.

Four modes

In leading the search for truth, the group therapist grapples with the *3 Rs*—strategies our patients (and ourselves) use for intrapsychic and psychosocial purposes. I propose that therapists, in struggling with these dynamic forces and actions, operate in four communicative modes or stances, captured under one or more of the rubrics: *diplomacy, integrity, sincerity*, and *authenticity*. These are tactics of discourse (Austin, 1962) or relational modes of speaking and listening, adopted with and without awareness. The modes are exhaustive but nonexclusive. They inform the interpersonal struggle to seek, confront, or modify ("slant") truth.

Since I believe that the psychology of the therapist remains central in all phases of group life, I deal primarily with characteristics that the therapist needs to struggle with and secondarily with engagement issues on the part of other members. The four modes are intimately inter-related, linked by communicative skills that we therapists strive to achieve in dealing with our patients and hope to model for them. These four categories supply conceptual references for the therapeutic stance one has adopted, allowing the therapist to be more aware of what he or she is doing, and why.

Exploring them could prove useful in disentangling and addressing some of the technical issues that concern the contemporary relational psychotherapist and that have been a focus of this and my earlier volume, *Relational Group Psychotherapy,* regarding topics of intersubjectivity, presentation of self, and self-disclosure.

In this final chapter, I present the four modes, the interrelationships among them, and their differing functions in the totality of the clinical situation. The chapter closes by applying the model to the larger group and the political leader: the recent presidency of G.W. Bush.

Diplomacy

Diplomacy is concerned with the uses and allocations of power, in establishing and maintaining relationships and alliances. Power needs to be shared; else there would never be a need to be diplomatic. Diplomacy works by creating or strengthening bridges between people or subgroups. These links have an associated affective range, from very warm to cold and distant. In the former, individuals are able to bond almost immediately and feel close with shared good feelings. Sometimes this is not possible, and the leader in diplomatic mode convinces the cold and distant parties that they have, at least, a common interest.

In being diplomatic, the therapist is both political and strategic: trying to influence the group to use its power in cooperative interrelationships rather than to express power in forms of retaliatory *rebellions* or *refusals*. Patience—timing and tact—would seem to characterize diplomacy; however, spontaneity, emotional openness, transparency (self-disclosure), and confrontation may be effective, even requisite, to bringing meaning to the group situation.

Diplomacy takes into account the motivations, affiliations, and beliefs among different people and subgroups and the roles they occupy. It may involve keeping channels of communication open so that the players can continue a search for communal or at least livable truths. Rather than one version of truth dominating another, differing positions of truth may compete, with positive outcome. Each may reveal strengths and weaknesses in the other. Each may stand alongside the other, confronting us with our personal biases and vulnerabilities in response to difference, the unfamiliar, or unknown. A new and better synthesis may emerge.

Leadership requires diplomacy

In psychotherapy groups, *diplomacy* relates to the clinician as leader, exercising authority and power, in regard to the group structure, process, and culture. The group therapist predetermines, defines, and enforces many of the essentials within the therapy, including boundary functions such as time, place, seating, duration of the session, and fee. Thoma and Kachele's (1994a) remarks apply to group as well as dyadic psychotherapy: "The analyst influences every phenomenon felt or observed in the analytic situation .... The course of therapy depends on the influence exerted by the analyst" (p. 7).

The group legitimizes the leader to lead and the members to be a part of the group (Alford, 1995). "Patients come to group because of the therapist's importance ... as an object of cathexis and dependence" (Slavson, 1992, p. 179). However, while the therapist sits in the seat of power in the center of the group process—being the symbolic "chair"—he or she must earn and maintain this position. In Shakespeare's *Henry IV*, Glendower brags: "I can call spirits from the vasty deep." Hotspur taunts: "Why so can I, or so can any man; But will they come when you do call them?" Leadership is a "performance art;" its inherently social nature involves influencing others to follow, by establishing a direction for collective effort and managing the collective activities accordingly (Bennis, 2007; Zaccaro, 2007).

The therapist's theory and technique bring power, control, and directionality to the psychotherapeutic experience, which privilege and prohibit types of interpersonal interactions (Hoffman, 1996). The mode of diplomacy includes, then, the therapist's monitoring and, if necessary, regulating or mediating power arrangements among members and subgroups to foster ideals of mutual respect and freedom of expression. The therapist must be able and available to protect vulnerable members and minority subgroups, to establish and maintain a climate of safety. Without such leadership, the members are more likely to form an *Establishment*, characterized by its mind-deadening, truth-evading qualities. Such groups are marked with inauthenticity, submission to authority, and conformity, "cold wars," impasses, and stalemates.

My position in this book has been that the search for truth is the primary function of the therapist and the group. In this first case example, I judged that bonding efforts were critical. Bonding essentially supports the search for truth, since we feel safer, and so more receptive, in the presence of allies.

Case example: Establishing leadership via bonding

I was invited to Israel to lead a two-day institute held in Jerusalem, prior to an international meeting of mental health workers on the topic of "Reconciliation." Israelis and Arabs formed the majority of the 13 participants; others came from Turkey, South Africa, and the countries that once comprised Yugoslavia. The first hour and a half passed as people talked about their cultural, geographic, and professional backgrounds and why the conference was important; several commented that they hoped to understand and achieve "passion," a reference to my work (Billow, 2003c).

The group seemed to have difficulty surmounting this introductory phase, and in response to increasing conversational lulls, I referenced Bion's (1979) powerful metaphor: That wherever and whenever people get together an "emotional storm" quickly develops. I suggested that a storm seemed likely to be brewing now and that it might be helpful to try to locate the sources of anxiety in oneself, and attempt to describe them.

I was pleased with myself for being able to introduce a sophisticated idea early on; after all, people were expecting me to interject didactic material into the experiential format, and I was glad to comply. However, a woman immediately responded that she was "perfectly relaxed." With a disingenuous smile, she suggested that it was I who must be feeling anxiety. Ignoring what I felt to be inexplicable hostility in her *refusal*, I acknowledged that indeed I did, and that I was attempting to use that source of emotional data to guide my comments. I analogized anxiety to pain receptors, as something positive, a mode of supplying information and hence links to self and others.

As if responding to my intervention—and sinking my good feelings about my intervention and my leadership—someone suggested it might be a good idea to return to the theme of the conference. "Everyone here wants peace, yet the process seemed so sad and difficult," another woman lamented. The Gaza residents talked about their difficulty getting past Israeli checkpoints even to attend a meeting on reconciliation; the Israelis countered with justifications for the barriers. Each side related stories of hardship, loss, and terror.

Attendees from other countries attempted to moderate the rising antagonism, and offered resolutions based on their history, such as the South African who spoke of the recent coming together of that strife-torn country. The Arabs and Israelis concurred that these suggestions were unfeasible, given the political climate in the Middle East and the influence of the "military-industrial complex."

After awhile, I said that, despite obvious ethnic and political tensions, the main barrier in the room appeared to be between everyone else and me. I could not locate, much less get through, a checkpoint and become part of this group. After some denials, reassurances, and hesitations, several members came forth with their doubts: I was an American, a visitor, and outsider; how could I understand their anguish and loss? I replied that it was probable that I understood less than anyone else and that I would learn and gain more than anyone else during our two days together. I made eye contact with those who spoke up or returned my gaze. I invited the group to deal with me directly if they felt I was "missing something," "off base," even, "out of it."

My verbal and behavioral interactions gave me a point of entry, and attention now turned to member-member configurations. Discrepancies in age, status, and political leanings were on peoples' minds: two students at a prominent Arab university tensely faced their senior administrator; an Israeli housewife and community organizer confronted what she assumed were bellicose attitudes of two high-ranking soldier-psychologists. Another woman complained about those—mostly the men—who were dominating the session with talk, but not with feeling. With each interaction, I encouraged the participants to respond to each other, and polled other members for their observations; feeling freer, I joined in the process.

During the morning of the second day, a heated discussion re-emerged between the Israelis and Palestinians. I commented that the anger and tears seemed directed to the tragic situation as much as to the participants in the room and that, perhaps for this reason, others did not feel a need to intervene. Still, I encouraged the others to participate. Later, I said that perhaps some progress had been made towards "reconciliation" when the participants related to each other as "people" rather than merely as representatives of hostile political entities. We could not be certain. And then, foreshadowing the afternoon's end of our group, I said, "We could mourn together."

Discussion

"All politics is local," Tip O'Neill (a longtime Speaker of the House in the U.S. Congress) purportedly declared. A group localizes itself by enacting *"equivalences"* (Hopper, 2003a). People bring sociopolitical configurations existing outside the group and enact them in the group. Actions, fantasies, object relations and affects that are occurring "there and now" (the sociopolitical environment), are brought to "here and now" (the group) via a process of projective and introjective identifications. The resulting interactive relationships—intrapsychic, interpersonal and immediate, are also historic, cultural, and involve the larger socio-political setting in which the group (including the therapist) is embedded.

Equivalences serve multiple goals: to expel, attack, and also, to achieve control and mastery over feelings of personal and social helplessness and powerlessness. Above all, they are attempts to communicate (Hopper, 2003a), often by replicating symbolically aspects of traumatogenic social experiences. As with other forms of enactments, they often are understood only in retrospect.

"What makes leaders successful depends not only on their message and their skill in getting it across, but also on their grasp of what followers want from them" (Maccoby, 2007, p. 1). Before the traumatized members could deal constructively with the "emotional storm" in which we were to be re-immersed, they needed to feel safe. This required a safe-enough leader.

Supplementing the typical paranoid/depressive dreads and excitements accompanying formation, then, our group was subject to specific determining influences: a collective, traumatic disillusionment with leaders, local, national, and international. Yet, a woman claimed to be "perfectly relaxed" when faced with my leadership. Since other members did not challenge her patent falsity or offer different emotional viewpoints, I could only assume that people were afraid of her, or of me. No one (but me) was anxious. As another woman asserted, "everyone here wants peace."

"Peace" would imply ignoring the active and passive *rebellion* against my leadership, a *defiant* inauthenticity, first masked by *fight/flight* subgroup dynamics. Calling attention to the aggression underlying the group's unresponsiveness to my leadership had the salutary effect of destabilizing the pre-existing ethnic subgroups—freeing members to relate to me, and then to each other, as individuals.

I let the participants know that I could tolerate their hostility without retaliating. This required confronting the group with their treatment of me and encouraging a verbal exploration of underlying rationales, such as my being an American outsider. At the same time, I both encouraged and modeled *bonding*, making eye contact, talking directly to individual members, and inviting authentic exchanges.

These included acknowledging my limitations—imagined, possible, and actual (see this chapter, on *authenticity*).

I have described *bonding* as a basic feeling of connectedness to other human beings, which the individual needs to establish and maintain. Bonding is an ongoing aspect of intersubjective experience, a type of mental relationship to oneself and others. As a mode of interpersonal behavior, bonding utilizes verbal and nonverbal communication primarily to establish connection between individuals. The affective experience involves a sense of mutual communication, in which the individuals feel satisfactorily recognized, cared for, and understood.

Although bonding interactions often involve words, they impact preverbal, non-rational use of verbal thinking and communication. These empathic, introjective-projective exchanges are "emotionally rewarding … [establishing] a sense of being in contact … a primitive form of communication that provides a foundation on which, ultimately, verbal communication depends" (Bion, 1967, p. 92).

Bonding provides a deep source of emotional truth regarding how safe others are and the extent to which they can be trusted to provide and protect. My actions were based on my belief that, most often, productive groups bond first to the leader; member-to-member bonds radiate from and depend on member-leader bonds.

Bonding also is mutual, and whereas the members needed to bond with me, I needed to bond to them as well. Bonding guides the clinical "feel" necessary in establishing leadership—securing adequate safety to maneuver and diplomatically advance cohesion, process, and progress. I had confidence that once we were and could remain sufficiently and mutually bonded, the group would display adequate sensitivity and concern for the individual and collective welfare.

Diplomatic maneuvers may be fair without treating all members or all contributions equally

In the diplomatic mode, the therapist may situate certain truths and not others as primary or ideal. Certain truths may be emphasized and explored, while others are minimized, shaded, or withheld. Diplomatic interventions are not always popular or balanced evenly among all participants. The following case vignette deals with the aggressive dynamics of exclusion that often accompanies entry of a new patient into an ongoing group. In my efforts to protect the new member, I was experienced as *rebelling* against the dominant group culture, that is, as suppressing the psychoanalytic agenda of exploring nonconscious dynamics, putting feelings into words, and taking chances with spontaneous interactions. I had confidence that the veteran members could benefit from the process of tolerating frustration, withholding themselves, and allowing a new member to unfold without interpretative challenge.

Case example: Maintaining an unstated agenda

Claire, in her early thirties and engaged to be married, recently joined our group but now had second thoughts. "Everyone here has children or is planning to. I don't want any; you're going to think something is wrong with me." Her declaration stirred interest and an incipient interrogation. "This is what I feared, that I would have to explain myself."

I too was interested in exploring the meanings behind Claire's decision, but there was truth in her apprehension, and I felt it important to call attention to it. "Yes, no one would question why one of us would want to have a child. 'Childless' seems to define something negative." Claire felt the support of my intervention, but several of the women took issue. "I feel you [the therapist] are suppressing me. I just want to learn about Claire." "Should I feel uncomfortable if I talk about being a mother and how wonderful it feels?"

Claire reassured the second speaker that she loved children and enjoyed hearing about them. But she was stung by the accusation of suppression, which she felt was directed to her: "I don't want to suppress you … " and she broke off, near tears but also frozen with her own anger.

Again, I heard truth in Claire's ostensible misidentification. The first speaker was angry with Claire for her position: announcing yet *refusing* to explore her decision. There also was justification in the first speaker's anger towards me for suppressing (as well as for my defending and therefore favoring Claire). I matter-of-factly acknowledged both standpoints, neither of which seemed untenable. Claire was not willing to have a child or to talk about it at this time. She had declared her turf, and I defended her right to it. I suggested that perhaps more than one person was angry, at me particularly. My summary statement served its purpose of cooling the situation sufficiently and the session proceeded with relatively peaceful co-existence.

Discussion

The strategy behind my assertion of power and authority was to forestall an open confrontation between a prematurely interpreting group and a member who would rebel and *secede* rather than abdicate a position of *refusal,* so as to prevent a fissure developing in group cohesiveness. In my evaluation, at this stage of the initiation of the new member, it was important to identify the mutual hostility but not encourage its exploration. In taking an active stance and a clear position *vis a vis* differing truth needs, I could deflect some of the anger to a safer target: me.

As Claire became integrated into group, we began to understand the transferential basis (the *resistance*) of her anti-interpretative stance. She told us about her wedding: "My mother was an embarrassment. She flirted and danced with Ben [the groom], as if she was taking him for herself." She reflected: "Nothing I had as a child seemed to belong to me. My friends became my mother's friends, and as soon as I was old enough, she would 'share' my clothes." Claire's feelings and beliefs belonged to her, and she did not want our group to rob her of them by intensive examination and interpretation.

I formulated that Claire feared a baby would do the same: deprive her body, her freedom, and her desire to remain, in her words, "an independent woman, not just a wife." I suspected that many of our clinically sophisticated group members reached similar psychodynamic hypotheses. For now, we kept our thoughts unspoken.

In the *diplomatic* mode, the therapist or other group member balances expressions of or requests for truth with pragmatic constraints. All object relations, internal as well as interpersonal, entail negotiating the not always resolvable divergences of interests and goals, and between what can be known about oneself and others, and what is safe to communicate. While ideally, empathic and truth-seeking needs of patients (and the therapist) will come to support one another, versions of truth, and even the need for truth, may continue to vary or even clash.

The dimension of self-interest in diplomacy

The interests and goals of the group may not be entirely congruent with those of some or even all of the constituencies. Regarding the therapist, they may be partially or entirely self-serving (as in issues of fee, vacation schedule, etc.) without necessarily being false or against the group's welfare. As we saw in the preceding vignette involving Claire, a member may need special accommodation despite the immediate consequences for group process, cohesion, and therapeutic alliances. In contrast, in the following example, the therapist supports and protects the group, at times at the seeming or actual expense of an individual member.

Case example: Dealing diplomatically with a monopolizing member

"How are you contributing to the group?" I asked Randy, cutting short his recount of an ongoing struggle with his wife involving his noncooperation with routine household tasks. "Maybe they [other members] can relate to their issues," Randy offered unconvincingly. Another man rejoined sarcastically: "It doesn't relate to me, I take out the garbage and don't have to be asked." Ignoring the group's resonance with this member, Randy continued. I interrupted again: "Randy, you're making yourself the butt of the group, it's not good for you and it's not good for the group. Isn't this what you do in your marriage?"

He launched once more into his story and I said he had to stop and respect my leadership. "But no one else is complaining, Rich. You're making me angry." I responded: "I understand that, but you'll have to control yourself and give other people a chance to talk." Randy: "You don't talk this way to other people." "I don't have to," I responded. Randy: "All you care about is your group, the big bucks." "Not 'all', but some," I acknowledged, "I care about the group and I care about supporting myself, now let's move on."

Discussion

"Diplomatic" is not synonymous with non-interventionist, "'nice," supportive, democratic, or non-confrontational. Not for the first time

I put Randy "on alert" for inserting himself as a relational obstacle. In the psychotherapy situation, the leader safeguards the group's emotional and interpretative impetus. Whereas I was willing once again to address Randy's entitlements and also acknowledge the truth in his identifying mine, my primary motivation was to "govern" the group system. My principles and practices served strategic purposes: in the service of the group, but also, of Randy's longer term therapeutic benefit: achieving self control. Finally, my actions were also self-serving, expressing my values and to some extent satisfying my own aesthetic, emotional, intellectual, and fiscal needs.

The use of falsity

We make distinctions between factual truth and emotional truth. At times, one may be valued over the other. For example, in most exchanges between people, emotional truth and understanding between them is more important than exact attention to facts. But if a point of fact is crucial to understanding, then the factual truth comes first. Emotional truth implies a degree of tactfulness: factual truth does not.

Perhaps alluding to diplomatic communications, Samuel Butler (1912–1951) penned, "Truth does not consist in never lying but in knowing when to lie and when not to do so." We may be honest but merciless, and must be careful how to ask for or volunteer truth when it can be hurtful. As we have asserted earlier, questions do not always seek truthful answers, and even when they do, minimization, shadings of feeling and meaning, even white lies, lubricate and may make possible beneficial social relations. Straying from what is exactly true and completely honest is not necessarily malicious, self-serving, or harmful to others. In the following example, I sorrowfully came to understand the depth of Butler's pithy statement.

Case example: Diplomatic falsity

"Rich, I better see you. I've been too embarrassed to come to group or make an individual appointment. I've been going for tests. I'm sorry to have to say this—they put me on Aricept and Namenda."

It was terrible news, although I was not surprised. I was intimately familiar with the trajectory of Alzheimer's: at age 57, my father had been a practicing physician who could no longer tell time. Dorothy had been complaining of memory problems for over a year. Her individual sessions were marred by references to group members with "what's her name? I can't remember." I had ceased attributing dynamic significance to her lapses. And now the medical data were emerging. "What should I do," she asked. "I guess I better go back and say good-bye."

"Do you want to leave?" I asked.

"No, not at all. I love the group, and I love you. I just feel I can't participate like the others."

"So what else is new?" This had been a typical complaint of Dorothy, who was a Midwesterner in a group with many members who were, in her words, "sophisticated New Yorkers." But my communication was not honest, since I knew that there was something "new" in her difficulty, which I ignored, and chose to mislead her.

Dorothy: "That's true."
Therapist: "Why don't you take your time and decide what feels comfortable for you. Would you like to stay?"
Dorothy: "Of course."
Therapist: "So stay."
Dorothy: "I don't want to appear 'out of it'."
Therapist: "Me either!" I interjected playfully. But, fearing what I believed to be the inevitable sequelae, I added seriously: "If you lose interest in the group, or feel that you're not connecting and we can't do anything about it, I'll help you leave."
Dorothy: "I'd hate that to happen."
Therapist: "Me too.

Discussion

I misled, evaded, and participated in collusion against factual truth. My pragmatic goal: to respond to what I felt was Dorothy's need (and perhaps my own), to feel comforted and cared for. I could tolerate the truth, but I felt it was in her best interest to forestall pointless pain, so that she could continue to benefit from group membership and the stimulation and support it provided. Dorothy had the freedom to make her own choice: when to embrace factual truth. There will be time later to mourn and to say good-bye, and for the extra-therapeutic contact that I am sure I and other group members will offer this beloved member.

Strategic qualifiers

I briefly call attention to introductory or concluding diplomatic statements typical of therapists and other group members: "You're going to hate this [what I'm going to say]." "Do you think maybe … " "I don't want to be a party pooper, but I'm having trouble with what you are saying." "I know this isn't your conscious intent … " " … I didn't mean to be insulting/argumentative/hostile." "I understand how you feel, but could we take a look at what you're doing with your feelings?" "You said you wanted honest feedback, so here it goes." "If I spelled out 'rules' you'd either comply and resent me or secretly go around them." "You're not on trial—just think about what people are trying to say and not rush to defend yourself." Such qualifications are strategic: They align with and serve to preempt the *3 Rs*—to encourage thinking about communications that might otherwise provoke *resistance*, *rebellion*, or *refusal*.

Integrity

In engaging from a mode of *integrity*, salience resides in the therapist's moral and ethical principles, in reference to his or her professional, political, ethnic and religious affiliations. Even in the face of pressure, *integrity* would seem, then, to present the least intrapsychic and interpersonal ambiguity concerning truth and falsity, since the therapist may refer to and rely on a clear set of conventions. But as I will emphasize, integrity involves strength and consistency, and also flexibility; it emerges not only from the therapist's principles, but how they are applied in the best interests of the group.

Integrity without judgment, self-examination, and relatedness, is not sufficient, and can be, in fact, inappropriate and even damaging. Integrity may manifest as rigidity, blindness to personal contingencies, and even be of questionable moral value. While integrity denotes being true to one's principles, such principles may be ill-chosen, ill-applied, or wrong. As the "Mayfair Madam," Sydney Biddle Barrows (1986) acknowledged: "I ran the wrong kind of business, but I did it with integrity."

Samuel Johnson (1759/1985) turns our attention to the truth function in issues of integrity by clarifying that "integrity without knowledge is weak and useless, and knowledge without integrity is dangerous and dreadful." As clinicians, we emphasize *self*-knowledge, of course, through which we also evaluate emotional truth and falsity and respond to the contributions of others.

In the following example, the group therapist, Jerome Gans (2006), carried out a painful introspection so that he could function with thoughtful integrity—truth with the small "t"—rather than respond moralistically and convey absolute "Truth." Gans first came to understand the truth that he, too, had an unethical part of his personality.

Case example: An unethical request

A group member: "My wife's insurance is paying for my therapy but it doesn't take effect until April. Could you bill the insurance company for eight sessions in April rather than the four we met in March and the four we met in April?" At one time Gans (2006) would have quickly responded, "No," motivated by unspoken moral outrage: "Who does he think he's dealing with, asking an ethical guy like me to participate in such underhanded shenanigans?" (p. 22).

Gans concurrently worked at a facility where many of the medical staff were double-billing their patients and finding other ways to inflate income. He found himself tempted, "frightened by the intensity of my own greed and the seeming ease with which I could rationalize it away" (p. 21). Getting in touch with his own fraudulent impulses provided crucial self-knowledge and stimulated curiosity about the member, rather than an internal rush to judgment.

Gans linked up the request with traumatic incidents of corruption in the patient's family history. When the patient brought up his request again, Gans responded: "How could you ever win with a request like that? If I do not comply with your request you will probably be annoyed with me and, if I do, you will have a corrupt therapist" (p. 22).

Discussion

Had Gans not, in his words, "metabolized superego countertransference leanings," his engaging from a position of integrity would have been premature and defensive. *Apropos* is Jacob's (1991) description of a "therapeutic screen," in which the therapist's narcissistic conflicts, needs, and biases are embedded within and concealed by well-accepted theory and technique (p. 654).

Hiding behind a screen of integrity is hypocritical, whereas engaging with integrity may include laying aside certain ethical or moral truths, in the service of developing meaning. A harder-won emotional honesty may emerge for all participants, the "sinners" and the "sinned against." As we see from the following case vignette, an appeal for integrity, while ideal in theory, may be false in practice.

Case example: A pretense of integrity

Alyssa and Linda were engaging in a heated exchange, and after an interlude in which they had become more than sufficiently nasty to each other, I intervened and invited group responses. Other members dolefully identified themselves as players in similar dramas they described as "dirty fighting," at which point the two women seemed to regain equanimity. Later, with a few minutes of the session remaining, Alyssa reintroduced conflict: "One other thing. I don't like the little private groups that go on. You [Linda] and Tom and, I think, Erica and maybe Mark too. Some of you talk to each other during the week and [turning to me] it's not fair."

Given that all the members mentioned were in combined psychotherapy, as was Alyssa, it was unlikely that I did not know about the subgroupings—the telephoning and e-mailings—typical of this group and occasionally if obliquely referred to in session. Indeed, Alyssa knew I knew since she had mentioned them several times in our individual work. Certainly, the enactments went against personal and group codes of our members: extra group contact, gossiping, and talking behind people's backs. Now I was being called to task for not dealing with these acts of *rebelliousness*.

Alyssa was within her rights to bring up these issues, and even, to frame them in ethical terms and to question my leadership. She was not upright in how, why, and when she broached them. She wanted to "score points," get the last word in, and create a cascade of guilt and self-recrimination among the targeted members, me included. None of this would work, however. In being superior, a "tattle-tale" and "guilt-tripper," she more likely fueled the very subgrouping behaviors she lamented, and guaranteed another round of mutual hostility with Linda.

I said to Alyssa: "Would you like to be part of a 'private group'?" She was surprised by my question, and softened and became teary: "I guess so."

"Who would you like in it?" I asked gently.

Now she smiled and with increasing confidence, named several members. Relieved of the pretense of integrity, and fortified with self-understanding, Alyssa was now linking honestly to her group cohorts.

Discussion

I had to consider multiple enactments that broke or seemed to have broken ethical norms: the degree of nastiness between two members, the covert alliances, and Alyssa's mode and reasons for exposing them. Each enactment could benefit from being made public, and subject to an ethical viewpoint, among other perspectives.

The therapist may demonstrate failure in integrity by omission as well as commission. In regard to the three unfolding enactments, I had to walk the fine line between a non-judgmental attitude and moral laxity. Let us consider them in turn. Regarding the Linda-Alyssa altercation, other members adequately addressed the mutual cruelty by identifying themselves with each of the participants and acknowledging their own guilt for similar "dirty" behavior.

The covert subgroupings via telephone and e-mails were enactments-in-progress, *resistances* hidden in plain sight. I believed it worthwhile to allow them to develop, to supply context from which we could generalize hypotheses about the group as well as relate to the members' histories, past and present. (see the extended case example referring to this group, *Chapter three*). Had I applied moral censure, I might have stimulated compliance, secrecy, or both, and defeated the meaning-making process that characterizes successful exploration of *resistance*.

Of my immediate concern was how to respond in the remaining minutes to Alyssa's appeal, which was moralistic and far from moral. Without being moralistic myself, I needed to protect Alyssa and the group, by countering what I took to be her spiteful intentions to sow discord and end the group session with *rebellious anarchy*.

My concluding intervention connected Alyssa to her underlying craving for love and acceptance, without attacking or blaming her for her hypocritical behavior. Group members could empathize with an honest expression of envy, but not duplicitous integrity.

As always, alternate frames of reference are useful for the therapist in order to think about and prepare interventions. I related the three enactments as corresponding to Bion's (1961) theory of *basic assumptions* and the *work group*. Illustrating the *fight/flight assumption*: two members express hatred of each other and are mutually hurtful; other members freeze or quietly take sides. Illustrating the *paring assumption*: ("sexual") alliances are formed; Alyssa, while envious, also becomes the spokesperson of the curious. Illustrating the *dependency assumption*: All eyes are on me. No other member satisfactorily defends or works with the warring participants, or acknowledges responsibility for taking part in the subgroupings, or ignoring them.

Rather than becoming truce-maker, moral arbiter, or solution-provider, I attempted to keep these issues open, even complicate them. I encouraged Alyssa—and by identification all members—to "join" alliances. Amoral desires to love, hate, and indulge curiosity are universal, they enliven our nonconsciousness and when brought to self-consciousness, provide emotional markers for a fair and balanced *work group*.

Judgments of integrity depend on perspective

Judgments of integrity depend not only on the principles and practices of the group leader, but also, how they interface with the ethical and moral beliefs of the culture and subcultures of the group participants and the larger social matrix.

Case example: Ethical controversy involving a controversial leader

The topic of the American Group Psychotherapy Association open session was "Passion and the therapist's use of self, in reference to the four modes of group leadership." The meeting began with my brief lecture setting up the conceptual categories, followed by an hour's demonstration group, led by a master clinician—male, prominent, and senior. A panel and audience discussion closed the session.

Early on in the demonstration group, the leader turned to Peter, one of the members, and noted what he thought Peter had said upon volunteering: "So, you wanted to be in group with Cathy [a female volunteer] because she was 'beautiful'."

"Bold and beautiful, I said," Peter corrected.

"'Bold and beautiful'" the group leader reiterated.

Cathy responded: "I'm glad you put them in that order!" She declared that she liked to be noticed, but not on looks alone.

"You're scary!" Peter interjected in response to her.

"You don't seem scared," the leader parried and then, to confront Peter with his attraction: "Cathy *is* quite beautiful."

Peter blushed uncomfortably and laughed (as did the other members of the demonstration group and the large professional audience). "I'm glad my patients aren't here, or my wife."

The leader [to group]: "What about you others, are you glad your patients and mates aren't here?" Several times, the leader returned to Cathy, calling attention to her attractiveness, and provoking discussion about her impact on two subgroups: males and females. Repartee among the men included sexual innuendo, playful reference to sexual arousal, and competition. The other women took on various roles, as cheerleader for Cathy, co-participant, or willing apprentice. Related themes, such as "taking chances," living in the present, and aging, were also developed meaningfully.

After the demonstration group, the three panelists opened the discussion by acknowledging the leader's exceptional skills. We agreed that, within just a few minutes, he had created an intense group process deeply involving the participants and also the observers. His use of humor and irony, and his ambiguously provocative presence demonstrated valuable personal qualities of group leadership and illustrated the four modes, and "passion" too.

However, when the discussion turned to the audience, a controversy emerged. Several women felt the leader had taken advantage of the females and had organized the male subgroup to similarly participate. They compared the leader's concentration on Cathy and her looks to the media's preoccupation with Hillary Clinton's physical characteristics and their discomfort with her "boldness." (Our meeting took place during the "primary" period preceding the 2008 presidential election in the United States, in which Hillary Clinton was competing against Barack Obama for the Democratic Party's nomination.)

Discussion

In a situation when new people are in a group, there will be heightened sexual tension. The leader has to make ongoing choices to ignore, reveal, or even provoke gender dynamics. Clinical decisions—while they revolve around the purpose of the group—involve many ethical factors. The status of the therapeutic alliance, timing and emphasis, and readiness of individual members remain central to beneficence (contributing to the good) and non-maleficence (doing no harm).

No one set of rules or principles can do justice to all group circumstances. Jonsen and Toulmin (1988) argued that practitioners must "fight off the bewitchment by the dream of an ethical algorithm—a universal and invariable code of procedures" (p. 7).

The professional context was educational: demonstration of leadership and leadership subjectivity. The leader practiced what he preached: taking chances and risking himself with the group of volunteers, and especially, with a critical audience of peers. He did not "bewitch" the audience by promulgating an "analytically purified" and hence false, subjectivity, or hide behind his seniority and status.

The leader thus practiced "virtue ethics" (Brabender & Fallon, 2009): living up to his ideals, exhibiting from this point of view courageous integrity in meeting the goals of the open session. However, from the perspective of the subgroup of audience dissenters, the leader has violated "feminist ethics" (Adleman & Barrett, 1990; Brabeck & Brown, 1997), privileging the men's experience over the women's and encouraging a hierarchical and competitive system of group organization.

In my opinion, the most incisive comment on the event came from a woman in the audience, perhaps representing a different subgroup. She observed, "Yes, the leader didn't act 'p.c.' [politically correct], but neither does the unconscious."

In the concluding case vignette, the therapist found herself caught between conflicting systems of ethics, her loyalty to the group member and respect for his confidentiality, and what she interpreted as state-mandated legal procedures. In her attempt to do the "right thing" and not act hastily, she shared her dilemma with the group member, with unanticipated consequences.

Case anecdote: The therapist's "will to a system of integrity" damages the therapeutic relationship

A long-standing group member occupied many sessions vilifying his wife, who had been, and possibly continued to be, unfaithful. Now he reported an incident in which his wife, tussling with their adolescent daughter over control of the television remote control, left a bite mark on her arm. The next day, the therapist telephoned and requested that he appear immediately in her office. She explained: "I was troubled all night by what I heard, and I think I might be required to call Child Protective Service to report abuse."

The group member became enraged and could hardly respond. "My wife and daughter have a great relationship! You know that! She's not an abusive mother. You must hate her as much as I do!" He stormed out of the office: "I don't know if I can continue treatment with you."

Although often reticent and even secretive about group, he shared this incident with his wife, who responded sympathetically. At the same time, she empathized with the therapist: "I'm sure I don't have the best reputation with her," and encouraged him to return to group and attempt to work it out. This did not entirely please the husband who, while somewhat mollified, now would have to present a different view of his wife to the group: Even when hearing falsities about herself as an unfit mother, she had remained steadfast, empathic to her accuser, and loyal to her husband and his need for therapy. However, the therapeutic alliance was damaged, and the patient *refused* individual sessions for over a year.

Discussion

Cohen and Schermer (2002) described the "moral order" of a group, referring to its norms, values, beliefs and ambience, and that it supplies a context for each member's group self and the group's collective conscience and ego ideal. The therapist most often personifies this ideal, and due to tendencies in one's personality as well to projective pressure, may reflexively take on a moralistic mantle. Rulebooks are ever-present, symbolic, but also real, sometimes in the bookshelves behind the circle of chairs in our offices. They guide but also may mislead us. We are all susceptible to a "law and order" mentality, and must assess our urges for fairness and "equal treatment for all," and wishes to advise and protect. Nietzsche (1889/1980) advised vigilance regarding orthodox adherence to text and the chimerical safety of dogma: "I mistrust all systematizers and avoid them. The will to a system is a lack of integrity."

Embedded in every group session then, and perhaps in the complexities of every psychological situation, are ethical dilemmas. In my view, an ethical therapist fosters the group's becoming a "friend" of a member's spouse, not only expressing compassion for the member. This is not to suggest that the group ignore a mate's illegitimate or dangerous behavior. Wickedness does exist, and it would be unfriendly to both marital participants to ignore its source as well as its targets. Still, no marital partner is likely without blame, and each needs to be understood.

But also, often and unknowingly, a group becomes the group member's "spouse," feeling and reacting similarly. In this example, the member had used the group as a receptacle for his negative perceptions (and projections) about his wife. The group, alienated by his unwavering disapprobation, in effect, abandoned him mentally as his wife had sexually. Now the member had to retrench, or else face disturbing real-time consequences. To be reconciled with the wife—and with the group and its therapist—all would have to inspect his mantle of moral outrage: his "truth" and how he misused it.

Sincerity

Sincerity conveys felt feeling and conscious intention. "One cannot both be sincere and seem so," Andre Gide (1902/1996) averred. *Sincerity* is categorical—either you are or not. In my conceptualization, sincerity derives from a developmental stage of idealization, the intersubjective platform of bonding and the establishment of trust, and which precedes the full-fledged working through of the "depressive position," as described by Melanie Klein. In this phase prior to emotional maturity, others are recognized and preserved mentally as loved objects, or hated and rejected. Splitting rather than mature thinking remains prominent as a mode of organizing experience ("either/or;" "good/bad," "in/out" thought and feeling).

When Freud described psychoanalysis as "in essence a cure through love," (Freud & Jung, 1974, pp. 12–13), he was referring to the patient's relationship to the doctor: "The process of cure is accomplished in a relapse into love ... and such relapse is indispensable, for the symptoms ... are nothing other than precipitates of earlier struggles connected with repression or the return of the repressed ... they can only be resolved and washed away by a fresh tide of the same passions" (Freud, 1907a, p. 90).

To a degree not expressed by Freud, love must be requited: The therapist also must love, and love sincerely. Writing on the analyst's stance toward the patient, Racker (1968) concluded, "to understand, to unite with another, and hence, also to love, prove to be basically one and the same" (p. 174). Racker emphasized that loving requires openness to all aspects of the patient, especially those that are split off or rejected: "Since the patient only lends his ear to the analyst while his positive transference is upheld, so too, in the case of the analyst, understanding shows its origin in love, since the analyst identifies himself with the patient's id and ego only while his positive countertransference is upheld" (1968, p. 63; see also, Balint, 1952, on "primary love" and Searles, 1979, on "therapeutic symbiosis").

Freud (1921c) attributed the formation of groups to a biological need to love and to be in harmony with others: "A group is clearly held together by a power of some kind: and to what power could this feat be better ascribed than to Eros, which holds together everything in the world?" (p. 92). In "uniting" with the other (and by extension, the group itself), the therapist bonds via the preverbal or "symbiotic" level characteristic of benevolent, infant-mother projective-introjective exchanges (Billow, 2000).

The loving contact, which sincerity generates, is communicated between and under the therapist's words. Bion contributed the model of the "*container-contained*" to describe how the therapist gathers in (introjects), deciphers, and communicates back to the patient/group aspects of its psychic experience that are communicated via projective mechanisms (Billow, 2003b,d). Such ongoing, pre- or nonverbal exchanges are "emotionally rewarding … [establishing] a sense of being in contact … [They are]a primitive form of communication that provides a foundation on which, ultimately, verbal communication depends" (Bion, 1967, p. 92; see also Beebe, Lachmann & Jaffe, 1997; Emde, 1990; Stern, 1995).

Our very devotion to our field, and its theories, techniques, and styles, may represent an at times inescapable ambition to "cure." And hence, even paradoxical, sarcastic, or ironic communications convey sincerity of intent; their surface, grammatical, or rhetorical style is complex, but the felt intention and goal concentrate on a single-minded purpose.

Sincerity may be felt and conveyed immediately, activated by the therapist's interest and compassion. It may be ongoing and constant, amplify over time, or be withdrawn. We may think we are being sincere without being so, for changes in our feelings often precede our own awareness, yet may be apparent to others. At other times, while we remain bonded, our level of sincerity is, feels, or is claimed to be insufficient to meet the relational needs of the group or of a particular member.

Case example: The therapist's sincerity guides understanding

In her first group session, Judy described a dream, in which she felt thwarted by my refusal to engage in sexual relations. She understood her creation as a group entry dream, expressing her disappointment in having to share me with other members.

A professional woman in her mid-thirties, Judy reported being desperate to be married, but attracted to unavailable men. Of her two current suitors, one was devoted, but "boring," and the other, "wild, wooly, and totally exciting," but a "player," involved with several women and not interested in a long-term relationship.

Our psychoanalytically savvy group members filled in Oedipal details. Judy's handsome and emotionally provocative father both attracted and scared her. The mother stayed in the background, perennially unhappy with herself and the other family members, particularly her husband.

An attraction flared between Judy and Tom, a recently divorced group member. She reported feeling complimented, but anxious and wanting to withdraw, which she did. Tom soon lost interest and their special bond evaporated. Judy connected Tom to her available suitors, and me to the "player" not solely interested in her, but involved with any group member who would have me.

The unfolding interaction integrated Judy into the group, which admired her courage in plunging into here-and-now group process. She came to enjoy and value her membership, yet remained teary, greatly distressed by her courtship travails, and easily wounded. At times, she expressed resentment towards the other women, with their easy group relations and access to the therapist, which she felt she could not have. This surprised other members, who affirmed my own subjective reactions: Judy's woefulness could irritate me, but I did not lose interest in her or feel unresponsive to her distress.

Indeed, it was because my "analytic libido" was relatively unwavering that we came to understand how she sabotaged relationships. During one group session I inquired if Judy was "pouting." Her smile at being recognized faded as group process shifted. I attended once again to her: "You don't seem to appreciate that I am as involved with you as with anybody else." Whereas I had intended to use the word "appreciate" to denote "understand," Judy heard an accusation that she was ungrateful and "bad," and her eyes filled. I clarified then elaborated on her interpretation. "If you transform your relationships to feel rejected, of course you cannot return gratitude."

The session was a turning point in her self-understanding and in modifying her presentation. "I guess I'm never satisfied and I make it known. You must feel like me when my mother is unhappy. She doesn't just invite me for dinner, she expects me to stay for the weekend, and when I don't, she makes me feel guilty, unloving, that I am an ungrateful daughter."

"I should be more grateful that you work with me," I said with light humor. And turning to the group, Judy continued the repartee: "Yes, you all should."

Discussion

The obvious truth involved Judy's sexualized relationship to her father. But the more significant truth involved the early maternal relationship, which emerged concurrently with the developing "paternal" transference-countertransference and the attendant *resistances*. Not sex, not aggression, but primarily, issues with bonding plagued Judy. On one intersubjective level, Judy and I had the requisite therapeutic or working alliance. On another, I was the unavailable and desired father. Yet, more basic was her fear and distrust of *sincerity*—of the dependability of her love as well as of others. Subtly, and often without her awareness or mine, she refused the introjective-projective processes wherein we could feel not only productive, but also accepted and special. This left her in a dual identification, both with her guilt-inducing mother and with her earlier "guilty" self. She quickly could feel needy and discouraged. All suitors, those momentarily exciting as well as "boring," ultimately were rejected.

Sincerity may represent a therapeutic achievement

Yalom (1995) stressed that "underlying all consideration of technique must be a consistent, positive relationship between therapist and patient. The basic posture of the therapist to a patient must be one of concern, acceptance, genuineness, empathy" (p. 106). I stress that the therapist may adopt this attitude without sincerely loving the other in a manner required by the relationship. In the following case example, I offered caring interpretations, and the patient reported "feeling better." Nonetheless, a particular developmental need to be considered as special, attractive, delightful was yet unsatisfied.

Case example: Insufficient sincerity

June (age 61) lamented to her group: "I don't feel you are excited to see me. People are delighted to see each other, but no one is delighted to see me." June was the respected "senior member" of the group; a slight limp from childhood polio added to her gravitas.

"You are 'soo' reserved," a group member responded truthfully, while a chorus of others added, ineffectively, "We care for you."

The theme continued in her individual psychotherapy. June: "I'm feeling blank, nothing. Weekend was pretty good, the kids brought the grandchildren, but not that exciting. I never have enough time. Always a stack of work on my desk, this committee and that. I can't enjoy myself because I think about all I have to do."

I reminded her of her feeling that I, and her group too, did not enjoy her. "Yes, it is not that you don't like seeing me. But I guess

I feel most people could take me or leave me." I asked whether she *believed* that I did not enjoy her, as well as *felt* it. She considered the question, and decided that she really believed it. "It's a matter of caring. You don't care that much. This is your job." She connected her feeling/belief with her memory of her parents. "They took care of me, maybe overprotected me when I got polio, but never made me feel pretty and that I could have that kind of effect on them."

"So that's what you want!" I replied, and then brought us into the reality of our heterosexual adult life: "You want me to find you sexually attractive." June did not directly respond, but I believe she had allowed me to offer and herself to receive a sexual thought. She ended the session without her usual tense facial expression and its trace of bitterness. I sensed that we both felt more relaxed and connected to each other.

The next individual session occurred after the weekend.

June: I feel out of sorts. Frank [her husband] and I sit at the table and do not talk. He seems to enjoy my company and feels it is all right not to say anything. I don't feel comfortable. I don't know where he is at and uncomfortable about saying anything about it. It is like being with my father, cold and distant, and my being scared, even though I know that Frank loves me very much and waits for me to eat with him. I feel safer with Frank, but he is not very exciting. Nothing unexpected goes on between us.

I dreamed about you. First dream about you in a very long time. First sexual dream. In the first part, you put your hand over mine. I liked it. Later, you brushed against my breasts and put your arm around me. You looked at me to see if I could deal with it. I found it very exiting and was wondering where we would go next.

June was pleased she had had a sexual dream, and that it involved me. She did not have many sexual dreams, and did not feel sexual often, she reminded us unnecessarily. Then, as an afterthought, she reported that she had had sex with Frank and had experienced a rare orgasm.

Discussion

Being "soo reserved" had had unfortunate consequences for June, since it signaled that she wished not to be touched with an erotic thought, fantasy, or flirtatious interaction. Her dream revealed otherwise: It exhibited her longing to be touched and to touch others—to "have that kind of effect." In June's dream, we engaged in a sexualized interaction: I touched her hand and shoulders and brushed against her breasts and she was excited and expectant. In her mental creation (co-occurring with the sexual encounter with her husband), June made erotic links to herself and to me. In communicating her dream, June enabled me to respond in kind. I now felt a sufficient erotic charge in our work, no matter the subject.

Despite June's obvious splitting and dissociation—"Nothing unexpected goes on between us" [June and her husband] and "I had an orgasm"—movement took place in June's fantasy life and the explicit erotic linkages it provided. June had expressed the elements of *passion*: frustration (*H*) and longing to be touched (*L*) and to be known (*K*) as an erotic object. The dream suggests that she intuited—or could imagine—my awakened desire, and by extension, the desire of other men, including her husband, and in turn, that excited her.

Beauty and its appreciation exists in every person, no matter how stifled by social forces or physical limitation. In Stephen Sondheim's musical play, *Passion*, a handsome visitor, Giorgio, arouses intense, encompassing love in Fosca, an ailing and homely woman. Her ardent declarations and pursuit prove irresistible to him, and he ultimately yields without regret. We cannot love, or love sufficiently, or effectively, without reciprocity of feeling, real or imagined. I, or our group alone, could not reignite June's libido from its embers. She too had to supply energy. Like Fosca, June took the chance to reconnect to her desire, which included her desire to be desired.

To the extent clinically appropriate (in terms of patient and also therapist readiness), the therapist's erotic mental relationship to the patient needs to be situated in the intersubjective analytic space—located as an object of mutual interest and verbal inquiry (Davies, 1998; 2001). Trauma in a patient's past (e.g., June's childhood polio) often influences countertransference (counter-*resistance*): I am alerted to trauma in a patient's life when I do not have evidence of such erotic mental activity in myself (as with June), when it becomes intense, arousing, or disquieting, or when I feel defensive about what I am thinking, feeling, or fantasizing.

I found it difficult to initiate in a sincere manner the topic of sex into our dialogue, and into our relationship when I felt her to be an unappealing sexual partner. She became more appealing and capable of serving as an erotic (mental) object when I could begin to feel her as emotional and interested in being experienced as sexual.

In being *sincere*, the therapist is sexual and not asexual, without being seductive. The maternal bonding model serves as the analogy. The mother, by "rousing her child's sexual instinct and preparing for its later intensity [she is] only fulfilling her task in teaching the child to love" (Freud, 1905d, p. 223). Derivatives of erotic feelings are natural and expectable, an enjoyable aspect of bonding with others. As with June, a patient's erotic history may be revealed in both modalities of combined psychotherapy, the derivatives being communicated verbally, nonverbally and motorically, as in stance, self-presentation, and responsiveness, and enactively, via group process.

Ruptures in therapeutic sincerity

We cannot will our feelings, and are rarely pure of heart and mind. Feelings spring from sources other than Eros and may conflict with therapeutic ideals and sincere intentions. Our love—openness to our patients and the group itself, interest, concern, and enjoyment—is revealed in the subtleties of timing, tone, and cadence, which amplify, modify, or even contradict what is verbally spoken (Chused, 1991; McLaughlin, 1991). We learn by ruptures, of course, and when opportune, we attempt to repair them.

Clinical anecdote: "Labeling" disables sincerity

A group therapist reported casually in supervision: "We [the group] were trying to reason with George [a member]. I got really annoyed. He battered away what anyone said. I realized how disturbed a patient he was, with his rationalizations and rigid attitudes, his obsessive defenses. I felt it better to sit back and let the group give up on its own."

Discussion

I was alerted to the rupture in sincerity not by the therapist's irritation, which was understandable and perhaps even a necessary component of the transference-countertransference. Rather, it was the conceptualization of George as "patient," the transformation from subject to diagnostically coded object, exiling George from the co-created intersubjective space of contemporary relational thinking. The therapist temporarily "gave up," withdrawing from the mutually generated, introjective-projective process girding sincere human relationships.

Case anecdote: Therapeutic competency disguises a rupture in sincerity

I return to a case I briefly described as the last example of *Chapter one*. After five years of intensive combined psychotherapy, the thrice-married Ralph began to grasp what I dubbed a "Fox News" dimension in his personality, a reference to the politically conservative American television network and its bullying commentators. But here he was again, bellowing and fiercely finger-pointing at Julie, a group member and wife-substitute, such that I had to intervene. In an attempt to exculpate himself, he reminded the group that he had not behaved this way in quite a while and that even his wife said he was better. That satisfied the members sufficiently to move on to other interactions.

Several weeks later Ralph asked me in an individual session whether something had changed between us. "You seem a little different, not distant or uninvolved, but maybe more work-focused or businesslike." I believe he meant that I focused on the material he presented with a so-called professional stance. I did not initiate or respond to the male-to-male banter that had previously been a cementing element in our relationship.

Associating to the incident in group and realizing the truth of his observation, I said: "I don't think I've recovered from the last 'Fox News broadcast'." My acknowledgment sounded to me defensively light-hearted, so that I added a corrective: "You're right. I don't feel the same way about you. I think you are going to have to repair our relationship."

"I apologized, what do you want! Now you're being hard-assed like Fox News," he retorted.

I wondered whether I was abiding by the talion principle, angrily paying him back for his hardness. I asked: "Did you apologize? It doesn't feel like one to me."

Ralph continued: "I checked it out with Julie after group, and we're okay."

"We're not okay, at least not yet," I acknowledged. Ralph had called attention to divergent senses of himself: his view and Julie's, and my own narrowed experience.

Ralph teased: "Oh, you're pouting. He doesn't want to fuck, just like my wife."

I acknowledged his insight, and did not hide my amusement with his homoerotic imagery. I smiled and offered what I understood to be the current state of my feelings: "Your being interested might help. I don't know yet."

Discussion

It took me awhile to realize that something had come alive again in our relationship: my *sincerity*, and I liked the feeling. I even liked saying: "I don't feel the same way about you," which I now recognize was true in my consciousness, but no longer true in my nonconsciousness. I had become one of Ralph's walking wounded, hurting from his ruthless treatment of Julie (and me, via my identification with her). Ralph felt my lack of involvement, and he pursued me, becoming playfully seductive, which apparently I needed in order to be able to love him again.

The limitations of sincerity

Wilde wrote, "All bad poetry springs from genuine feeling" (in Trilling, 1971, p. 119). *Sincerity*—in its direct transportation of a feeling—is always simple, and sometimes simplistic. Consciousnesses of sentiment and its public expression do not necessarily advance relationships. The target of our love may be unready, or undeserving, and in not moderating or holding our emotional response in thoughtful abeyance, we may distract or obscure that which is cogent. Alceste, the protagonist of Moliere's *Le Misanthrope*, declared, "my chief talent is to be frank and sincere" (in Trilling, 1971, p. 17). Alceste's "remorseless of outspokenness on behalf of truth" (Trilling, 1971, p. 17) revealed hubris and a lack of regard for the needs of others and the status of the intersubjective relationship.

Cordelia, in *King Lear*, similarly was blinded by her own rigid standards of sincerity. Unlike Alceste, she spoke too little rather than too much. She asserted that to be "true" [Act I, Scene 1, line 109] she could not "heave/My heart into my mouth" [lines 93–94] and declare her love in terms that her father could understand, no matter his plea to "mend your speech a/little" [lines 96–97]. When wedded to historical analytic or Tavistock technique, the group therapist may, like Cordelia, say "nothing" [line 91], and be needlessly depriving and detrimental. *Sincerity* has its risks. One can be sincere yet self-deceptive, ineffective, inappropriately seductive, willful, misleading.

Case example: Sincerity has unpredictable therapeutic effects

A senior therapist had established a warm working relationship with Helene, a patient in combined treatment. Helene had endured several miscarriages and, nearing 40 years old, she feared remaining childless. Being the trusted witness to Helene's travails, the therapist felt increasingly uncomfortable withholding her own parallel experience. At a moment she felt it particularly beneficial to the distressed Helene, she disclosed that she also had married in her late thirties, and described similar difficulties in childbearing. Helene seemed reassured when the therapist revealed that she was the mother of two thriving teenagers.

Now, pregnant again and half way to full term, Helene came into a group session announcing that the fetus had died, and she would have to have an abortion. The therapist cried along with the patient, which touched the members, who concurred that the therapist "really cared."

Was she crying for Helene or for her earlier self?, the therapist wondered. She felt herself to be false, undeserving of the credit for "caring," since the group did not know of her own reproductive struggles and identification with Helene. And, in her atypical display of emotion, the therapist was concerned that she drew attention to herself, depriving the anguished Helene. The patient had a different take; much later, Helene revealed apologetically that, if she could not deliver a healthy child, she would be a disappointment to the therapist.

Discussion

"Enactments are ... [the therapist's] expectable lot" (McLaughlin, 1991, p. 613). We (co)create them nonconsciously by our activity (and inactivity) and deliberately, such as in this example, by personal revelation and frank expression of feeling. However, no matter how sincere our feelings and intentions, and how directly we express them, we cannot be fully aware or certain of our motivation, meanings, interpersonal consequences and therapeutic effects (Frank, 1997; Greenberg, 1995). In expressing truths that are felt immediately, we may omit others and falsify ourselves.

The therapist appreciated that she was not responsible for the patient's transference, which contributed to her countertransference, and the resulting enactments. But Helene had not inquired about the therapist's personal history, and she felt guilty for burdening Helene with unneeded stimulation. She was disappointed in herself; support and caring could have been conveyed without unbidden personal testimony and what the therapist evaluated as her emotional laxity. Helene also felt herself to be a disappointment, the therapist realized. She was alerted to the strong identification with Helene, and to her participation in cycle of the introjection-projection that underlies *sincerity* and may cloud other modes of therapeutic engagement.

There was no harmful intent in the therapist's behavior, but any long-term consequences remain unknown. The evolving interaction did uncover significant emotional truths: Helene's transference fantasy of being a "disappointment" and the therapist's countertransference predilection to feel similarly. Yet the therapist remained haunted by the reality that her self-disclosures might have burdened and complicated Helene's emotional situation when she had wanted to sooth and simplify. The therapist's *sincerity* had opened up important issues, but might another way, and another time, have been better?

Authenticity

In contrast to *sincerity* is *authenticity*, in which struggle exists among competing motivations. Authenticity remains an uncertain, incomplete process: mentally integrating conflicting feelings, thoughts, wishes, and motives, directed to loved objects and also to those we find troublesome and wish to reject. It represents, then, the achievement of working through the depressive position, its hallmark being the toleration of ambivalence while maintaining a balanced and humane outlook.

Sincerity and authenticity can coexist, but authenticity monitors the expressions of sincerity such that idealizations and devaluations do not predominate. Translated into Bion's (1961) group terminology, sincerity remains wedded to *basic assumption* mentality while authenticity encompasses *work group* thinking as well.

Whereas *sincerity* is categorical and simple, *authenticity* is dynamic and complex: Tension exists between self-awareness and expression. Authenticity bears upon how the therapist approaches and avoids truth, in the context of theory, technique, and experience-based wisdom. The group therapist's communications are mediated by appreciation of the dimensionality of emotion, the influence of interacting nonconsciousnesses, and the inescapability of social role.

In his monograph, *Sincerity and Authenticity*, Trilling (1971) analyzed the differences between these terms. *Authenticity* suggests "a more strenuous moral experience than 'sincerity' does, a more exigent conception of the self and of what being true to it consists of, a wider reference to the universe and man's place in it, and a less acceptant and genial view of the social circumstances of life" (p. 11).

Trilling's conceptualization implies that authenticity is difficult and remains ambiguous. It requires "strenuous" mental activity, an "exigent" (i.e., demanding) standard of being true and of representing truth. A "less acceptant" view of human interaction is requisite for authenticity: the recognition that neither therapist nor group member can simply love and remain sincere. Uncongenial circumstances of social life inevitably get stimulated by group process and must become part of an authentic group experience.

Remorse and reparation: The pathway from sincerity to authenticity

Immersion in the projective-introjective process of intersubjective relations stimulates covetous, angry, and censorious feelings, thoughts, and behaviors, even towards those we love; so we feel guilt and sorrow (Klein, 1975). The commitment to the therapeutic process becomes an act of reparation (Racker, 1968), efforts to repair the harm we have caused, both imagined and real. The therapist moves from the mentality and mode of *sincerity* to *authenticity* as he or she tolerates the working through process involving the "depressive position." He or she thereby becomes informed by the "painful bringing together of the primitive and the sophisticated that is the essence of the developmental conflict" (Bion, 1961, p. 159). That is, authentic therapeutic leadership involves synthesizing the pre- and irrational, rational, truth and falsity, the narcissistic and socialistic, the blunt and cultivated aspects of our personality. He or she accepts the dynamics of the *3 Rs*—attempting to understand the manifestations, derivatives, and particularly, the intersubjective motives underlying the shifting and overlapping processes of *resistance, rebellion* and *refusal*, as they exist in self, group, and organizational life.

Case anecdote: Struggling towards authenticity

Three months into a new year, Seth summoned courage to report that he had felt "ambushed" when I began January with the announcement of a raise in group fee. "I had no choice," Seth protested. "It would be fairer if you had discussed it first in group." Other members disagreed: "This is what other doctors do." "Besides, it wouldn't make a difference, it is Richard's right to set the fee, we don't have to stay."

I was surprised and became interested in Seth; he spoke up forcibly and *rebelliously*, rather than be his usual agreeable and conformist self. He had made a fair point and, despite my support from other group members, I felt slightly embarrassed, and remorse for hurting him. But I was also annoyed, as if he was being ungrateful for making so much of the issue. After all, my rates were not exorbitant and he was benefiting from my efforts. I knew that aspects of my conflictual response involved *resistance*, that is, "primitive" and irrational, and that I needed to remain "sophisticated" as well. My act of reparation involved tolerating the mix of pleasant and unpleasant feelings towards Seth and supporting his efforts at being *authentic* (as well as my own). I responded by saying that I had not realized that he had felt ambushed, and that I would do as he suggested next time, even if no one else seemed to care. Seth was delighted, for he had anticipated my *refusal*: "I didn't expect to be heard."

Discussion

In struggling towards a mutually authentic relationship, Seth had become less "acceptant" (Trilling's term) and genial. He now required others (myself particularly) to recognize and anticipate our effects on him, and thereby, modify our behavior, no matter how we might feel or wish to behave in the interactive moment. Seth had become a person capable of "*passion*"—a concept I have revisited several times in this volume and in *Relational Group Psychotherapy*.

Passion

Whereas sincerity expresses love, *authenticity* strives for "*passion*," which represents an integration of "the primitive and the sophisticated" that Bion (1961) earlier had identified as essential for growth of the individual and the group. Bion (1963) introduced the term and defined it ambiguously, but he was clear to mean something not limited to sensuous or sensual experience: an integrated emotional experience "derived from *L*, *H*, and *K* ... an emotion experienced with intensity and warmth though without any suggestion of violence" (pp. 12–13). By "violence," he meant undue intensification or intrusion into one's own or another's physical or mental space.

Passion involves being receptive to the derivatives of our basic emotions, the primal affects involving loving, hating, and curiosity (*LHK*), as we link to our own mind and to the minds of others: "Passion is evidence that two minds [or more] are linked" (Bion, 1963, p. 13). Passion in this sense is crucial in both the therapist's and group members' evolution of knowing—that is, to the dynamics of discovering and transforming truth. As an intense mode of "experiencing experience," passion involves more than merely "thinking about" or "reacting" to experience. One's emotional consciousness is both concentrated and wide.

Passion requires the individual to think thoughts and feel feelings that are "not nice"—evaluated by the mature self as too needy, aggressive, immoral, or primitive. The passionate dimension of intersubjective experience is uncomfortable to acknowledge to oneself, much less to admit publicly.

A suitable term to describe the metapsychology of passion is *primal receptivity* (Billow, 2003c). The individual is able to escape (sufficiently) the influence of historical internal and external objects, and so freshly think about oneself, other group members, and the group itself as *contemporaneous, versatile, affect-provoking, mental objects*. In this optimal, if often anxiety-laden situation of passion, one has achieved the mental clarity and "moral freedom" (Racker, 1968) to feel, if not say, anything.

Etymologically, "passion" draws on its Latin derivation, meaning suffering or submission. Tolerating and trusting gut truths, which arise partially from the primitive, nonconscious, or irrational part of oneself, is not easy. Meaninglessness and confusion are part of the relational process, along with the foreboding that the emotional emergent (*LHK*) will be dreaded and resisted by patient and therapist alike.

Group therapy rests on the bedrock of *sincere* bonding experiences (*L*), making tolerable its interfering (*H*), and challenging aspects (*K*), which allow therapist and group member to be not only or always *sincere*, but *authentic*. The putting-in-words process, whether initiated by therapist or other group member, spoken or held internally, connects the individual to others and supports the emotional bonding characteristic of *sincerity*. However, when these words carry significant truth, they also disrupt the secure emotional links characteristic of *sincerity*. *Authenticity* necessarily separates the participants from prior connections—existent emotional states of knowingness and knownness.

In wearing "two faces" (*Chapter three*), the therapist supports the secure connections and bonding relationships characteristic of *sincerity*. In striving for *passion*, he or she must also disturb them. To drive change and stimulate creative growth, we endure and encourage others to tolerate the breakdown of pre-established and safe emotional attitudes, upsetting the comfortable arrangements we make with others and ourselves. The therapist, and not only one's patients, suffers through the often irrational, disorganizing, even frightening feelings and thoughts aroused by *passion*. Paranoid and depressive anxieties are unavoidable, and hence, there are always elements of pain, including social anxiety. For these reasons, the therapist who is *authentic* aggresses against the self and the other, and hates and dreads (*H*) the group and its members for being subjected to the very group he or she creates, nurtures by understanding (*K*), and loves (*L*).

Case anecdote: Risking passion

An anguished Peter described a weekend visit to his parents' lavish country home. After sharing some expensive wine, his father suggested playfully that they give up their careers to set up a vineyard. "After all," Peter's father declaims, "you're a metrosexual." Peter felt "labeled and objectified," and "put down" by his competitive father for being a successful young professional.

The group responded empathically.

Joanne: "I feel sorry for the way you get treated."

Lori: "Your father means well, he wants to be close in his way."

David: "As a child, I was so angry that I would go to neighbor's property and dislodge decorative stones and make a mess. You're beyond that."

We all resonated with David's encouragement of the mature or "sophisticated" outlook, and it took me a moment to apprehend my distress and to separate from a comfortable sense of bonding with the group. I confessed that I was not "beyond that," and that I was filled with rage and wished to retaliate. Peter said he could understand my reaction, that he had some of those feelings but pushed them aside.

I turned to David: "Peter is not beyond vandalism. He is a 'pre-vandal'."

Several people wondered if I meant that Peter should have told his father off. Peter assured the group that he did not just take his father's parries, but struck back several times: "No Dad, I'm not metro, I'm homo, just like you." His father enjoyed the ribbing.

I rejoined: "You liked what you said, but it didn't really do it for you. We're not talking about action, but a state of mind."

Peter: "I'm afraid to bring a vandal mind to group."

Joanne responded: "I wish you would. I feel I have to take care of you."

Peter: "What you and Lori do feels condescending, 'poor Peter,' I hate it and it makes me angry, but I don't express myself and then feel misunderstood and even angrier at the group, and I keep that to myself, and I feel ignored and put down. I invite the reaction to me that I don't want and then don't do anything about it—maybe that's why my parents still feel they can control me."

Discussion

"Passion" requires acknowledging, valuing, and integrating the "primitive" or vandal element in one's state of mind. For Peter, as well as for the group and its leader, that meant tolerating separation from bonding attitudes and behavior—the comforts that typify the not-always authentic realities of family and social life. "To thine own self be true" (Shakespeare, 1961, *Hamlet*, 1, 3, line 78 advised the paternalistic Polonious. But in Peter's mind, someone could not tolerate even thinking about truth—was it his father, group, himself?—he could not be sure.

The influence of the nonconscious

Sincerity as feeling is spontaneous. As a mode of communication, it may be deliberate or not. *Authenticity*, while always deliberate, involves conscious and nonconscious influences, yet happens without full awareness or certainty. Authentic clinical communications are mediated by forethought, enhanced by clinical theories and experience. But retrospectively, in reevaluating our words, actions, and feelings (omissions as well as commissions), we may discover what we really consider to be true. Merleau-Ponty (1964, p. 88) captured an aspect of this process when he wrote: "My spoken words surprise me and teach me my thoughts."

As we discussed in *Chapter five*, the nonconscious and irrational parts of our personalities are not merely storehouses of archetypal and archeological truths, or passive, merely receiving and eventually rebroadcasting repressed, split-off, or inherited and prototypical mental contents, as Freud and Jung conceived. As a "truth releasing mechanism" (Grotstein, 2000), the nonconscious protects the self as well as others from being "blinded" by too much truth, too soon, by making itself known through the disguises and indirections of *resistance*, via symbols, myth, condensations, displacements, dissociations, and enactments. Nonconscious and pre- and irrational thinking are essential to the "bringing together" process, supplying a "binocular" or correlative perspective to consciousness (Bion, 1962, p. 53; Matte-Blanco, 1988), informing our intersubjectivity of truths both primitive and sophisticated.

We are humbled by the awareness that our words and actions are partially derivatives of an unfolding (and evolving) conscious-nonconscious, and that we cannot fully understand ourselves before or even after we communicate. Authentic communications represent the therapist's most profound insights and powerful intentions. Yet, they remain only "best guesses" of "truth"—what we feel, think, and decide is appropriate to express—to be reevaluated and revised as we continue to participate in here-and-now clinical experience.

The inescapability of social role

As therapists, we function with and propagate contractions. "Be real" is an unstated message. Yet, as Nietzsche asserted (in Trilling, p. 119), "every profound spirit needs a mask." Therapist and group members wear masks, that is, roles that are social and mutually contracted, and which allow us to talk to each other in ways not otherwise possible. Within our respective roles, therapist and group members participate in and bear witness to the struggle to develop and communicate truth. In the course of effective group psychotherapy, the group member moves from a mask that conceals to one that reveals, from falsity to sincerity and finally, to authenticity.[1]

Authenticity necessitates embracing multiple roles in group, while eschewing role-playing. Most prominent are the "two faces" (*Chapter three*) of the therapist, who is both conservator and challenger of group process and organizational culture. He or she introduces principles and practices that normalize group relations and provide a sense of identity, regularity, and security. In this role, however, the therapist risks generating an *Establishment*, becoming too comfortable in a professional identity as well as in the overt and

---

[1]In developing a "real relationship" (see Greenson, 1967), the therapist intentionally and unintentionally reveals aspects of the personal self without dropping the mask, and so losing the potential for authenticity.

covert diplomatic alliances and compromises of the group. In the role as powerful agent of change, the therapist encourages examination of group culture, process, and leadership, disturbing the very status quo that he or she works to establish.

Case segment: The four modes in interaction

In the therapist's striving for authenticity, the modes of diplomacy, integrity, and sincerity also come into play. In this report of an eight-year combined individual-group treatment, I describe a series of clinical interludes with a young woman who consistently challenged my therapeutic engagements in all four modes.

Lori entered combined treatment after a series of medical procedures failed to conclusively diagnose or treat varying and inconsistent vaginal and bladder symptoms. She had a complicated family background, with a journalist mother often gone on assignments, leaving Lori with a beloved maternal grandmother and a housekeeping staff. Her socialite father showed little interest in his daughter and wife, or in his other children from this and a previous marriage, and he was openly involved with other women.

A professional woman in her late twenties, Lori was relatively sophisticated psychologically, quick, bright, and often sarcastic. The group members took to her immediately, but she doubted that we really respected her, particularly when she complained about her physical pain and her doubts about psychoanalytic theories and methods. She often skipped group when symptomatic, fearing that the members would "lose patience," or professing her own impatience with group process or particular individuals. During several intervals, she sacrificed group sessions to undergo invasive medical interventions and supplementary physical therapies. Ameliorative effects were temporary at best.

"Do you know what it is like to have to pee every minute!" she remonstrated, submitting to my encouragement to return to group. Rhetorical questions like these beg for responses that are not answers, and at different moments I along with other members would sympathetically affirm her right to be angry and frustrated, encourage her to explore the implication that I was uncaring and resolute, or challenge her scapegoating me. She typically did not rejoin directly, but would plead in a self-consciously childish voice: "Are you sure this is going to help? Tell me I'm going to get better, and that this is the way, the only way."

Lori greeted my return from a short vacation with the news that her vaginal burning had disappeared. She joked in the group session that she no longer needed me, since she did better in my absence. But soon afterwards urinary urgency returned. I suggested that perhaps her jocular remarks regarding my leaving her covered over other feelings that were reemerging physically: "gut-level" abandonment anxiety and "burning" anger. She gave intellectual assent: "It makes sense, fits in with my transference, my 'traumatic childhood' as you like to call it. I still can't believe that I'm so reactive every time you go out of town. [And with humor] Are you that important, or do you need this for your ego?"

The group greeted the quip warmly, but missed its significance, which I expanded on. Parents are supposed to exist for a child, and not vice versa, but in Lori's experience, her importance, and their interest, rested on the whims of their egos. My interest as well, Lori insisted, returning to the subject in an individual hour: "Do you really care when you're 'off duty?' You don't have to answer, because I won't believe you if you say yes, you'd be 'therapeutic,' and besides, you can't."

With brief periods of remission, her physical distress remained, and in the fifth year of our work, she scheduled a consultation with a female therapist with an international reputation for treating psychosomatic disorders. "If you had a daughter who had to pee every time she wanted to leave the house, would you tell her to see a psychoanalyst or a specialist who treats neurotics with gynecological disorders?"

When the group questioned her implication that I discouraged her from considering other treatment approaches, she defended me: "Rich has been open, very open, but I don't believe him. [To me] You think your way is the best. I want you to think that way, I don't want you to have doubts, too."

The burning and urgency stopped immediately after her first visit to the other therapist. "There's something about Elisabeth [the psychotherapist]. So warm. She didn't say anything you haven't said. Maybe it is seeing an older woman. But I don't care, I feel wonderful."

A month passed, and Lori had to decide between therapists: "It's great to get my life back. But I don't know what to do. I don't want to stop seeing you, I would see you both, if I could, but Elisabeth won't let me. I can continue in group for awhile." I said I understood, that "chemistry" is important between patient and therapist, and that we really cannot be sure what makes the process work.

Lori: "Maybe because I know that she is a 'healer.' I feel instantly relaxed, like with yoga, but it lasts."

She knew that her reasoning was weak and easy to dismantle. "If one of my friends talked this way to me I would think she was a complete loser, and you probably think that of me." She asked if I felt hurt, maybe angry. She would be devastated if she were me, particularly being exposed in a group, and would want to "get even." I said that I thought I was handling my feelings without taking them out on her, but that I was interested if she agreed.

Lori softened: "I know you care about me and want the best. I wish I could be so generous towards people. No matter what anyone says, I still feel like an ungrateful child, a spoiled brat. My parents were right after all!"

She maintained attendance in group for the following three months, with an uncharacteristically low profile, and I expected a termination announcement. Instead, I heard a sheepish message on my answering machine: "It's me, I'm baa-ck. When will you see me for an individual [session]?"

Lori seemed breathless when I returned her call: "I'm just where I was. Elisabeth was great until she wasn't, her 'warmth' got annoying, and my burning came back. I'm such a 'borderline'."

Reporting on Elisabeth's quirks—making fun of what now she evaluated as being a trite "earth-mother" or "guru"—Lori had little to add about her disillusioning experience other than that it confirmed our familiar hypotheses regarding anger, longing, anxiety, and so forth. In the three years since returning to combined treatment, however, Lori often thinks more soberly and allows herself to elaborate on these hypotheses.

For instance, I called attention to the urgency of her communications, analogizing her tendency to jump from one therapy to another, or even, from thought to thought, to "little squirts" of urine. "Yes, I get 'pissed off' easily, and want to get rid of it," Lori added with typical flippancy. But then, with feeling: "Low frustration tolerance. Sometimes I feel I can't hold my ideas in, or my feelings. You've made me realize that I am anxious all the time, much more than I or anybody else understands. It tightens my pelvic floor, I know it now. I have to get it right, show how clever I am in group, or else I could 'blow it' with you. That was the ticket to attention in my family."

"Ticket to love?" I asked.

"I'm not even sure. Was I loved? Can I love? Only sometimes, maybe [I'm] like my father, and you, 'loving' me when we're in session [sarcastic] and then you get on to the next patient you love."

With my own sarcasm: "Yes, I am the 'love-therapist'."

"I can't say that you act that way in group," she acknowledged. "You treat everyone differently, and fairly. That's another thing I don't like about you. You know what you are doing. Whether you are being easy or tough, say a lot or a little, I can't trust that you are being 'you'."

"Are you being 'you'?" I asked.

Lori: "Being 'me?' You got me there. Only when I'm relaxed and not trying too hard—'squeezing' [reference to bladder muscles] to be good, or maybe 'great'."

Discussion

There are, of course, many different ways of thinking about, organizing, and analyzing the clinical data of this summary of a combined treatment. In concentrating on the four modes of engagement, and their relationship to *resistance, rebellion* and *refusal,* I necessarily neglect or minimize other important interpersonal and intrapersonal factors.

Diplomacy

I met the *rebelliously defiant* Lori with good humor, but challenged her persistent, if often nonconscious, maneuvers to sabotage the treatment. Lori attempted to wear down her listeners by various strategies of *refusal*: abruptly shifting subject matter (not the same as free association), varying loyalties from group to individual psychotherapy, or vice-versa, proclaiming loss of interest or availability, or interrupting insistently with a lengthy stream of words. Her sarcastic rejoinders, charming and amusing in their effect on the group, were designed to make me—and our profession's theories and techniques of combined psychotherapy—seem foolish. Hence, they were instances of *rebellious anarchy* by sowing (temporary) group disorganization.

I thought the best tactic to disarm Lori was to detect, uncover, and investigate her hidden "weapons of mass destruction." I alerted her when I felt she was "pissing on us," i.e., derailing constructive communication. Touching on underlying processes and the derivatives of *resistance*, I repeated how and when she was reaffirming hostile familial identifications. When she disparaged me as "too serious," "sensitive," or "you're pissed, admit it, and you're going to turn the group against me," I reminded her that she herself had been similarly belittled by family members, who teased her for being "too serious," "[overly] sensitive," and "always angry and unhappy." These *diplomatic* maneuvers were essential in preserving the treatment.

While she sometimes felt exposed and chastised, particularly in the group, she also seems reassured. Lori needed me, and by extension, the group, to survive her attacks on psychoanalytic thinking and psychotherapy, hence her plea: "You think your way is the best! I want you to think that way, I don't want you to have doubts, too."

Integrity

Lori sought psychoanalytic treatment with two interrelated goals: to seek psychic and physical relief. She wanted to learn about herself and work through psychological conflicts that might be causing or contributing to her gynecological difficulties, but she should expect, in time, reduction of physical pain. Whenever she believed an alternative or supplementary treatment could cure her somatic symptoms, she protested and even *refused* our treatment, sometimes resorting to unilateral action.

I found her expectation reasonable and fair, and therefore, my response to her skepticism, defiance, refusals, and rebellious acts were, as far as I can determine, sympathetic and noncensorious. Even if my hypotheses were correct in explaining the psychosomatic *resistance*, that is, the psychogenic roots of her pain, psychoanalytically oriented combined psychotherapy might not cure it. I could not be sure that medical or physical procedures would be unnecessary or insufficient, or that "chemistry" with another practitioner might not be better. When she planned and instituted a new therapeutic regime with Elisabeth, I thought it fair to acknowledge and validate her point of view. As well, my values require that I behave with *integrity*, and I believe that this helped Lori's establishing trust in me over time.

Lori was impressed by my willingness to support her *revolutionary* act—overthrowing the leader's unique authority by moving from combined to conjoint treatment—without pressuring her to stay, undermining the other therapist, turning the group against her, or "lording" over her when she returned. But at the same time, she continued to distrust my "ego." Regarding seeing Elisabeth: "You have been open, very open, but I don't believe you." But for other members of the group, my being sympathetic to doubting patients, acknowledging that I did not have absolute certainty, and that other forms of therapy and other therapists might be better, seemed to reaffirm the group's trust in my *integrity*.

Sincerity

Among other motives, Lori attempted to overthrow the combined therapy because in her mind I was insincere. At any moment I could withdraw love and abandon her, and in her nonconscious, I already had. I was her detached and ineffective mother, a failure at empathic recognition: "Do you know what it is like to have to pee every minute!" I was her impatient mother, rushing her through her therapy hours, to move on to other interests. I was also the greedily demanding mother, subjecting Lori to disdain and dismissal. "I have to get it right, show how clever I am in group, or else I could 'blow it' with you." On some occasions, I was her seductive, two-timing father: "'loving' me when we're in session and then you get on to the next patient you love."

However, a therapeutic aura of *sincerity* was not the virtual cure Lori had hoped for. The "warm" Elisabeth failed in her role as "healer," returning Lori to deal with her group and me. Apparently, we remained bad-enough good objects for her to learn about and struggle with the emotional truths represented by her *resistances*, *rebellions*, and *refusals*.

Sincerity is essential for *bonding* to occur, but as Lori's experience with Elisabeth shows, sincerity is necessary but perhaps insufficient for deep change.

Authenticity

Lori intuited the difference between *sincerity* and *authenticity*. *Sincerity* involves "caring for patients." The essence of *authenticity* is "being oneself," while also the professional. Merely caring, being a "love therapist" (an epithet eventually applied to Elisabeth) was not enough. Being "relaxed and not trying too hard" is not an accomplishment of beginners. Authentic work remains, in Trilling's words, "strenuous" and "exigent," and as our forebears, Bion and Foulkes, have emphasized, it takes years of training and experience to deal (inter-) subjectively with the complexities of the emotions, thinking (conscious, nonconscious, and the states in-between), and the multiplicities of social role.

Remorse, reparation, and "passion"

Lori conveyed the pure reality of physical pain. Caring for her aroused my rescue fantasies and ambitions, and an inescapable, although irrational, sense of guilt for failing at fulfilling them. Lori played her part in stimulating my *resistances*, of course. An intersubjective drama of masochistic rebellion and submission played out on the "theater" of her body (McDougall, 1989), and hence, impinged on the transference-countertransferences and the resulting enactments. Her insistent, imagistic language of bodily pain had as one purpose to "capture the analyst through the power of the image" (Bollas, 2000, p. 95). I was to become hostage—a remorseful witness to the distress that I caused and could/would not relieve. My punishment was to submit to her wearisome recitation of physical pain and the implicit and explicit reminders of my failure to provide relief.

She tested my *authenticity* in assessing whether I could become informed but not overwhelmed by these subjective reactions. She needed me to be more (and less) than "warm"—capable of hosting and integrating ambivalent feelings (*LHK*), some "primitive" and others "sophisticated." Authentic engagement is conveyed by *passion*, demonstrated in both individual and group modalities by the therapist's emotional capacity "to treat everyone differently, and fairly," by firmness and consistency, yet sufficient flexibility to be "easy or tough, say a lot or a little."

Despite Lori's diversions and provocations, I believe I succeeded in staying and guiding our group to remain accepting and interested

(*L* and *K*), and also challenging (*H*). To some extent, Lori has found a maternal home. Yet our group and I have not renounced a paternal presence, or repudiated phallic qualities. We maintain an interpretative stance that is penetrating without being unduly seductive.

The influence of the nonconscious

To engage authentically, the therapist must think consciously and nonconsciously. Relating with forethought, the therapist appreciates that an ongoing process of nonconscious communication co-exists and may be understood retrospectively. To the extent of her psychopathology, Lori nonconsciously "became" her symptom of painful bladder, a dysfunctional container: the model of a mind not able/willing to carry out the functions of emotional thinking. And I, without conscious forethought, became an improved version of Lori's bladder and urethra.

When her associative flow needed to remain open and affective, she would *refuse* and close it, squeezing out drops of premature and unintegrated thoughts and feelings. I encouraged her to take her and the group's time to speak. At other times, to promote delay rather than immediate discharge, as well as ensure the participation of others, I broke into Lori's disjointed verbal stream: "Hold back for a moment, let's try to reflect on what you've just said." I assessed how intense were her distress and felt need for relief—when it was appropriate for her to empty her psychic body, and when she could wait and attend to mental functions that could interest her and delay or even replace her reliance on verbal evacuation, a primary mode of *rebellion* and *refusal*.

Metaphorically carrying out bodily functions with and for Lori, I became an improved version of her parents too. As the parental "container," I "took in" her painful anxiety, such that I could feel and come to understand nonconsciously—before I could represent conceptually aspects of *resistance*—the psychic truths displaced into the surface and interior of her body.

The inescapability of social role

Lori experienced parental failure in negotiating social roles. Her mother too early and too easily forsook Lori for professional commitments, substituting for maternal roles a grandmother and housekeeping staff. Her father was inconsistent: warm and charming, or angry and dismissive; neither mood conveyed interest in any of his children. Who was Lori to him?, she wondered. And who was he?

The masks of authority were flimsy and transparent, hiding egotistic egos, hence Lori's derision of analytic jargon and any hint of *Establishment* pretension, motives for *rebellion* and *refusal*. She challenged and tested each mode of therapeutic engagement before she could begin to accept that I could be both "therapeutic" and trustworthy: "You don't have to answer, because I won't believe you ... you'd be 'therapeutic'."

At the present state of our work, Lori struggles with granting either of us legitimacy, emotionally integrating the reality that my wearing "two faces" is an aspect of being an authentic self. "You know what you are doing. I can't trust that you are being 'you'. ... Being 'me'? You got me there. Only when I'm relaxed and not trying too hard." In these moments of increasing frequency, when she is "being" herself, and allows me and other group members to "be," we progress with the analysis of *resistance*.

The four modes applied to political leadership: Evaluating George W. Bush

The four modes extend and may be applied to any group situation, dyadic, small, large, or political. I thought it would be interesting to evaluate the leadership of the former president of the United States according to these categories.

George W. Bush was and remains a controversial figure, stimulating polarized opinions, provoking uncooperative dissention between the two major political parties, and antagonizing emotional attitudes. For my purposes here, I will refer to "'Bushies" and "anti-Bushies," and red and blue states, respectively. This classification is not exact, as there were conservatives who objected to Bush's interventionist foreign policy, as well as his domestic fiscal policies. Likewise, some liberals favored the war in Iraq. However, the two groups have differed markedly in their evaluation of Bush as a leader and in his relationship to truth.

Diplomacy

Bush's style of *diplomacy* eschewed compromise. The "Bushies" applauded his confrontational, "meeting the enemy there rather than here," "with us or against us" style of engagement. He was the "decider" (his word), entitled to appoint officials who served "at the pleasure of the president." He boldly asserted authority with tough rhetoric ("bring it on"), threats, ultimatums, and powerful follow through. His "or else" to Saddam Hussein sowed *rebellion* in that country. Bush promised *revolutionary* support and soon delivered.

The "anti-Bushies" decried the president's *refusal* to engage in many softer or engaging diplomatic maneuvers, such as talking and negotiating with one's enemies rather than name-calling ("the axis of evil": Iran, Iraq, and North Korea), and nurturing rather than alienating long-term allies ("old Europe"). They saw Bush's diplomacy as self-serving, satisfying his allegiance to various special interests.

Some political thinkers analyzed Bush diplomacy in terms of *resistance*, hypothesizing Oedipal dynamics behind the strategy of "getting the job done" in Iraq. In overthrowing President Hussein, Bush, our 43rd president, also toppled his father, President George H.W. Bush ("41"), vanquishing his policies of compromise and containment.

Integrity

Bush supporters perceived a man of *integrity*. Ethical, moral, and religious principles guided his political philosophy and decision-making. His belief in democracy, his understanding of the sanctity of life, freedom from excessive government regulation, and Bible-supported (heterosexual) norms motivated how he engaged, as in overthrowing an oppressive dictator, nominating conservative Supreme Court justice candidates, opposing stem cell research and abortion, and promulgating an anti-gay marriage stance.

Bush's antagonists decried an ideologically based, wrongheaded, and hypocritical assertion and application of moral and ethical principles. They characterized as anti-democratic and not humane Bush's incursion into civil liberties (increased surveillance), violation of international norms via the Patriot Act (suspension of habeas corpus and use of torture), neglect of the poor and disenfranchized

(Hurricane Katrina and New Orleans), and obstruction of national and international attempts to address global warming (e.g., denial of California's right to regulate carbon emissions).

Sincerity

Some agreement between the "reds" and the "blues" existed in the evaluation of President Bush's *sincerity*. He was perceived as straightforward in articulating how he understood key concepts he favored: God, Jesus, freedom, democracy, life, and heterosexual norms. To advisors and their advice, he remained steadfastly consistent and loyal (e.g., Secretary of Defense Rumsfeld, "Heck of a job" Brownie of Homeland Security, Attorney General Gonzalez, Putin of the Russian Federation), even when his positions and alliances were unpopular with constituents on the right.

To a significant extent, Bush's appeal rested in his *sincerity*. One knew what he believed, how he thought, and what he felt, and could be confident that he would adhere to and act on his convictions. To supporters, Bush's sincerity made him affable and trustworthy. Adhering to stances unpopular with some conservatives, on immigration, budget deficits, and Iraq, was proof of Bush's sincerity and courage, and so admirable.

By dividing the world into simple categories, such as good/bad, Bush persuaded constituents to love (and hate) accordingly. To opponents, *sincerity* made the president odious and dangerous. They judged that by idealizing certain people and certain ideas (e.g., "freedom" for Iraq, "protection" of stem cells), Bush detracted from, falsified, *rebelled* against, and *refused* that which was cogent but more complicated.

Authenticity

Bush prided himself on being a categorical, not complex thinker. No evidence exists in his history of "strenuous" mental activity (an indifferent student, failed businessman, casual governor). He valued short work hours, physical exercise, and lengthy vacations, even in times of national and international crisis. For wisdom and direction, he relied on an evangelical reading of the Bible, "feelings of conviction," and the minds of others (a conservative brain trust, including Wolfowitz, Perle, Rove, and Cheney, and their military, legal, and industrial cohorts).

Bush denied making mistakes or wishing to have made different decisions; hence guilt and reparation would have seemed unlikely to impinge on this leader's consciousness. (We cannot know what impinged on his nonconsciousness, for as he was a public, mostly scripted figure, we are not privy to derivatives, which would be revealing. If consciousness and nonconsciousness are dissociated, authenticity is obviated.)

The lines of "we" versus "they" were obvious. For supporters, conspicuous single-mindedness was one of the qualities that made G.W. Bush a trustworthy and unifying leader. When choices are clear, and the demarcations between good and bad, right and wrong, are simple and unambiguous, there should be no demarcation between modes of *sincerity* and *authenticity*.

For his detractors, Bush was guided by simplistic thinking and unexamined emotion, *refusal*, and not by *passion*, which involves tolerating and integrating a complex of tensions, even contradictory feelings and attitudes. They cautioned that a deliberate, "go slow" reflective stance is not the same as "waffling" or being paralyzed by indecision or over- analysis. In concluding that invading Iraq was going to be quick, cheap, and easy, he disregarded available but unwelcome information about the mental and emotional life of individuals and their ethnic, religious, and political subgroups: the complexities and ambiguities of truths of an alien society.

They saw Bush as inauthentic—false and posturing—serving at the pleasure of the religious right, oil industry, and big business, and instituting a misguided war (aimed at Iraq rather than Afghanistan) based on pretenses, untruths (the existence of weapons of mass destruction), and wishful thinking. The president who is authentic must lead with "two faces," once conveying the reassuring, patriotic image of conservator of the republic, but the other, the firm countenance of a leader who brings difficult truths to the public, and in making it think, secures the republic's vitality, perhaps even, its future.

Summary

In the leader's striving for *authenticity*, the modes of diplomacy, integrity, and sincerity also come into play. G.W. Bush believed his truths and to this extent he was *sincere*. Whether he had been sufficiently complex in his thinking, diplomatic, and ethical in his behavior remains controversial. Certainly, his modes of leadership contributed to the current polarization of the country into two antagonistic camps—typical of *fight/flight basic assumption*—that have difficulty communicating and forming a *work group*.

Concluding remarks

Leadership involves holding the tension of truth as best as one understands it, and deciding how, when, and how much to convey, and to whom. Values and practical considerations exist in tension. We rarely live up to the "should books" provided by theorists and writers such as myself. To lead well, we must live with paradox, attempt to find balance without definitive solutions, and accept the nonexistence of the perfect option, flawlessly applied. Growth remains possible and likely, if the leader remains thoughtful, invitational to feedback, and self-critical as to what is achieved.

Diplomacy, integrity, sincerity, and *authenticity* describe modes of relating to others as well as to truth itself. The four modes are navigated to cement bonding, build trust, allow relationships to evolve and resolve, and strengthen the abilities to think creatively and relate constructively to impasses and challenges. Perforce, dynamics of *resistance, rebellion* and *refusal* are at play. The four modes represent the therapist: how he or she approaches, and avoids, truth in the context of the *3 Rs*. As the leader meters truth, significant truth about him or herself is revealed to all.

EPILOGUE

Putting it together

Piece by piece.
Bit by bit, putting it together.
Piece by piece, only way to make a work of art.
Every moment makes a contribution,
Every little detail plays a part.
Having just a vision's no solution,
Everything depends on execution.
Putting it together, that's what counts!
Ounce by ounce, putting it together.
Small amounts, having it can make a work of art.
First of all you need a good foundation,
Otherwise it's risky from the start. …
But without the proper preparation,
Having just a vision's no solution,
Everything depends on execution. ...
The art of making art
Is putting it together, bit by bit.
(Lyrics by Stephen Sondheim, *Sunday in the Park with George*)

I begin and end this volume with a lyric from Sondheim's *Sunday in the Park with George*, describing the creative process—applicable to clinical leadership. "The analyst has to be an artist—he has to make constructions of what is going on" (Bion, 1987, p. 76).

There are infinite psychic "bits" in a group session—derivatives in word, look, action, and most importantly, our (inter-) subjective reactions. We piece together inferences concerning *truth, falsity, resistance, rebellion* and *refusal,* test interpretative themes, and enact interactional strategies, involving modes of *diplomacy, integrity, sincerity,* and *authenticity*. Such are our constructions—everything we do (and do not do). Every moment makes a contribution; every detail plays a part. The process of putting things together, making truth, holds the group, and allows it to benefit its members.

Group is risky—a bold and adventurous enterprise for all participants. First of all the therapist needs a good foundation, built from experiences as group member and leader, from texts, didactics, and supervision. Without the proper preparation, having a vision is no solution. No matter how intuitive, empathic, spontaneous we may believe ourselves to be, group therapists are constrained by principles, discipline, and the professional and social contexts that shape our material—form, process, and content.

Everything depends on the therapist's execution. The specific therapeutic quality of a group "is embodied in the conductor … he has created the group and his influence remains decisive from the beginning to the end" (Foulkes, 1964, p. 160). I am less concerned with a group leader's failures in efforts to find truths not obvious, than with a passive therapist who does not attempt to bring shape and meaning to a session. The art of making art is revealed in the therapist's earnest and persistent application of thought and feeling conveyed to the group and each member. The group as creative entity requires the therapist's *authenticity*, arousing, participating in, and making useful its *resistances, rebellions*, and *refusals*.

APPENDIX I

Basic concepts: Relational group psychotherapy

1. States of mind: Intrapsychic-interpersonal-transpersonal (group level)

Kleinian theory postulates two basic states of mind, the "psychotic" or primitive, and the neurotic or normal. The former consists of two *"positions"* (plus the enduring *manic defenses* against both positions) that inform our emotional outlook: *paranoid-schizoid* and *depressive.* The positions must be tolerated and processed, informing and vitalizing the learning and growing self/group with pre-rational levels of feeling and thought. Similarly, Bion described two states of mind in a vital group that must *interact*—the *basic assumption* and *work group* mentalities. The *work group* needs the *ba's* to learn from experience. The therapist fosters primitive-sophisticated interactions via bonding, confronting, and interpreting (*"container-contained"*).

Bion's three types of *basic assumptions* associate with *"psychotic positions"* and *manic defenses* (and to *LHK*, see below).

a. BaF/F The *fight/flight assumption* refers to the *paranoid-schizoid* outlook in which others are experienced as potentially dangerous.

b. BaD The *dependency assumption* refers to the *depressive* outlook, involving a preoccupation with "oral" supplies (i.e., nurturance and love).

c. BaP The *pairing assumption*, a type of *manic* defense, removes the group from its immediate emotional concerns via voyeuristic curiosity with a "copulating pair" (e.g., one member or more trying to "cure" another).

Summary

The therapist aids the group (and vice-versa) in embracing our "animal inheritance" ("prewired" or basic reactions, "instincts," desires, etc.) to learn from experience. The *psychotic positions* (paranoid-schizoid and depressive, and the manic defense) underlie and inform neurotic/normal character structure and functioning. The *basic assumptions (F/F, D, P)* underlie and inform *work group* structure and functioning.

2. Basic conflict: To think, not to think, or to anti-think

a) Metapsychology of thinking

Humans bring inborn, pre- and irrational intellectual and emotional categories ("*premonitions*") to "raw" experience (creating "*beta elements*"). They anticipate events and place "primitive" cognitive-emotional schemata upon experiences both before and when they occur. The task is to feel, think about, and use these "protomental" categories in our confrontation with reality, making higher-level mental "transformations" (into "*alpha elements*") such that meaning may be created and we learn from experience. Bion called this necessary process the "*alpha-function.*" The ongoing transformation of *beta* into *alpha elements* provides consciousness and nonconsciousness with symbols, nameable affects in the form of feelings and emotional thoughts of increasing complexity that may be expressed in fantasy, dreams, art, science, mathematics, etc. Alpha function links individuals to themselves and others, and thus, extends relational awareness.

Summary

"Primitive" or "*psychotic*" (pre-rational) self meets experience—stimulating the development of un-understood mental elements (*beta*).

Beta elements are transformed into *alpha elements*—"alphabetized"—symbols, words, ideas, which may be thought about consciously/nonconsciously, to produce meaningful experience.

b) Thinking hurts

Thinking inherently involves an exchange of painful, primitive feelings creating often unwanted thoughts. This exchange involves a recapitulation of the earlier development shifts from *paranoid-schizoid* to *depressive positions* into moment-to-moment processes of oscillation between disintegration and reintegration (symbolized as *Ps↔D*). (*Manic defenses may serve against either* or both.) As patterns of painful emotional-cognitive experience, *Ps↔D* oscillations participate in all other learning experiences in complex arrangements with *"container-contained"* processes, and with the processing of basic affects, *LHK* (see below).

Summary

Thinking is *persecutory*: Learning involves partial disintegration of what is known until a state of ignorance is regained, and meaninglessness and confusion is tolerated.

Thinking is *depressing*: In (re-) integrating, one risks ever-greater separation from established, conventional relations with others, as well as with one's previous ideas, feelings, and identity (see below, on *"premonitory anxiety"* and *LHK*).

c) Psychotic part of the personality

A universal component of personality evades or grossly modifies learning by experience when threatened with mental pain. As an "anti-ego," the psychotic part defends against innate tendencies to tolerate the movement *Ps↔D*, to link to others via the *"container-contained,"* and to develop and integrate the basic affects, *LHK*. The psychotic part underlies all neurotic and characterological disturbances, and partakes in *basic assumption* group activity.

Summary

We defend against experience by evading or even attacking the mental linking processes by which we come to know and integrate our thoughts and feelings, to the extent to which we wish to avoid frustration and other forms of mental pain. We thus starve ourselves of "food for thought" ("truth" with the small "t") and cannot grow.

3. Role of internal/interpersonal object relations: The container-contained

The container-contained represents a transformatory process of the mind—one mind or many minds—reaching (or evading/attacking) emotional awareness. Three types of intrapsychic and interpersonal relationships support (or undermine) the individual's drive to think, develop meaning, and learn from experience.

a) "Symbiotic" or bonding relationships

In human development, container-contained processes initially are *symbiotic*, based on early infant-(m)other projective-introjective exchanges. The normally empathic (m)other gathers in (introjects), deciphers, and communicates back to the infant aspects of its psychic experience beyond its current cognitive and emotional capabilities. By containing the infant's primitive feelings, and interesting the infant in them, the receptive (m)other fosters the development of a *"normal" part* of the infant's personality that concerns itself with psychic quality. Bonding relationships remain important throughout life as we test, establish, and re-establish trust in our own thoughts and the thoughts of others. In group, symbiotic communications involve verbal and nonverbal bonding behaviors, heightened projective activity, enactment, and benevolent forms of acting-out.

b) "Commensal" or abstract/symbolic relationships

To an increasing degree, the child becomes able to contain feelings while in the (m)other's absence, and to transform them into images and rudimentary prototypes of sophisticated thought. These internal containers develop that which previously was split off and/or projected. Symbols and thoughts now serve the functions to transform preverbal emotional meaning, functions once provided primarily by the other. *Commensal* relations are established with one's own mind and the minds of others. In group, members apply reason to emotions, stimulating symbolic processes such as those involved in dream thoughts and language, which in turn furthers emotional development which must then be contained by new thought and the exchange of ideas.

c) "Parasitic" or destructive relationships (anti-linking)
Because of traumatic early failures in infant-caregiver relationships, the individual (or the traumatized part of the personality) comes to experience containing and being contained as untrustworthy, painful, and dangerous. Social feedback in the form of *commensal* communications, as well as empathic projective-introjective symbiotic exchanges, are feared and distrusted. When *parasitic* dynamics prevail, the *container-contained* represents a hostile and destructive process. Thinking—and thinkers—must be avoided or attacked, and thought and language are employed to evade or even destroy meaning rather than establish and further thinking processes in self and other. *Parasitic* communications may be provocatively direct, as well as subtle and not immediately identifiable, as when a member utilizes projective identifications to "numb" the receivers' thought processes, or withdraws projective identifications to emotionally starve the group.

Summary

The *container-contained* is a complex model which describes processes of human development, internal and external object relations, affect integration, symbol formation, individual, dyadic, and group functioning, and learning from (and resisting) emotional experience. It draws attention to how we hear and think about another's communication, how we convey our experience back, and how this communicative interplay impacts the participants and the immediate future of one's own thinking and of the relationship.

4. Basic affects (LHK) and "Passion"

According to Klein, the infant first comes to know about the world through its basic affects ("drives"), dividing the world into good and bad mental categories on the basis of them. Bion turned attention to a third mental category of affective experience, curiosity, and offered an alphabetic shorthand: *L*—our need to love and be loved; *H*—to hate and be hated; *K*—to know others emotionally and to be known.

a) "Premonitory anxiety" and "not nice" feelings

LHK may first intrude as premonitions, emerging into consciousness with vague awareness and anxious dread. Derivatives of *LHK* may be felt as "not nice," irrational, primitive, and amoral feelings, wishes, or desires, and rather than tolerated and integrated, they may be projected and enacted in the group setting, depositing *"beta elements" into group process and provoking a basic assumption* mentality."

b) "Minus" LHK and basic assumptions

A group may be amplified with intense feelings yet fail to progress emotionally. When not developed into integrated emotional thoughts, *LHK* exist as *minus*, misinforming via affective exaggeration and/or omission. *Basic assumptions* easily become saturated with "minus" affects: *BaD (or -L); BaF/F (or -H); BaP (or -K)*. To be utilized productively, as *"plus,"* these affects need to be "linked" together via *work group* mentality.

c) Passion

A meaningful experience requires a particular sequence of thinking, involving tolerating primal affects. The goal is *"passion,"* in which *LHK* may be experienced largely in nonsplit, holistic, and integrated ways. An optimal expression of maturity at any developmental level, passion exists in a warm, human context, balanced and without excessive emotional intensification.

d) Therapist's passion

Leaders feel group tensions that relate not only to complementary and concordant identifications, but also, from *LHK* activated by social participation. Through these affects the therapist represents, mentally organizes, and responds to the group and its members. By maintaining a self-conscious curiosity (*"primal receptivity"*) about one's own *LHK*, the therapist provides an internal boundary, from which he or she can integrate multiple intersubjective perspectives, and participate emotionally and interpretatively. *Primal receptivity* (to *LHK*), while also participating in transference-countertransference, represents a different dimension of experience.

Summary

LHK are the foundation of relational awareness: how we feel about others and ourselves and how (we think) others feel about us. *LHK* emerge as affects, drives, or unavoidable desires, fantasies, wishes, etc., to inform us and to be utilized productively in the intersubjective situation. To develop personal meaning and learn from group experience, *LHK* must be claimed within the here-and-now relational context, made mentally available, and linguistically expressible.

Passion occurs in realizing, integrating, and engaging one's basic and important emotions during the meaning-unfolding process. In every session, each individual needs to feel "not nice," experiencing love, hate, and curiosity regarding one's own evolving emotional experiences with the group and its other members. Like other group members, the therapist approaches thinking with trepidation, and consequently makes (coconscious-nonconscious) "decisions" at various moments to evade, modify, or modulate the mental pain arising from tolerating emotional experience. It requires effort, discipline, and courage to allow one's thought to reach the full vibrancy of *passion*.

APPENDIX II

Basic concepts: Resistance, rebellion and refusal

Basic premises

- The development of the individual and the growth of the group occur through mentation: the generation, pursuit, and articulation of truth that is appropriate and legitimate to its human context.
- The dynamic conflict: truth-falsity, rather than consciousness-nonconsciousness. Group organization and activity conceptualized as a series of moves and countermoves to express, redirect, modify, or block the search for emotional truth.
- Traditionally, all efforts to counter psychotherapeutic work have been captured under the umbrella term, *resistance*. However, the assumptions, methods, and goals of therapeutic work may be challenged metapsychologically, philosophically, ethically, pragmatically, and politically. Hence, *rebellion* and *refusal*.
- *Resistance, rebellion* and *refusal* may not signify maladjustment or pathology, or antagonism to all emotional thinking and manners of pursuing it, but rather, to the particular approach or purpose of the endeavor, which may be experienced and evaluated as false.

- *Resistance*, *rebellion* and *refusal* sit in interpersonal contexts and their locus and legitimacy must be judged by psychosocial circumstance and viewpoint.

Resistance: What is psychically unfolding and formulating; how do I think/feel?

- *Resistance* entails therapeutically a gradual elaboration of nonconscious, preconscious, and partially conscious experience. In group therapy, what is resisted is mentalized nonconsciously and symbolically: thought about and communicated, often without awareness.
- Utilizing metaphor, symbols, myth, dream, condensations and displacements, and participating in nonverbal communication and enactments, each member broadcasts resisted versions of emotional truth, which are received, evaluated, and responded to by other group members.
- Subjective experience/group process: promotes thinking and feeling, tension, suspense, and surprise. The individual or group becomes immersed in process, and working with and through resistance intensifies interpersonal intimacy.

Rebellion: Why are power arrangements being challenged and what are the options?

- Group members feel intersubjective tensions that arise from differences in beliefs about how their group should function, and at times they rebel against the group process. *Rebellion* denotes a strategy of social action, adopted by a faction, when other avenues of influence seem futile or unattractive, a judgment that depends on the group's genuine receptivity to discussion and change (*diplomacy*), and equally, on the state of mind of the rebelling faction.
- *Rebellion* may activate and focus consciousness: What kind of group is this and is it acceptable? Unlike *resistance*, the ideas and feelings that are expressed, and the behaviors that are planned or enacted, are not to be considered primarily in terms of nonconscious levels of meaning, or interpreted as symbolism.

The basic premises and values of the group—its truth and falsity—are at the center of the controversy, to be acknowledged, and first addressed on that level.

- Subjective experience/group process: *Rebellion* may be mentally challenging (*defiance*), it also stimulates anxieties and a sense of danger, related to rejection and abandonment (*secession/ exile*), confusion, misunderstanding, and disruption (*anarchy*), and/or to the anticipation of change (*revolution*). It involves mental opposition and emotional antagonism, and may threaten self-esteem and group cohesion.

Four pathways of rebellion

1. *Defiance.* Palpable and continual or phasic pressure exerted against ongoing group process and content. The group has become issue focused, and progressive development is problematic without frank acknowledgment and some attempt at resolution.
2. *Secession/Exile.* Rupture between one or more individuals and the main group threatens reciprocal allegiances and attachments. When the contentious faction withdraws or is ejected from membership, the rebellion is suspended or quelled. Controversial issues may remain unresolved and continue to impact the group.
3. *Anarchy.* A consequence of effective psychotherapy is emotional disturbance and a breakdown of core defenses. The anarchically inclined do not commit to this type of productive and necessary breakdown and promote crises of miscommunication, misunderstanding, and confusion.
4. *Revolution.* The premises of the rebelling faction come to overpower and dominate the group, propelling a new phase.

Refusal: Why non-thinking and how to readdress?

- A willful nonparticipation in offering or responding to material that can be symbolized, and even in social relationships. The individual, subgroup, or group blocks access to or invalidates the communicative instruments used to uncover *resistance* and *rebellion*: feeling, fantasy, thought, and language. *Refusal* thus establishes a mental boundary between what is considered appropriate and inappropriate for intrapsychic or interpersonal dialogue.

- All communication has an element of *refusal*: one path is chosen and others are precluded. *Refusal* occurs at various levels of awareness, intensity, and legitimacy. Internal or interpersonal dialogue, free association, insight, confrontation, or interpretation—each is more or less relevant, authentic, or well timed, and so represents a compromise between advancing and averting mental collaboration, i.e., between emotional truth and falsity.
- Subjective experience/group process: The mentation process is stalled. Initially one may feel mentally or emotionally provoked; *refusal* may eventuate into irritation, boredom, and psychic "deadness." In creating a temporary impasse or resilient stalemate, refusal affirms separateness, without necessarily annihilating relationships, an ever-present danger in certain pathways of *rebellion*.

Three categories of refusal

1. *Refusal to perceive external experience*. Distortion, narrowing of affective interest or cognitive focus, characterological "not seeing" (e.g., the truth in positive interpersonal interactions), physical or emotional withdrawal.
2. *Refusal to think about what one knows*. Refusal to think about relevant "facts," memories, attitudes, and behaviors; established truths of psychotherapeutic work (e.g., transference-countertransference patterns) forgotten or made meaningless. Painful scenarios may be remembered, dreamt about, and enacted in group, but remain, in effect, mentally "frozen." Their significance may be discounted, or treated as insurmountable and a rationale for entitled behavior.
3. *Refusal to think about what one does not know*. Refusal to think about and develop incipient feelings and thoughts—a muted receptivity to "fresh" or "unformulated" internal and external experience. Meaning accepted intellectually without emotional integration. Also, a legitimate stance (e.g., refusal to engage in treatment-destructive maneuvers).

APPENDIX III

Basic concepts: Diplomacy, integrity, sincerity, and authenticity

Basic premises

- The development of the individual and the growth of the group occur through mentation: the generation, pursuit, and articulation of emotional truth that is appropriate and legitimate to its social context.
- Group organization and activity may be conceptualized as a series of moves and countermoves to express, redirect, modify, or block the search for emotional truth. Hence *resistance, rebellion* and *refusal*: *the 3 Rs.*
- *Diplomacy, integrity, sincerity,* and *authenticity* are modes of relating—how the group therapist uses self to build relationships, establish cohesion, foster process, generate meaning, and respond to challenges and impasses. They describe the leader in interaction: how he or she approaches emotional truth. "*Passion*" exists in the mode of authenticity.
- All interventions may be captured under these overlapping rubrics, which are exhaustive but nonexclusive, and are influenced by intersubjective group processes. They supply conceptual references for the interactional stance one has adopted,

allowing the therapist to be more aware of what he or she is doing, and why.

Diplomacy

Diplomacy is concerned with power and with establishing and maintaining relationships and alliances. The therapist situates certain emotional truths and not others as salient in the immediacy of the clinical situation. He or she remains cognizant of the motivations, affiliations, and beliefs among members and subgroups and the roles they occupy. Diplomacy may involve keeping channels of communication open so that the players can continue a search for communal or at least livable truths. Diplomatic interventions are not always popular or balanced evenly among all participants.

Integrity

Integrity resides in the therapist's moral and ethical principles, in reference to one's professional, political, ethnic, and religious affiliations. It emerges not only from principles, but how they are applied. Samuel Johnson penned that "Integrity without knowledge is weak and useless, and knowledge without integrity is dangerous and dreadful." *Self*-knowledge is the lens through which the therapist evaluates emotional truth (and falsity) and responds to the contributions of others, representing morality while eschewing a moralistic attitude.

Sincerity

Sincerity conveys the leader's positive emotionality. "One cannot both be sincere and seem so" (Andre Gide). *Sincerity* is categorical—either you are or not. "A group is clearly held together by a power of some kind: and to what power could this feat be better ascribed than to Eros, which holds together everything in the world" (Freud). Freud described psychoanalysis as "in essence a cure through love," referring to the patient's relationship to the doctor. To a degree not realized by Freud, love must be requited: The therapist also must love, and love sincerely. "To understand, to unite with another, and hence, also to love, prove to be basically one and the same" (Racker).

In "uniting," the therapist bonds via the preverbal or "symbiotic" level characteristic of benevolent, infant-mother projective-introjective exchanges, communicated by and also between and under the therapist's words.

Authenticity

Sincerity is categorical and simple, *authenticity* is dynamic and complex: Tension exists between self-awareness and expression. "Every profound spirit needs a mask" (Nietzsche). Therapist and group members wear masks, that is, roles that are social and mutually contracted, and which allow us to talk to each other in ways not otherwise possible. *Authenticity* bears upon how the therapist approaches truth, in the context of frame, technique, and propriety. The group therapist's communications are mediated by appreciation of the dimensionality of emotion (*LHK*), the influence of the nonconscious, and the inescapability of social role.

Sincerity expresses love; *authenticity* strives for "*passion*:" a relational process of realizing and engaging basic affects (*LHK* and attendant paranoid-schizoid and depressive fantasies and thoughts), establishing and maintaining links from one's mind to the minds of others. In this optimal situation, the therapist achieves the mental clarity and "moral freedom" to feel and to think—if not say—anything.

Addendum: Basic affects (LHK) and "passion"

According to Klein, the infant first comes to know about the world through its basic affects ("drives"), dividing the world into good and bad mental categories on the basis of them. Bion turned attention to a third mental category of affective experience: curiosity, and offered an alphabetic shorthand: *L*—our need to love and be loved; *H*—to hate and be hated; *K*—to know others emotionally and to be known. *LHK* are the foundation of relational awareness: how we come to feel about others and ourselves and how (we think) others feel about us.

Group therapists feel group tensions that relate not only to complementary and concordant identifications, but also, from *LHK* activated by social participation. Through these affects the therapist represents, mentally organizes, and responds to the group and its members. In operating with and promulgating *passion,* the therapist claims *LHK* within the here-and-now relational context, such that they are contained, developed, and made mentally available and linguistically expressible. Without *passion,* a group becomes mired in *basic assumptions,* as affects remain exaggerated and "minus:" *BaD (-L); BaF/F (-H); BaP (-K).*

REFERENCES

Agazarian, Y.M. (1994). The phases of group development and the systems-centered group. In: V.L. Schermer & M. Pines (Eds.), *Ring of fire: Primitive Affects and Object Relations in Group Psychotherapy* (pp. 36–85). London: Routledge.

Agazarian, Y.M. (1997). *Systems-centered Therapy for Groups*. New York: Guilford.

Alford, C.F. (1995). The group as a whole or acting out the missing leader? *International Journal of Group Psychotherapy, 4*: 125–141.

Aron, L. (1991). The patient's experience of the analyst's subjectivity. *Psychoanalytic Dialogues, 1*: 29–51.

Aron, L. (1996). *A Meeting of Minds: Mutuality in Psychoanalysis*. Hillsdale, NJ: Analytic Press.

Austin, H. (1962). *How To Do Things With Words*. Oxford: Clarendon Press.

Balint, M. (1952). *Primary Love and Psycho-analytic Technique*. New York: Liveright, 1965.

Barrows, S.B. (1986). Quoted by Marian Christy: "'Mayflower Madam' Tells All." *Boston Globe*, September 10.

Beebe, B., Lachmann, F. & Jaffe, J. (1997). Mother-infant interaction structures and pre-symbolic self and object representations. *Psychoanalytic Dialogues, 7*: 133–182.

Bellak, L. (1980). On some limitations of dyadic psychotherapy and the role of group modalities. *International Journal of Group Psychotherapy, 30*: 7–22.

Bennis, W. (2007). The challenges of leadership in the modern world: Introduction to the Special Issue. *American Psychologist, 62*: 2–5.

Bennis, W.G. & Shepard, H.A. (1956). A theory of group development. *Human Relations, 9*: 415–437.

Berg, D. (1998). Resurrecting the muse: Followership in organizations. In: E. Klein, F. Gabelnick & P. Herr (Eds.), *The Psychodynamics of Leadership* (pp. 27–52). Madison, CT: Psychosocial Press.

Billow, R.M. (1977). Metaphor: A review of the psychological literature. *Psychological Bulletin, 84*: 81–92.

Billow, R.M. (1999a). Power and entitlement: Or, Mine versus yours. *Contemporary Psychoanalysis, 35*: 475–489.

Billow, R.M. (1999b). An intersubjective approach to entitlement. *Psychoanalytic Quarterly, 68*: 441–461. [Translated and reprinted in *Aperturas Psicoanalíticas* (http://www.aperturas.org), No. 6, 2000.]

Billow, R.M. (2000a). From countertransference to "passion." *Psychoanalytic Quarterly, 69*: 93–119.

Billow, R.M. (2000b). Bion's "passion;" the analyst's pain. *Contemporary Psychoanalysis, 36*: 411–426.

Billow, R.M. (2000c). Relational levels of the container-contained in group. *Group, 24*: 243–259.

Billow, R.M. (2002). Passion in group: Thinking about loving, hating, and knowing. *International Journal of Group Psychotherapy, 52*: 355–372.

Billow, R.M. (2003a). Rebellion in group. *International Journal of Group Psychotherapy, 53*: 331–351.

Billow, R.M. (2003b). Relational variations of the container-contained. *Contemporary Psychoanalysis, 39*: 27–50.

Billow, R.M. (2003c). *Relational Group Psychotherapy: From Basic Assumptions to Passion*. London: Jessica Kingsley.

Billow, R.M. (2003d). Bonding in group: The therapist's contribution. *International Journal of Group Psychotherapy, 53*: 83–110.

Billow, R.M. (2004). Truth and falsity in group. *International Journal of Group Psychotherapy, 54*: 321–345.

Billow, R.M. (2005a). The two faces of the group therapist. *International Journal of Group Psychotherapy, 55*: 107–187.

Billow, R.M. (2005b). Truth seeking and abandonment: group processes of resistance, rebellion and refusal. *Group*: *29*: 453–467.

Bion, W.R. (1961). *Experiences in Groups*. London: Tavistock.

Bion, W.R. (1962). *Learning from Experience*. London: Heinemann. [Reprinted in: *Seven Servants: Four works by Wilfred R. Bion*. New York: Aronson, 1977.]

Bion, W.R. (1963). *Elements of Psychoanalysis*. London: Heinemann. [Reprinted in: *Seven Servants: Four works by Wilfred R. Bion*. New York: Aronson, 1977.]

Bion, W.R. (1965). *Transformations*. London: Heinemann. [Reprinted in: *Seven Servants: Four works by Wilfred R. Bion*. New York: Aronson, 1977.]

Bion, W.R. (1966). Book review: Medical orthodoxy and the future of psychoanalysis, by K.R. Eissler. *International Journal of Psychoanalysis, 47*: 575–579.

Bion, W.R. (1967). *Second Thoughts*. London: Heinemann.

Bion, W.R. (1970). *Attention and Interpretation*. London: Tavistock. [Reprinted in: *Seven Servants: Four works by Wilfred R. Bion*. New York: Aronson, 1977.]

Bion, W.R. (1975). *Bion's Brazilian lectures 2: Rio/Sao Paulo, 1974*. Rio de Janeiro, Brazil: Imago Editoria.

Bion. W.R. (1979). Making the best of a bad job. In: F. Bion (Ed.), *Clinical Seminars and Four Papers*. Abingdon, England: Fleetwood, 1987.

Bion, W.R. (1987). *Clinical Seminars and Four Papers*. F. Bion (Ed.). Abingdon: Fleetwood.

Bion, W.R. (1992). *Cogitations*. F. Bion (Ed.). London: Karnac.

Bird, B. (1972). Notes on transference: Universal phenomenon and the hardest part of the analysis. *Journal of the American Psychoanalytic Association, 20*: 267–301.

Blake, W. (1977). Auguries of Innocence (Poems from the Pickering manuscript). In: A. Ostriker (Ed.), *The Complete Poems*. London: Penguin Classics.

Bloom, H. (1997). *The Anxiety of Influence: A Theory of Poetry (2nd ed.)*. New York: Oxford University Press.

Blum, H.P. (1985). *Defense and Resistance: Historical Perspective and Current Concepts*. New York: International Universities Press.

Boesky, D. (1988). Comments on the structural theory of technique. *International Journal of Psychoanalysis, 69*: 303–316.

Bollas, C. (1999). *The Shadow of the Object: Psychoanalysis of the Unthought Unknown*. New York: Columbia University Press.

Bollas, C. (2000). *Hysteria*. London: Routledge.

Brabeck, M. & Brown, L.S. (1997). Feminist theory and psychological practice. In: J. Worell & N. Johnson (Eds.), *Shaping the Future of Feminist Psychology: Education, Research and Practice* (pp. 15–36). Washington, DC: American Psychological Association.

Brabender, V. & Fallon, A. (1993). *Models of Inpatient Group Psychotherapy*. Washington, DC: American Psychological Association.

Brabender, V. & Fallon, A. (2009). Ethical hot spots of combined individual and group therapy: Applying four ethical systems. *International Journal of Group Psychotherapy, 59*: 127–147.

Bromberg, P. (2001). *Standing in the Spaces: Essays on Clinical Process, Trauma, and Dissociation*. Hillsdale, NJ: Analytic Press.

Brown, D. (2003). Pairing Bion and Foulkes: Towards a metapsychology? In: R. Lipgar & M. Pines (Eds.), *Building on Bion: Roots* (pp. 153–180). London: Jessica Kingsley.

Bucci, W. (1997). *Psychoanalysis and Cognitive Science; A Multiple Code Theory*. New York: Guilford.

Burroughs, W. (1985). On coincidence. In: *The Adding Machine*. Cited in *The Columbia World of Quotations*. New York, Columbia University Press, 1996.

Butler, S. (1912) *Samuel Butler's Notebooks*. E.P. Dutton, 1951.

Calef, V. & Weinshel, E. (1981). Some clinical consequences of introjection: gaslighting. *Psychoanalytic Quarterly, 50*: 44–67.

Caligor, J., Fieldsteel, N. & Brok, A. (1984). *Individual and Group Therapy: Combining Psychoanalytic Treatment*. New York: Basic.

Caper, R. (1999). Group psychology and psychoanalytic group. Internet publisher: International Psychoanalytic Association, Committee on Interregional Conferences (http://www.ipa.org.uk/CIRC/Caper-m1.htm).

Chused, J. (1992). The patient's perception of the analyst. *Psychoanalytic Quarterly, 63*: 161–184.

Cohen, B. & Schermer, V. (2002). On scapegoating in therapy groups: A social constructivist and intersubjective outlook. *International Journal of Group Psychotherapy, 52*: 89–109.

Dalal, F. (2000). *Taking the Group Seriously*. London: Jessica Kingsley.

Davies, J. (1998). Between the disclosure and foreclosure of erotic transference-countertransference: Can psychoanalysis find a place for adult sexuality? *Psychoanalytic Dialogues*, 8: 747–766.

Davies, J. (2001). Erotic overstimulation and the co-construction of sexual meanings in the transference-countertransference experience. *Psychoanalytic Quarterly*, 70: 757–788.

Desmond, R. & Seligman, M. (1977). A review of research on leaderless groups. *Small Group Behavior, 8*: 3–24.

Dickinson, E. (1960). Tell all the truth but tell it slant. In: T.H. Johnson (Ed.), *The Complete Poems of Emily Dickinson*. Boston: Little, Brown.

Durkin, H.E. (1964). *The Group in Depth*. New York: International Universities Press.

Eissler, K. (1958). Remarks on some variations in psychoanalytic technique. *International Journal of Psychoanalysis, 39*: 222–229.

Emde, R. (1990). Mobilizing fundamental modes of development: Empathic availability and therapeutic action. *Journal of the American Psychoanalytic Association, 38*: 881–913.

Ettin, M.F. (2003). Bion's legacy to median and large groups. In: R. Lipgar & M. Pines (Eds.), *Building on Bion: Branches* (pp. 29–69). London: Jessica Kingsley.

Ettin, M.F. & Cohen, B.D. (2003). Working through a psychotherapy group's political cultures. *International Journal of Group Psychotherapy, 53*: 479–504.

Ezriel, H. (1950). A psychoanalytic approach to group treatment. *British Journal of Medical Psychology, 23*: 50–74.

Foucault, M. (1978). *History of Sexuality: An Introduction.* New York: Pantheon.

Foulkes, S.H. (1964). *Therapeutic Group Analysis.* London: George Allen & Unwin.

Foulkes, S.H. (1971). Access to unconscious processes in the group-analytic group. *Group Analysis, 4*: 4–14.

Foulkes, S.H. (1983). *An Introduction to Group-Analytic Psychotherapy.* London: Maresfield Reprints.

Foulkes, S.H. & Anthony, E.J. (1957). *Group Psychotherapy.* New York: Penguin.

Frank, K. (1997). The role of the analyst's inadvertent self-revelations. *Psychoanalytic Dialogues, 7*: 281–314.

Freud, S. (1894a). The neuro-psychoses of defence. *S.E., 3.* London: Hogarth.

Freud, S. (1900a). *Interpretation of Dreams. S.E., 5.* London: Hogarth.

Freud, S. (1904a). Freud's psycho-analytic procedure. *S.E., 7.* London: Hogarth.

Freud, S. (1905d). Three Essays on the Theory of Sexuality. *S.E., 7.* London: Hogarth.

Freud, S. (1907a). Delusions and dreams in Jensen's *Gradiva. S.E., 9.* London: Hogarth.

Freud, S. (1907c). The sexual enlightenment of children. *S.E., 9.* London: Hogarth.

Freud, S. (1909d). Notes upon a case of obsessional neurosis. *S.E., 10.* London: Hogarth.

Freud, S. (1910k). Observations on wild analysis. *S.E., 11.* London: Hogarth.

Freud, S. (1911c). Psycho-analytic notes on an autobiographical account of a case of paranoia. *S.E., 12.* London: Hogarth.

Freud, S. (1912b). The dynamics of transference. *S.E., 12.* London: Hogarth.

Freud, S. (1912e). Recommendations to physicians practicing psycho-analysis. *S.E., 12.* London: Hogarth.

Freud, S. (1912–1913). Totem and taboo. *S.E., 13.* London: Hogarth.

Freud, S. (1914d). On the history of the psycho-analytic movement. *S.E., 14*. London: Hogarth.

Freud, S. (1915d). Repression. *S.E., 14*. London: Hogarth.

Freud, S. (1915e). The unconscious. *S.E., 14*. London: Hogarth.

Freud, S. (1916d). Some character types met with in psycho-analytic work. *S.E., 14*. London: Hogarth.

Freud, S. (1916–1917). Introductory lectures on psycho-analysis: 17th and 28th Lectures. *S.E., 16*. London: Hogarth.

Freud, S. (1917e). Mourning and melancholia. *S.E., 14*. London: Hogarth.

Freud, S. (1919a). Lines of advance in psycho-analytic therapy. *S.E., 17*. London: Hogarth.

Freud, S. (1920g). Beyond the pleasure principle. *S.E., 18*. London: Hogarth.

Freud, S. (1921c). Group psychology and the analysis of the ego. *S.E., 18*. London: Hogarth.

Freud, S. (1923b). The ego and the id. *S.E., 19*. London: Hogarth.

Freud, S. (1924b). Neurosis and psychosis. *S.E., 19*. London: Hogarth.

Freud, S. (1924e). Loss of reality in neurosis and psychosis. *S.E., 19*. London: Hogarth.

Freud, S. (1925h). Negation. *S.E., 19*. London: Hogarth.

Freud, S. (1927e). Fetishism. *S.E., 21*. London: Hogarth.

Freud, S. (1937c). Analysis terminable and interminable. *S.E.*, 23. London: Hogarth.

Freud, S. (1940a). *An outline of psycho-Analysis. S.E., 23*. London: Hogarth.

Freud, S. & Breuer, J. (1895d). *Studies on Hysteria. S.E., 2*. London: Hogarth.

Freud, S. & Jung, C. (1974). *The Freud-Jung letters*. R. Manheim (Trans.). Princeton, NJ: Princeton University Press.

Fromm, E. (1963). The revolutionary character. In: *The Dogma of Christ*. New York: Holt, Rinehart & Winston.

Gabbard, G.O. (1995). Countertransference: the emerging common ground. *International Journal of Psychoanalysis, 76*: 475–485.

Gans, J. (2006). My abiding therapeutic core: Its emergence over time. *Voices, Winter*: 14–29.

Gayle, R. (2009). Co-creating meaningful structures within long-term psychotherapy group culture. *International Journal of Group Psychotherapy, 59*: 311–333.

Gediman, H.K. & Lieberman, J.S. (1996). *The Many Faces of Deceit: Omissions, Lies, and Disguise in Psychotherapy.* Northvale, NJ: Aronson.

Gerson, S. (1996). Neutrality, resistance, self-disclosure. *Psychoanalytic Dialogues, 6*: 623–645.

Gerson, S. (2004). The relational unconscious: A core element of intersubjectivity, thirdness, and clinical process. *Psychoanalytic Quarterly, 73*: 63–98.

Gide, A. (1902/1996). *The Immoralist*. R. Howard (Trans.). New York: Vintage.

Gill, M.M. (1994). *Psychoanalysis in Transition*. Hillsdale, NJ: Analytic Press.

Goffman, E. (1972). *Presentation of Self in Everyday Life*. New York: Doubleday.

Gotta, H. (2005). The group wants to party. *Group, 29*: 435–445.

Green, A. (1999). *The Work of the Negative*. A. Weller (Trans.). London: Free Association.

Green, A. (2000). The intrapsychic and intersubjective in psychoanalysis. *Psychoanalytic Quarterly, 69*: 1–39.

Greenberg, J. (1995). Self-disclosure: Is it psychoanalytic? *Contemporary Psychoanalysis, 31*: 193–205.

Greenberg, J. (1996). Psychoanalytic words and psychoanalytic acts: A brief history. *Contemporary Psychoanalysis, 32*: 195–213.

Greenson, R. (1967). *The Technique and Practice of Psychoanalysis*. New York: International Universities Press.

Grotjahn, M. (1993). *The Art and Technique of Analytic Group Therapy*. Northvale, NJ: Aronson.

Grotstein, J.S. (2000). Some considerations of "hate" and a reconsideration of the death instinct. *Psychoanalytic Inquiry, 20*: 462–480.

Grotstein, J.S. (2003). Introduction. In: R.M. Billow, *Relational Group Psychotherapy: From Basic Assumptions to Passion*. London: Jessica Kingsley.

Grotstein, J.S. (2004). The seventh servant: The implications of a truth drive in Bion's theory of "O." *International Journal of Psychoanalysis, 85*: 1081–1101.

Hanly, C. (1999). On subjectivity and objectivity in psychoanalysis. *Journal of the American Psychoanalytic Association, 47*: 427–444.

Hendin, H. (1981). Psychotherapy and suicide. *American Journal of Psychotherapy, 35*: 469–480.

Hobdell, R. (1991). Individual and group therapy combined. In: J. Roberts & M. Pines (Eds.), *The Practice of Group Analysis*. London: Tavistock/Routledge.

Hoffman, I.Z. (1983). The patient as interpreter of the analyst's experience. *Contemporary Psychoanalysis, 19*: 389–422.

Hoffman, I.Z. (1992). Expressive participation and psychoanalytic discipline. *Contemporary Psychoanalysis, 2*: 1–14.

Hoffman, I.Z. (1994). Dialectical thinking and therapeutic action in the psychoanalytic process. *Psychoanalytic Quarterly, 63*: 187–218.

Hoffman, I.Z. (1996). The intimate and ironic authority of the psychoanalyst's presence. *Psychoanalytic Quarterly, 65:* 102–136.

Hoffman, I.Z. (2006). The myths of free association and the potentials of the analytic relationship. *International Journal of Psychoanalysis, 87:* 43–61.

Hopper, E. (2003a). *The Social Unconscious: Selected Papers.* London: Jessica Kingsley.

Hopper, E. (2003b). *Traumatic Experience in the Unconscious Life of Groups: The Fourth Basic Assumption: Incohesion: Aggregation/Massification or (ba) I:A/M.* London: Jessica Kingsley.

Hopper, E. (2009). Building Bridges between Psychoanalysis and Group Analysis in Theory and in Clinical Practice. [Plenary lecture.] *Bridging Identities, Clinical Impact of Groups.* Prague, Czech Republic: 4th EFPP Group Section Conference.

Isaacs, S. (1952). The nature and function of phantasy. In: M. Klein, P. Heimann, S. Isaacs & J. Riviere (Eds.), *Developments in Psychoanalysis* (pp. 67–121). London: Hogarth.

Jacobs, T. (2001). On misreading and misleading patients. *International Journal of Psychoanalysis, 82*: 653–669.

Jacobson, E. (1959). The "exceptions:" An elaboration of Freud's character study. *Psychoanalytic Study of the Child, 14*: 135–154.

Jaques, E. (1955). Social systems as a defense against persecutory and depressive anxiety. In: M. Klein, P. Heimann & R. Money-Kyrle (Eds.), *New Directions in Psychoanalysis* (pp. 478–498). London: Tavistock.

Johnson, S. (1759). *The History of Rasselas, Prince of Abissinia.* England: Penguin Classics, 1985.

Jonsen, A. & Toulmin, S. (1988). *The Abuse of Casuistry: A History of Moral Reasoning.* Berkeley, CA: University of California Press.

Kauff, P.F. (2009). Transference in combined individual and group psychotherapy. *International Journal of Group Psychotherapy, 59*: 29–46.

Kernberg, O. (2000). A concerned critique of psychoanalytic education. *International Journal of Psychoanalysis, 81*: 97–120.

Klein, M. (1975). *Love, Guilt and Reparation.* New York: Delacorte Press.

Lacan, J. (1977). On a question preliminary to any possible treatment of psychosis (1957–1958). In: *Ecrits* (pp. 177–225). A. Sheridan (Trans.). New York: Norton.

Langs, R. (1978). Some communicative properties of the bipersonal field. *International Journal of Psychoanalytic Psychotherapy, 7*: 87–135.

Laplanche, J. (1976). *Life and Death in Psychoanalysis.* Baltimore, MD: Johns Hopkins University.

Laplanche, J. & Pontalis, J-B. (1973). *The Language of Psycho-Analysis*. New York: Norton.

Louw, F. & Pitman, M. (2001). Irreducible subjectivity and interactionism: A critique. *International Journal of Psychoanalysis, 82*: 747–765.

Lowental, U. (2000). Defense and resistance in the psychoanalytic process. *Psychoanalytic Review, 87*: 121–135.

Maccoby, M. (2007). *The Leaders We Need and What Makes Us Follow*. Boston: Harvard Business School.

Maltsberger, J.T. & Buie, D.H. (1973). Countertransference hate in the treatment of suicidal patients. *Archives of General Psychiatry, 30*: 625–633.

Matte-Blanco, I. (1988). *Thinking, Feeling and Being*. London: Tavistock/ Routledge.

McGuire, W. (Ed.) (1974). *The Freud/Jung Letters: The Correspondence between Sigmund Freud and C.G. Jung*. R.F.C. Hull & R. Manheim (Trans.). Princeton, NJ: Princeton University Press.

McLaughlin, J. (1996). Power, authority, and influence in the analytic dyad. *Psychoanalytic Quarterly, 65*: 201–235.

Merleau-Ponty, M. (1964). *Signs*. Evanston, IL: Northwestern University Press.

Mitchell, S. (1988). *Relational Concepts in Psychoanalysis*. Cambridge, MA: Harvard University Press.

Mitchell, S. (1993). *Hope and Dread in Psychoanalysis*. New York: Basic.

Modell, A.H. (1976). "The holding environment" and the therapeutic action of psychoanalysis. In: R. Langs (Ed.), *Classics in Psychoanalytic Technique* (pp. 489–498). New York: Aronson, 1981.

Motherwell, L. & Shay, J. (Eds.) (2005). *Complex Dilemmas in Group Therapy—Pathways to Resolution*. New York: Bruner-Routledge.

Nietzsche, F. (1980). *Sämtliche Werke: Kritische Studienausgabe*, Vol. 6, p. 63. G. Colli & M. Montinari (Eds.). Berlin: de Gruyter, 1889. [In *Twilight of the Idols*, "Maxims and Arrows," section 26.]

Nitsun, M. (1996). *The Anti-Group*. London: Routledge.

Ogden, T. (1997). Some thoughts on the use of language in psychoanalysis. *Psychoanalytic Dialogues, 7*: 1–21.

O'Leary, J. & Wright, F. (2005). Social constructivism and the group-as-a-whole. *Group, 29*: 257–276.

Ormont, L.R. (1992). *The Group Therapy Experience*. New York: St. Martins.

Pfeifer, G. & Spinner, D. (1985). Combined individual and group psychotherapy with children: An ego developmental perspective. *International Journal of Group Psychotherapy, 35*: 11–35.

Pollack, L. & Slavin, J.H. (1998). The struggle for recognition: Disruption and reintegration in the experience of agency. *Psychoanalytic Dialogues, 8*: 857–873.

Porter, K. (1980). Combined individual and group psychotherapy: A review of the literature 1965–1978. *International Journal of Group Psychotherapy, 30*: 107–114.

Porter, K. (1993). Combined individual and group psychotherapy. In: H. Kaplan & B. Sadock (Eds.), *Comprehensive Group Psychotherapy (3rd Edition)* (pp. 314–324). Baltimore: Williams and Wilkins.

Praper, P. (1997). A case of combined therapy: some developmental and object-relations phenomena. *Group Analysis, 30*: 331–348.

Psychoanalytic Psychology (2006). The Relevance of Sigmund Freud for the 21st Century. Vol. 23.

Racker, H. (1968). *Transference and Countertransference*. Madison, CT: International Universities Press.

Raps, C. (2009). The necessity of combined therapy in the treatment of shame: A case report. *International Journal of Group Psychotherapy, 59*: 67–84.

Reich, W. (1933). *Character Analysis*, T. Wolfe (Trans.). New York: Orgone Institute Press, 1945.

Renik, O. (1993). Analytic interaction: Conceptualizing technique in light of the analyst's irreducible subjectivity. *Psychoanalytic Quarterly, 62*: 553–571.

Rescher, N. (1987). *Forbidden Knowledge and other Essays on the Philosophy of Cognition*. Dordrecht, Germany: Reidel.

Rosenthal, L. (1994). *Resolving Resistance in Group Psychotherapy*. Northvale, NJ: Aronson.

Roth, B. (2009). Some problems with treatment: Destructive enactments in combined therapy. *International Journal of Group Psychotherapy, 59*: 47–66.

Roth, B., Stone, W. & Kibel, H. (Eds.) (1990). *The Difficult Patient in Group. Group Psychotherapy with Borderline and Narcissistic Disorders*. Madison, CT: International Universities Press.

Rowan, A. & Harper, E. (1999). Group subversion as subjective necessity—Towards a Lacanian orientation to psychoanalysis in group settings. In: C. Oakley (Ed.), *What Is A Group? A New Look at Theory in Practice* (pp. 168–203). London: Rebus.

Russell, B. (1927). *An Outline of Philosophy*. London: Allen and Unwin, 1970.

Rutan, J.S. & Alonso, A. (1982). Individual, group, or both? *International Journal of Group Psychotherapy, 33*: 3–16.

Rutan, J.S., Alonso, A. & Molin, R. (1984). Handling the absence of group leaders. *International Journal of Group Psychotherapy, 34*: 273–287.

Rutan, J.S. & Stone, W. (2001). *Psychodynamic Group Therapy. 3rd Edition*. New York: Guilford.

Schachter, J. (1988). Concurrent individual and individual-in-a-group psychoanalytic psychotherapy. *Journal of the American Psychoanalytic Association, 6*: 455–480.

Scheidlinger, S. (1974). On the concept of the "mother group." *International Journal of Group Psychotherapy, 24*: 417–428.

Scheidlinger, S. & Porter, K. (1980). Group therapy combined with individual psychotherapy. In: T. Karasu & L. Bellak (Eds.), *Specialized Techniques in Individual Psychotherapy*. New York: Brunner/Mazel.

Searles, H. (1979). *Countertransference and Related Subjects*. New York: International Universities Press.

Shakespeare, W. *The Tragedy of Richard the Third*. In: *The Complete Works*. New York: Harcourt, Brace, 1961.

Shakespeare, W. The Tragedy of Hamlet, Prince of Denmark. In: *The Complete Works*. New York: Harcourt, Brace, 1961.

Slater, P.E. (1966). *Microcosm*. New York: John Wiley.

Slavson, S.R. (1957). Are there "group dynamics" in therapy groups? *International Journal of Group Psychotherapy, 7*: 131–141. [Reprinted in: K.R. Mackenzie (Ed.), *Classics in Group Psychotherapy*. New York: Guilford, 1992.]

Slavson, S.R. & Schiffer, M. (1975). *Group Psychotherapies for Children*. New York: International Universities Press.

Spence, D. (1982). *Narrative Truth, Historical Truth*. New York: Norton Spence.

Spezzano, C. (1996). The three faces of two-person psychology: Development, ontology, and epistemology. *Psychoanalytic Dialogues, 6*: 599–621.

Stern, D.B. (1997). *Unformulated Experience: From Dissociation to Imagination in Psychoanalysis*. Hillsdale, NJ: The Analytic Press.

Stern, D.B. (1990). Courting surprise: Unbidden perceptions in clinical practice. *Contemporary Psychoanalysis, 26*: 452–478.

Stern, D.N. (1985). *The Interpersonal World of the Infant*. New York: Basic.

Stolorow, R.D. (1997). Principles of dynamic systems, intersubjectivity, and the obsolete distinction between one-person and two-person psychologies. *Psychoanalytic Dialogues, 7*: 859–868.

Strachey, J. (1957). Editor's note. *S.E., 14* (pp. 161–165). London: Hogarth.

Swiller, H.I. (1988). Alexithymia: Treatment utilizing combined individual and group psychotherapy. *International Journal of Group Psychotherapy, 38*: 47–60.

Symington, J. & Symington, N. (1996). *The Clinical Thinking of Wilfred Bion*. London: Routledge.

Thoma, H. & Kachele, H. (1994a). *Psychoanalytic Practice, 1: Principles.* Northvale, NJ: Aronson.

Thoma, H. & Kachele, H. (1994b). *Psychoanalytic Practice, 2: Clinical Studies.* M. Wilson (Trans.). Northvale, NJ: Aronson.

Thoreau, H.D. (2008). *Collected Works of Henry David Thoreau.* Publisher: Amazon.com.

Trilling, L. (1971). *Sincerity and Authenticity.* Cambridge, MA: Harvard University Press.

Twemlow, S. & Parens, H. (2006). Might Freud's legacy lie beyond the couch? *Psychoanalytic Psychology, 23*: 430–451.

Vella, N. (1999). Freud On Groups. In: C. Oakley (Ed.), *What Is A Group? A New Look at Theory in Practice* (pp. 8–38). London: Rebus.

Whitaker, D. & Lieberman, M. (1964). *Psychotherapy Through the Group Process.* New York: Atherton.

Wilke, G. (2002). The large group and its conductor. In: R.M. Lipgar & M. Pines (Eds.), *Building on Bion: Branches* (pp. 70–105). London: Jessica Kingsley.

Winnicott, D.W. (1960). Ego distortion in terms of true and false self. In: *The Maturational Process and the Facilitating Environment: Studies in the Theory of Emotional Development* (pp. 140–152). New York: International Universities Press, 1965.

Winnicott, D.W. (1971). *Playing and Reality.* London: Tavistock.

Wong, N. (1979). Clinical considerations in group treatment of narcissistic disorders. *International Journal of Group Psychotherapy, 27*: 325–345.

Wright, F. (2004). Being seen, moved, disrupted and reconfigured: Group leadership from a relational perspective. *International Journal of Group Psychotherapy, 54*: 235–250.

Wurmser, L. (1977). A defense of the use of metaphor in analytic theory formation. *Psychoanalytic Quarterly, 46*: 466–498.

Yalom, I. (1995). *The Theory and Practice of Group Psychotherapy (4th edition).* New York: Basic.

Zacarro, S.J. (2007). Triad-based perspectives of leadership. *American Psychologist, 62*: 6–16.

INDEX

For Product Safety Concerns and Information please contact our EU representative GPSR@taylorandfrancis.com Taylor & Francis Verlag GmbH, Kaufingerstraße 24, 80331 München, Germany

Batch number: 10726011

Printed by Printforce, the Netherlands